LOST SOUL

To Melissa

Best Wishes

Les Rolston

9/18/10

Library of Congress Cataloging-in-Publication data:
Rolston, Les, 1954-
Lost soul: the Confederate soldier in New England/Les Rolston
    p. cm.
    Includes bibliographical references.
    ISBN 0-916489-88-4
    1. Postlethwaite, Samuel, 833-1876. 2. Confederate States of
America. Army. Mississippi Infantry Regiment, 21st Biography.
3.Postlethwaite, Samuel, 1833-1876—Death and burial. 4. Soldiers—
Mississippi Biography. 5. Woodville Region (Miss.) Biography. 6. River
point (R.I.) Boigraphy. 7. Postlethwaite family. 8. Greene family. I. Title.

E589.5 21st.R65 1999   99-25079
                                                                    CIP

Copyright 1999
Ancestry.com Incorporated
P.O. Box 990
Orem, Utah 84057

First Printing 1999
10 9 8 7 6 5 4 3 2 1

Printed in the United States of America

LOST SOUL

THE CONFEDERATE SOLDIER IN NEW ENGLAND

Les Rolston

Ancestry®

DEDICATION

For Jane

ACKNOWLEDGMENTS

I N 1991, WHILE HAVING DINNER WITH MY FRIEND MARK Johnsen-Harris, I told him the tale of a mysterious grave I had found. When I was finished he said to me, "You'll have to write a book about this, you know." This book would not have been possible without the kind help and encouragement of Mark and Mrs. James "Honey" Gross of Woodville, Mississippi. Thanks to both of you for helping me tell "Sam's" story.

Special thanks to the Cardin family, the Postlethwaite family, Ms. Mabel Clark, Mr. Ralph Ciaramello, Mr. John Wrona, Rep. Joe McNamara, Rep. Leona Kelly, Mr. Donald Estes, Ms. Genevieve Barksdale, Ms. Catherine Brandon Morgan, Mr. Vidal Davis, The 2nd South Carolina String Band, Ms. Cam Wiener, Ms. Elva Wirth, Ms. Vivian Hartnett, Ms. Marie Dick, Ms. Blair Greene, Mr. John S. Lewis, Sen. Claiborne Pell, Mr. Dilmond Postlethwaite, Ms. Marie Hays, Ms. Peggy Palmer, Mr. Dale Fleming, Ms. Cherry Bamberg, Mr. Patrick J. Griffin III, Ms. Rosalind Colley, Mr. Donald Garrett, Dr. Nicholas Bellantoni, Ms. Jane Duggan, Ms. Linda Byrne, Mr. Jim Ruck, the United Daughters of the Confederacy, the Daughters of the American Revolution, the Mississippi Department of Archives and History, Ms. Judy Bolton of the Louisiana

State University Library, the Virginia Historical Society Library, the Rhode Island Historical Society Library, Ms. Susan Dunn and Ms. Cynthia Archambault of the Warwick Public Library, Boston Public Library, West Warwick Public Library, Providence Public Library, the National Archives, the Department of Veterans Affairs, the Louisiana State Archives, the Rhode Island State Archives, the National Park Service, *Civil War* magazine, the *Civil War News*, the Sons of Confederate Veterans, Ms. Lou Szucs, Ms. Jennifer Utley, Ms. Rebekah Thorstenson, Mr. Matt Grove, Mr. John Tolman, and "Sam's" friends everywhere.

CONTENTS

PROLOGUE

THE KAWASAKI FOUR-WHEELER WHIPPED THROUGH knee-high Mississippi grass. Seated behind my wife Jane and our guide, Vidal Davis, I dangled from the edge of the seat like a reluctant rodeo cowboy. As we scaled fallen trees and other obstacles it became evident that if we were to reach our destination it would only be by such a mode of travel.

Overgrown, barely passable paths yielded little evidence of a thriving plantation from 150 years past. Each avenue dead-ended in thicket; Vidal found it hard to conceal his growing doubts about finding the little cemetery somewhere in the surrounding wilderness. He had stumbled upon the ruins ten years earlier while hunting in these same woods, never expecting to take visitors there. But I had traveled more than a thousand miles hoping to find a brick-walled burial ground on the remnants of a plantation known as Mount Independence.

A foray of more than two miles into the woods had thus far yielded nothing more noteworthy than a terrified armadillo. Without a word Vidal suddenly cut the ATV's engine, dismounted, and began walking uncertainly into a particularly dense portion of forest. I followed a few paces behind. About thirty yards ahead the shape of a modest headstone emerged through the shadows and light. "There it is!" I cried to Jane, who had remained with the vehicle. Vidal smiled with relief as I, impressed, patted him on the back.

Mount Independence Cemetery was devastated. Ravaged by time, nature, and careless logging, every stone was toppled or broken; the remains of brick walls lay in heaps. Nevertheless, I was thrilled; I had found another key piece of a Civil War soldier's life story.

The stone tablet that was the object of our search lay broken in five sections. Gently repositioning the stone and coating it with a light layer of dirt, I deciphered this inscription:

This Monument Was Erected By
W. D. Postlethwaite To The Memory Of His Beloved Wife,
SUSAN
Who Departed This Life On The
10th of Sept. A. D. 1835, Aged
21 Years, 4 Months & Four Days
The Loveliest In This World Of Sadness Are
Destined To Decay The First, And Those Whose
Fate Seems Woven Of Gladness Are Mournful
Victims Of The Worst.
So She Like Roses Rudely Torn
In Graceful Fragrance From Their Stem.
Bloomed Like Her, Emblems Of A Morn.
Then Crushed And Withered Like Them.

The young wife of William Dunbar Postlethwaite had died six days after giving birth to her second child, Susan. Little Susan's life was to span a gold rush in the West, a civil war, Reconstruction, and the advent of the automobile. Long after the days of King Cotton and the grandeur of plantation life had become distant memories, Susan would live her last days alone at the plantation her father had built for her mother. She was a true steel magnolia.

The elder Susan hadn't lived to spend a single day at

Westmoreland plantation, but William would remarry and raise seven more children with his second wife, Sophia Carter, on its 1,800 acres. Only daughter Susan, refusing to leave, would reside on Westmoreland's remnants at the dawn of the twentieth century. By that time Westmoreland's scale had been diminished by the sale of much of its acreage and by sharecropping, which continued at what is now known as Westmoreland Farms as late as the 1970s.

Susan came into sole possession of Westmoreland upon the death of her only full sibling—a brother named Samuel. Two years her senior, Susan's brother died at forty-three years of age in the unlikeliest of places for a plantation owner: a thousand miles away in the quiet village of Riverpoint in the industrialized, seafaring state of Rhode Island.

Samuel Postlethwaite's grave had been marked by a simple stone bearing the inscription "S.P." This tiny monument did not survive the years, but in 1995, twelve decades after Sam Postlethwaite's death, one hundred people would convene at the mansion of Rhode Island's Civil War governor to honor him. A nearly forgotten soldier, a lost soul, sadly symbolic of so many soldiers whose deeds and sacrifices have been forgotten, was finally to have his dignity restored with a marked grave.

This is Sam's story and the story of the scores of people who put aside differences and came together as Americans to rally on his behalf.

*Top: The stone tablet of Sam's mother, Susan.
Bottom: Mount Independence Cemetery where
Susan is buried.*

CHAPTER ONE

Three Generations

In 1991, on a frozen Sunday afternoon, I began to contemplate where I might vacation if summer were kind enough to someday return. As a child, I had come to the age of awareness at the time of the murder of a young president and as America commemorated the centennial of a brutal civil war. Now, at thirty-seven years of age, it occurred to me that although I had explored Europe and the West Coast of the United States extensively, I had never ventured south of Washington, D.C.

My intention was to tour several battlefields of the American Civil War. Limited to two weeks, I decided to visit a local library to research the sites I wanted to see and plan the most efficient travel route. This casual visit to the library was the inadvertent first step in unraveling a complex and compelling story.

One book in the library's Civil War collection suited my needs perfectly. It was a detailed, state-by-state guide to the Civil War published in the early 1960s. I began by glancing through the Rhode Island section of the book and was struck by a particular reference that seemed completely out of place: "Greenwood Cemetery has the grave of a Confederate soldier, Samuel Postlethwaite. At *present the grave site has an unmarked stone to the right of the William Rogers Greene stone."*

A Confederate? Was he a Rhode Islander? Why was his grave marked in such an undignified manner? Out of simple curiosity, I decided to visit the cemetery and see the humble grave for myself.

The cemetery was much larger than I had expected, and finding the stone of William Rogers Greene seemed hopeless in the gathering darkness. The only other visitors turned out to be the cemetery owner and his wife, who took a moment with me to point out the graves of several Union soldiers. The gentleman had no knowledge of a Confederate soldier buried there. His wife agreed to check their records for me, but she was unable to find any documents dated earlier than 1920.

I didn't know that I was embarking on a research project that would consume several years and require at least a dozen trips to the South. A story would slowly emerge, and I would speak with and explore sources throughout the United States. I would walk the battlefields on which this soldier had fought and the fields he had plowed. Gradually, "Sam," as I began to call him, would come to life for me, a fascinating figure who by accident of fate became part of one of Rhode Island's most famous families and whose story became entwined with mine.

I N RHODE ISLAND, THE FIRST THREE WEEKS OF AUGUST 1876 were very hot and dry. The drought was so severe that many mills were forced to shut down by low water levels. The weather was a preoccupation, and Rhode Islanders were still abuzz over the demise of General George Custer and his men somewhere in the West.

But Sunday, 20 August, was a day for recreation and enjoying the company of friends and family. The day was cool and breezy, much more like October than mid-summer. There were picnics and baseball games and several

family outings at a bayside park, known as Rocky Point.
Many Rhode Islanders were enjoying Narragansett Bay,
digging clams, or setting out to vacation at Block Island, a
new resort spot. At half past four that afternoon, on the
estate of his half-sister Mary and her husband, William
Rogers Greene, Samuel Postlethwaite died. The official
cause of death was consumption, which Samuel had developed after being wounded in the lungs during the Civil
War. He was forty-three years old.

The next day, Samuel's body was taken from Mr.
Greene's estate, Corotoman Farm, and buried in
Greenwood Cemetery across the street. A small stone with
the inscription "S.P." marked the grave. Father Cocroft of
St. Andrews Episcopal Church performed the funeral
service. In one sense, the saga of the only Confederate soldier known to be buried in Rhode Island had begun.

As late as 1876, many Rhode Island men were still suffering and dying from the wounds they had received a decade
and more earlier. What makes Sam's story unique is that
he had been a Confederate soldier. Like most Southern
soldiers, Sam had fought in what he believed was the
"Second War of Independence;" it would become known
as the Lost Cause. And like most Southern soldiers, Sam
had been drawn into the conflict simply to defend his
state. Although this is his story, it is also the story of two
families whose sons fought on opposing sides through
our greatest national tragedy.

Three Generations:
The Greenes and the Postlethwaites

In the early 1700s, the Greene family was already a force
in Rhode Island business and politics; it would play a
prominent role in the coming war for independence. The
Greenes had produced two of the colony's governors and
one of the state's founding fathers.

Many of the Postlethwaite clan had emigrated from England in short order, attaining significant stature in Virginia and Pennsylvania. During the Revolutionary War, men of the Postlethwaite family served in the Carlisle Pennsylvania Militia. Captain John Postlethwaite was married to the daughter of Charles Scott—one of George Washington's generals.

Several of the Greenes saw military service during the revolution. Few soldiers experienced such a remarkable ascent in rank as did Nathaniel Greene. In civilian life, Nathaniel Greene had managed his father's successful iron foundry. He walked with a noticeable limp, but his physical limitations did not prevent him from joining the Rhode Island State Militia. His natural gift for military strategy was soon appreciated, and in a single promotion he was transformed from a private to commander of the state militia.

At the outset of the American Revolution, Greene was made responsible for the defense of Long Island. Later, he would command the Continental Army in the Carolinas, where to this day he is regarded as highly as he is in his native state. His coolness and ability to make and justify unpopular decisions won George Washington's respect and trust. On several occasions, he persuaded Washington not to attack the British or suggested retreat to the dismay of Washington's battle-seasoned generals. History has shown that these engagements would have been disastrous for the Continental Army and could have led to total defeat.

Nathaniel Greene was rumored to have been Washington's successor in the event of the unthinkable. He retired at the rank of general, remembered best for his long marches and his ability to divide his army and confuse the enemy. Nathaniel died at the age of forty-four in 1786, sunstroke cheating the war hero of a promising political career. He twice declined the position of secretary of war; one can only conjecture upon what his political aspirations may have been.

At the end of the eighteenth century, Nathaniel Greene's widow joined struggling Virginia plantation owners in commissioning an inventor to produce a device that would make the harvesting of cotton more efficient. It took Eli Whitney only a matter of weeks to develop a machine that enabled one slave to do the work of several by separating the lint from the seed mechanically. Cotton production increased dramatically as did the slave population. The cotton plantations' dependence on slavery was cemented by the advent of the cotton gin.

At the beginning of the nineteenth century, the territory that would eventually become Mississippi was under the control of Spain. The governor of what was known as the Natchez District was Gayoso de Lemos. The town of Natchez sits high above the Mississippi River and its massive bluffs hover above its port, which is simply known as "under the hill." The river provided for limitless commerce between the Louisiana territories and the United States.

The area was rich in raw materials, such as cotton. Natchez was very attractive to entrepreneurs in the North, who began to settle in the area in hopes of building fortunes. One of the earliest settlers was Sam's grandfather, Samuel Postlethwaite, who descended the Ohio and Mississippi rivers from Pittsburgh on a flatboat. Upon arriving in Natchez, he sold the flatboat and began a career as a merchant. He became so successful that by his early thirties he was advising other settlers on financial matters and, some believe, developing a close relationship with Gayoso.

Gayoso sought Postlethwaite's opinion on a wide range of issues and often mediated between the settlers and the Spanish regime. The people of Natchez, who believed him to be a fair and reasonable governor, respected Gayoso. In 1792, he was able to avert a war between Choctaw Indians and Northern settlers who were encroaching on the tribe's hunting grounds. The Treaty of Natchez guaranteed the Choctaws a protected area for their tribal needs. Gayoso also protected the rights of farmers and cattlemen by enacting strict trading regulations. A man ahead of his time, Gayoso even implemented one of the first anti-pollution laws in North America.

Through his business success and ties with the Spanish governor, Samuel Postlethwaite soon stood at the highest rung of the local social and economic ladder. In 1805, he married Anne Dunbar, the daughter of wealthy settler William Dunbar. (The ruins of Dunbar's massive plantation, The Forest, are visible on Highway 61 North, six miles south of Natchez.)

Two years later, a child, Matilda Rose, was born, and on 24 September 1810, William Dunbar Postlethwaite came into the world.

When France took the vast territory of Louisiana from Spain, the emperor Napoleon promptly sold the land, which stretched as far north as Canada, to the United States. According to Postlethwaite family lore, as Gayoso and the Spanish left the territory in 1803, Samuel Postlethwaite's successful career continued. He was named captain of the Natchez Artillery and served as an executor of several plantations, each of which was turning a profit. Samuel capped his remarkable success by becoming president of the Mississippi Bank.

Upon Matilda's marriage, Samuel presented her with the gift of an estate called Manse, complete with seventy slaves. But Samuel didn't limit use of his wealth to his family; he gave freely to the poor, becoming a true friend to the needy people of Natchez.

A yellow fever epidemic struck Natchez in the mid-1820s, taking a vicious toll. On 25 October 1824, the newspaper *Ariel* reported:

> That we have a morbid or infected atmosphere there can be no doubt. The news from Natchez respecting the disease is truly melancholy. Numbered among those who have died since the last *Ariel* was . . . Samuel Postlethwaite, (52), President of the bank.

Samuel Postlethwaite is entombed in Natchez Cemetery.

The tomb of Samuel Postlethwaite (elder) at Natchez Cemetery in Mississippi.

Simon Henry Greene was born on 31 March 1799, in Centreville, Rhode Island, the youngest of Job and Abigail Greene's four children. Job Greene was the eldest son of Nathaniel Greene's cousin, the late Colonel Christopher Greene, who had died a hero in the American Revolution. While Colonel Greene was distinguishing himself in the war, the duties of managing the massive mill estate of the Greene family had been placed in the hands of young Job.

The family had inherited the mills and several farms from Christopher's father in 1761, when Philip Greene decided to divide much of his wealth among his children. This property extended from Coventry to the forks of the Pawtuxet River and included a section of a manufacturing village known as Riverpoint. Philip presented Christopher with a mansion that stood on almost five hundred acres. Much of the remaining Riverpoint property was bequeathed to grandsons Job and Jeremiah.

Barely twenty-five, Job Greene quickly exhibited a natural talent for management and administration. His abilities were akin to those of a much more experienced businessman. As with many of the Greenes, Job's success in business went hand in hand with civic responsibilities. A commander of the Kentish Artillery, he also served as a lieutenant in the 2nd Regiment of the Rhode Island State Brigade. Job held a seat on the Warwick Council and served in the Rhode Island House of Representatives and, later, the state Senate.

Simon Henry Greene was nine years old when his father, Job, died in 1808. Along with a brother, Christopher, and two sisters, Susannah and Mary Ann, Simon grew up in an environment of wealth and privilege tempered by devotion to the state and nation. The four children were given the finest educations and were well-traveled. The oldest child, Christopher, had all the attributes for carrying on the Greene legacy, and by his early twenties he was an accomplished writer and orator. At the age of twenty-six, Christopher became one of the first of the Greene family to seek adventure and fortune in the South, becoming a successful merchant in Charleston, South Carolina. He married Mary Ann Lehre of Charleston and fathered one child, who survived only a few days. Soon after, Christopher contracted Scarlet Fever, and he died on 6 November 1825. He was thirty-nine. Mary Ann would join him in death three years later. Simon lived to tell his own children about the brother who dared to go south, never to return.

As the only surviving son, Simon became the heir to the Riverpoint mills. By 1838 he had moved from Providence with his wife and family to Clyde, Warwick, where he built a house. Clyde is a village in part of the city of Warwick, which is now the town of West Warwick. Adjacent to Riverpoint, it was here that Simon would establish a new mill.

Simon had married Caroline Aborn, a granddaughter of Roger Williams, the founding father of Rhode Island, in 1822. As Simon's business, the S. H. Greene Company, grew, so did his family. Twenty years after the move to

Simon Henry Greene moved from Providence to Clyde,
Warwick, Rhode Island where he built a house for his family.
Pictured is the home as it stands today.

Warwick, Simon and Caroline had seven surviving children, all sons. The oldest was Edward, followed by Henry, Christopher (Kit), William Rogers, John, George, and baby Francis. Simon adored his children, and a close friend observed that the home on Main Street had an atmosphere of "peace and harmony" with much "pleasantry and humor." Caroline Greene enjoyed the daily transformation of her husband when he returned from the mill and became "one with his boys."

Simon Henry Greene, father of William Rogers Greene, who is buried next to Samuel Postlethwaite at Greenwood Cemetery in Rhode Island.

Simon Greene was an avid reader of religious philosophy. He was influenced by the teachings of Emmanuel Swedenborg, who advocated a more liberal and practical interpretation of the Holy Scriptures than more conventional Christian orders. Swedenborg was an inventor, mathematician, and philosopher who wrote essays on the functions of the brain that were not fully accepted for more than one hundred years. He devised plans for a flying machine not unlike the Wright brothers' twentieth-century invention. He claimed to have visions of heaven and hell and the second coming of Christ, sometimes going into a trance for days.

Simon Greene was instrumental in the construction of the Providence Society of the New Jerusalem Church, which was sited across the street from the main gate of his mill. Simon often led Sunday services himself. His religious beliefs affected every aspect of his life, and in business and politics he conducted himself as a gentleman.

Simon was committed to improving education in Rhode Island and was instrumental in restructuring it.

He developed a new system that featured a superintendent of schools and quickly became a model for the rest of the country. Simon never actively sought public office, but he believed it was the duty of every citizen to bear this responsibility if called upon by the community. He ran unsuccessfully on a statewide ticket with the prominent

The New Jerusalem church where Simon Greene often led Sunday services. Today it is a cellular phone store.

attorney Sullivan Ballou and served two terms in the Rhode Island General Assembly in the early 1840s; then the death of a business partner forced him to devote more time to his business.

Upon his marriage in 1832, Mrs. Anne Dunbar Postlethwaite presented to her son William a gift of one thousand acres situated between the waters of the middle branch of Thompson Creek and the Mississippi River. Twenty-year-old William began construction of a home on the land; it would become Westmoreland Plantation, named for the Pennsylvania county where Postlethwaites had settled a century earlier and where Samuel had lived as a boy.

William had fallen in love with eighteen-year-old Susan Smith, daughter of a wealthy planter named Israel Smith of Mount Independence Plantation. As construction continued at Westmoreland, William and Susan spent their first year of marriage at Mount Independence, the plantation owned by Susan's family.

It was at Mount Independence on 6 April 1833, that Susan Postlethwaite gave birth to a son, Samuel, who was named for his grandfather. Shortly after his arrival the happy family moved to its own sprawling estate. Like the Greene children, young Samuel was born into a family of wealth and influence and a life of opportunity and good fortune.

Westmoreland Plantation sat a few miles south of Woodville, Mississippi; it was actually located in West Feliciana Parish (county), Louisiana. Although Woodville was the nearest community, most of the Postlethwaite family ties were to Natchez, thirty-five miles to the north. Westmoreland Plantation covered hundreds of acres; scores of slaves worked the cotton fields.

In Rhode Island, the business of Simon Henry Greene was also tied to plantation life, as Simon produced various fabrics made from cotton grown in the South. Rhode Island's mills had quietly developed a unique trade relationship with plantation society, becoming the world's leading manufacturer of "Negro cloth," which was sewn

into slave uniforms. Rhode Island's industry also capital-
ized on slavery by producing manacles and leg irons at a
brisk pace.

Susan Postlethwaite gave birth to a second child, a
daughter, on 4 September 1835. But the joyous atmosphere
at Westmoreland dimmed as the twenty-one-year-old
mother suffered complications following the birth. She
fought for life for six days before succumbing. In a brutal
turn of events, William Dunbar Postlethwaite became a
widower with two small children: Sam, two years old,
and an infant, Susan.

William Dunbar Postlethwaite remarried on 2 August
1838. His new bride was Sophia Carter, a distant relative
of George Washington. She would bear William seven
children: Anna Beverly (Nancie), Mary Carter (Mollie),
Amelia, William Dunbar (Will), Frances Beverly (Fannie),
Helen Dunbar, and Georgiana Carter (Georgie). The family continued to live and work at Westmoreland along
with a nanny, a private tutor, and scores of slaves
throughout the 1840s and 1850s. The Postlethwaites,
along with many other families in the Natchez area, had
many friends and relatives living in the North. They had
mixed feelings about the continuing states' rights debate
and the first serious discussion of secession.

As with the Postlethwaites, the household of Simon
Greene was filled with children. Any large family has its
share of tragedy, and the Greenes were no exception. A
month after her fourth birthday, Caroline Cornelia Greene
died. Her death came less than a year after six-month-old
George Frederick Greene had died. In 1838, another son
was born; he was also named George Frederick Greene.
Another infant, Charles, died in 1841 at the age of three
days. Francis was born in 1842, and three years later
Caroline gave birth to her last child, Abby Susan, who lived
only five weeks. By 1850, Simon and Caroline had seven
surviving children; the youngest was Francis (Frank).

In the mid-1850s, twenty-five-year-old William Rogers
Greene decided to try his hand as an independent business-

man in the South. As he was the fourth of Simon's sons, it was obvious that any success he might experience in the S. H. Greene Company would be limited. His father had doubtless told his boys tales of Uncle Christopher's adventures in the South in the 1820s, and the idea likely appealed to young William.

Venturing south was a risky proposition in a country beginning to burst at the seams, but William was determined to make the skills he had inherited from many generations of Greene mill operations pay off. After some initial success, brothers Kit and George joined him. The W. R. Greene Company soon had mercantile operations in St. Louis, Memphis, Vicksburg, and New Orleans.

While William's oldest brothers, Edward and Henry, were immersed in their father's business, younger brother John may have been tempted to go south as well. But he was still in his teens, so this decision was not his to make. Tragedy intervened when a fire broke out at the mill; John became trapped when a chimney collapsed on him. Although severely burned over most of his body, he survived. His health would be impaired throughout his life; he was lame and "exceedingly deaf," which may explain why he was struck and killed by a train at the age of forty-one.

As 1859 drew to a close, nine-year-old Harry Greene received a letter from his Uncle William. Dated 20 December, it had been mailed from St. Louis. The letter displayed the kindheartedness for which William was known throughout his life.

My Dear Harry,

I was very much pleased to receive a few days ago a letter from you and was quite surprised to see that you could write so well, as I cannot think of my little nephew as any other than the little fellow that I left five years and more ago. I hope to have letters often from you, and will always be prompt in my replies; your letter found me on a sick bed, as I

was confined to my room for several d
chills and fever. Today I am out again bu.
I am weak and my hand trembles very m.
write; yet by writing I strike out tolerably
Please give my love and kisses to Sarah and Ed.
also to your mother and father (William's brothe.
Edward and his wife Hannah), and say to them that
I shall write soon.

I have often thought about that horseback ride
that we are to take some time, as it has been so long
delayed, I think that we ought to enjoy it very much
when the time does come. I have not ridden horseback for a long while. On one occasion since my
residence in the West I rode by buggy and horseback nearly twelve hundred miles, 700 of which I
rode horseback. Don't you think that a long ride?

I met with many adventures, as my route was
mostly through a comparatively unsettled country,
where there were no regular roads and no bridges
and when it came to the rivers, I would generally be
obliged to ford them but oftentimes (as it was winter) I could cross on the ice and one time as I was
most over I felt the ice give way and down my horse
went, but I succeeded in jumping off and did not
get wet and fortunately as the water was but 3 or 4
feet deep, got my horse out without much trouble,
but the question was how I was to get myself and
horse up the bank of the river, as there did not
appear to be any other place where I could do so,
but I found a place where I concluded to make the
attempt. I crawled up the snowy, slippery bank
(leading my horse who came after me). I finally
regained the top of the river bank, and was urging
my horse to do the same. As he made a spring to
jump up, down he slipped and I having the halter
around my hand, we both rolled down the bank to
the ice again but fortunately it did not break
through and on the third attempt we succeeded in

getting on firm land again. This is one of the many adventures I met with. I hope to relate to you others on some other occasion. I must now close with much love from your

Uncle William

I intended to say that your Uncle George was confined to his room all last week with a bilious attack. He is now getting better. Did he know I was writing he would send his love.

In July 1860, in the midst of the presidential campaigns, William again wrote from St. Louis to his nephew.

My Dear Harry,

You must excuse me for not answering your kind letter before this as I had fully intended—but circumstances have prevented. I presume from what your father writes that you must have enjoyed your recent trip to Brookline very much, the sailing especially must have been very delightful. How much I wish that I could enjoy such a sail, as I formerly enjoyed them so much, and six long years have passed since I have had such a pleasure. I had promised myself a visit East this summer, and had anticipated pleasant times fishing and sailing, attending clam bakes, etc., entering into it with such great zeal as a six year would cause one to, that formerly enjoyed such things so much. I often think whether those that I left would know their Uncle William and whether their Uncle William would know them. Many pleasures had I anticipated (and I find it a pleasure to anticipate even though I fail to realize), but my plans are indefinitely postponed in consequence of poor George's protracted illness. He continues to improve and goes down stairs daily, using crutches of course, and yesterday walked to the gate and back, by resting in a chair two or three times that they carried beside him that he might rest as he wanted. The understanding seems to be now that they will leave for home, that is, Father and Mother accompanied by George, probably by Monday the 16th and go by easy stages home.

Please tell your father that we had a rousing ratification meeting Saturday night for Bell and Everett. We believe we can carry Missouri for them. They are my first choice and Lincoln and Hamlin next. Our meeting was the largest and most respectful of any of the political meetings that I have been holden here. It was comprised of our best citizens and Americans at that. It seemed like a good old conservative Whig meeting.

I have just received from the Post Office your Father's letter of the 5th and notice what he says about the Sulpher Springs and will look for another letter from him by next mail, but the probability is, that they will go directly home, thinking that as George is daily improving, he may recover as rapidly at home as anywhere else and in case he does not recover the use of his leg he could then go to such of the Sulpher Springs as shall seem the most desirable. Give my best love to Papa and Mama as well as to Sarah and Eddy—reserving a share for yourself from

Your Uncle William
(Greene Letters, 1850-1870.)

Before Harry would receive another letter from his uncle, their lives, and the world, would be very different.

CHAPTER TWO

The National Fuse

Smitten by curiosity, I returned to Greenwood Cemetery the next weekend and this time found the grave of William Rogers Greene with relative ease. But to its right, where the Confederate soldier was supposed to be buried, there was no sign of a marker—only grass. I decided to call the author of the guidebook that had led me to the cemetery.

Speaking from her home in Chicago, the author explained that she had lost many of her records and had forgotten how she had heard of the grave. Not long after our conversation another Rhode Islander, at my request, wrote to the author inquiring about the grave. I was quite surprised when the author referred the person to me. Sadly, the reference to the grave has been deleted from subsequent editions of the book. I couldn't help but feel that Samuel Postlethwaite had somehow been cheated, and in a sense I felt responsible for him. His very existence had suddenly been denied, and it was partly my fault. My

The empty space next to the grave of William Rogers
Greene at Greenwood Cemetery, Rhode Island, provoked
the search for information about Sam's identity.

curiosity had begun to evolve into a sense of purpose; to
me, Sam became symbolic of forgotten soldiers of all
wars—a lost soul.

As time allowed, I began checking with local historical
societies; none of them knew of any Confederate soldier
buried in Rhode Island. Considering the beautifully
marked Union graves throughout our state, the plight of
this lone, lost veteran was to me be both sad and a
gnawing mystery. Who was he? What did he see in the
war? Why was he buried with Mr. Greene? Was he really
buried there at all?

Determined to learn of Sam's military experiences and
civilian life, I spent the late winter of 1991 grasping at aca-
demic straws. Which former Confederate state had he come
from? With no other options available, I compiled the
names and addresses of more than one hundred newspapers, universities, and historical societies throughout the
South.

I had a name and knew that it belonged to a
Confederate soldier; that was all. I sent a brief form letter
seeking information on "Confederate soldier Sam
Postlethwaite" to each institution. During the ensuing
weeks, replies to my query filled my mailbox, and I grew
accustomed to negative responses. I became convinced

that my needle-in-a-haystack method of research would be fruitless; it seemed that Sam would remain a mystery. But the last week of March brought a surprise and a major breakthrough. John Ferguson, state historian of Arkansas, contacted me and related that "Samuel Postlethwaite was a private in Company D, 21st Mississippi Infantry." The state of Mississippi would now be my prime focus.

A T THE BEGINNING OF THE 1830S, ANDREW JACKSON was president of the United States. Noah Webster had published his *American Dictionary*, the first passenger train service in America had begun operating, and Samuel Morse invented the telegraph.

Over the next few years, Texas would declare itself independent of Mexico, and the slaughter of a garrison of Texans at a little-known place called the Alamo would follow. Native Americans would be brutally pushed off their land by settlers moving west. The push to the West and the attendant conflict with Mexico took center stage in American politics while a steady undercurrent of divisiveness rolled just beneath the surface.

Unabated expansion in the Western territories had soured the United States' relationship with Mexico. Although the importation of slaves had been outlawed since 1808, thousands of slaves entered the United States each year, helping both the plantations in the South and the mills in the North to flourish. South Carolina, whose slave population exceeded its white population, had declared its right to ignore Federal law. In Virginia, a slave rebellion led by Nat Turner had taken the lives of more than fifty whites. Turner was captured, tried, and executed.

The argument over the abolition or expansion of slavery and the debate over states' rights were the worst of the young nation's many growing pains. The Southern states saw slavery as the key to their economic survival. They feared that as new states were brought into the Union, the power of individual states would be diminished and superseded by Federal law, endangering both states' rights and slavery. Slavery existed on a much smaller scale in the North, and Northern abolitionists were determined to make certain that there would not be an expansion of slavery in the West.

By the 1850s, a war with impoverished Mexico had come to a glorious conclusion, producing a slew of heroes and the coronation of the United States as the only major power in the Americas. But the United States paid a high price—the loss of its innocence. In his memoirs, President Ulysses S. Grant would note that the Mexican War was a classic example of a rich, powerful nation shamelessly crushing a smaller, weaker one. And while the war had produced a groundswell of patriotism, the victory was tempered by the possibility of one or more of the Southern states declaring itself independent of the Union. Many believed that as the country expanded, it would inevitably disintegrate into separate nations.

The differences between the Northern and Southern states were physically recognizable. Northern skylines were becoming crowded with smokestacks, while the Southern cities were unchanged from the era of George Washington and the American Revolution. The ports of the North and South were crammed with merchant ships from around the world; the ships departed daily loaded with strikingly different cargos. The docks of New York, Philadelphia, and Providence bustled with activity as products from mills and foundries filled the hulls of foreign ships. In contrast, the Southern ports of Charleston, Savannah, and New Orleans were crammed with tobacco, sugar and, of course, cotton. While the North embraced the Industrial Revolution, "King Cotton" had brought Southern prosperity to heights unimaginable just a few decades before.

The success of Northern industry and Southern agriculture was built on the back of the poor mill worker and the slave. The average mill worker in the North fared far better than the Southern slave, but his or her life was abysmal nonetheless. Low wages, long hours, dangerous machinery, and no opportunity for advancement were accepted realities. Workers, many of them children, were provided with few rest breaks and often no sanitary facilities. Wages barely covered the cost of housing, food, and clothing, and these were often owned and controlled by the mill owner. Those who were fortunate enough to develop a marketable skill, such as blacksmithing or carpentry, and those gifted in the arts, escaped the drudgery of the mills. Others had little chance of breaking out of a cycle that passed through generations.

The California Gold Rush of the late 1840s brought the issue of states' rights to center stage. Statehood for California was the only means of protecting her riches from the rest of the world. But the debate over slavery had reached an emotional peak. The South insisted that if slavery were outlawed in a state of California, it would become increasingly difficult to argue for it in other territories, such as Utah and New Mexico. Abolitionists based their argument on the same theory.

Two senators, a Northerner and a Southerner, proposed a compromise that wouldn't please either side but would preserve the Union. President Fillmore signed into law Daniel Webster and Henry Clay's bill, which prohibited slavery in California but took a hands-off approach to the issue in the new territories of Utah and New Mexico. The Great Compromise also called for stricter enforcement of the Fugitive Slave Law, which had been mostly ignored in the North; Federal troops would be used, if necessary, to capture and return runaway slaves to their owners. Many Americans were relieved, but statehood was inevitable for territories in the Midwest and the Southwest. The debate over slavery would not go away.

Harriet Beecher Stowe's popular novel about slave life, *Uncle Tom's Cabin*, caused Northern empathy for the slaves to soar. Her book provided the average American with a rare glimpse into plantation life, and suddenly everyone had an opinion on slavery.

In 1854, the not-so-united United States tried once again to sidestep the issue of states' rights. With the creators of the Great Compromise gone, the mood in the Senate chamber was foul; the new Senate replaced reason with anger and confrontation. This time the battleground was Kansas. One of the most powerful figures in the Senate was Stephen Douglas of Illinois, a Northern Democrat and owner of nearly 150 slaves. Aware that a strong decision on slavery in Kansas might have a negative impact on Illinois and possibly hinder the railroad he hoped to build there, Douglas pushed for a new "compromise" that left the decision of slavery in Kansas and Nebraska up to their settlers.

The shortsightedness of this agreement was immediately evident. Many Kansans believed they could settle the question for the entire nation. Pro-slavery men from Missouri began pouring over the border into Kansas and attacking anti-slavery settlements. Fanatical abolitionist John Brown organized a militia in Kansas and led an attack against an encampment of Missourians. The seeds of the American Civil War had been planted.

The violence in mid-America even reached the Senate floor when Senator Charles Sumner of Massachusetts was nearly beaten to death by a colleague from South Carolina, Preston Brooks. Two days earlier, during a passionate discourse on the evils of slavery, Sumner had insulted a senator from South Carolina who wasn't present. Brooks bludgeoned Sumner with his cane, and several witnesses claimed that the burly, intimidating figure of William Barksdale of Mississippi prevented anyone from intervening. Others claimed that Barksdale had played no part in the incident—but he would play a role in the events that followed.

The next year, the United States Supreme Court ruled in the Dred Scott case that a slave was not free simply because he had lived on free soil in Missouri for several years, and that any slave traveling through a free territory was still the property of his master and could not seek protection from the Federal government. Chief Justice Roger Taney further declared that the Federal government could not ban slavery from any territory and that, due to the black person's "inferior order," blacks could not become citizens.

To much of the nation, Stephen Douglas represented a serious threat to the cause of abolition. His power in the Senate was beyond the control of the anti-slavery North, and he appeared to be unbeatable for re-election. But the upstart Republican Party would provide Douglas with noble, if not threatening, opposition in 1858 in the person of Abraham Lincoln, a successful lawyer who had dabbled in politics with only middling success.

Opposing the Mexican War and the expansion of slavery into new territories, Lincoln had lost a bid for the Senate in 1855 and resolved to retire from politics. But in 1856 the Republican candidate for president was John Fremont, an explorer of California and the Rocky Mountains who had earned the nickname, the Pathfinder. Lincoln campaigned enthusiastically for Fremont and was once again bitten by the political bug. He decided to end his short-lived political retirement and run for the Senate again. Although he seemingly had little chance of defeating Douglas, the lively debates between the two men served to air the nagging problem of slavery. During the debates Lincoln gained national recognition.

As a lame-duck president, James Buchanan seemed to wish simply to survive the events of the late 1850s rather than to shape them. His approach to avoiding the dissolution of the Union was to surround himself with Southerners and to support many pro-slavery causes. This position angered Republicans and many other Americans, who believed that the slavery question needed to be addressed before the violence seen in Kansas engulfed the country. With every new crisis, each more dangerous than the last, Buchanan did virtually nothing. He seemed determined not to let anything prevent him from enjoying the remainder of his presidency.

The name John Brown, which became synonymous with the anti-slavery movement three years earlier when Brown and his sons murdered five pro-slavery men, captured the national spotlight once again in October 1859. Outraged by the Supreme Court's fugitive slave ruling, Brown believed that slaves could only escape their bondage through violent uprisings against their owners. To set an example, Brown led a small contingent of men (including five blacks) to Harpers Ferry, Virginia, where they seized a Federal arsenal and planned to distribute arms to the local slave population.

Fearing retribution from their owners and for the most part unaware of what was taking place, the slaves of Harpers Ferry failed to respond. But the local white population did respond, and in great numbers. In the ensuing battle, two of Brown's sons were killed and a black man was mutilated by the angry mob. This time Buchanan did act; he ordered a unit of marines commanded by Colonel Robert E. Lee to Harpers Ferry. Lee and his men overpowered Brown, who had lost half of his force, and delivered him to Virginia authorities. He was swiftly tried and convicted and, six weeks after the raid, hanged. The execution was a spectacle, and the newly formed Virginia 1st Militia was present as a show of the state's strength. (A man named John Wilkes Booth joined the unit, ensuring that he would get a view of the event.) Before his death, Brown predicted that the sins of nation could only be "purged with blood."

Talk of secession was heating up in some of the Southern states. In addition to the issues of slavery and states' rights, there were many cultural differences gnawing at the South's bonds to the North. Although many Southern men vehemently opposed secession, their first loyalty remained with their states, regardless of the state's status in the Union.

As early as 1851, Mississippi had rivaled South Carolina as the leader of the states' rights movement. Nevertheless, Union loyalty prevailed when Jefferson Davis was defeated by pro-Unionist Henry Foote in the race for governor that year. Relations with the North became further strained, however, when Northern leaders insisted that the right of secession was prohibited by the Constitution. A line had been drawn.

Despite the Federal government's hard line on secession, the policy was essentially toothless. Most states had a militia of some sort, but the United States Army barely existed, totaling a mere twenty thousand men. The Southern states had no army at all. This peculiar military situation made it easy for each side to bluster and threaten as though it had a massive army behind it. Few could foresee these imaginary armies becoming reality.

In command of the United States Army was Lieutenant General Winfield Scott. Scott had been a national hero in the Mexican War, but by the late 1850s he was a shell of his former self. Obese, in his seventies, and suffering from chronic diarrhea, he was a vision of "ruined magnificence." In a crisis, he might need to be replaced, despite his experience.

President Buchanan sought Scott's counsel, but Buchanan preferred to let the next election decide policy. In 1860, the road to the White House was unlike any election before or since. The Democratic Party was paralyzed over the slavery issue, while the Republicans stood united against slavery but stopped short of calling for its abolition.

The Democrats fielded two candidates: pro-slavery, John Breckinridge of Kentucky and Stephen Douglas, whose platform promised self-determination for the new territories. So split were the Democrats that they held two separate conventions, each claiming to spawn the real nominee. Both conventions were so heated that the survival of the party itself was in doubt. Still, the Democrats hoped that even as a divided party they could defeat any Republican challenger, who would have no chance of carrying the South.

The scene became even murkier when a fourth party, the Know-Nothings, entered the race offering a conservative alternative, John Bell of Tennessee. The Republicans held their convention in Chicago; Rhode Island delegate Simon Greene voted for Salmon Chase on the first ballot and later cast a vote for Abraham Lincoln.

When the general election ballots were in, Abraham Lincoln could claim only forty percent of the popular vote, but he had won a clear majority of the electoral vote. He had carried every free state except New Jersey. The North had given Lincoln a mandate on slavery; the South determined that the new president was undoubtedly its nemesis. As his running mate, Lincoln had selected Hannibal Hamlin of Maine. Hamlin's dark complexion led many to suspect that he was a mulatto, which only added fuel to the already broiling slavery debate.

Lincoln's election terrified many in the South. South Carolina began preparing for secession from the Union. In Sunflower County, Mississippi, successful businessman Benjamin Humphreys' concern for his state caused him to begin organizing local militia companies. Humphreys' military experience was limited to having been expelled from West Point after a Christmas Day prank backfired and the entire academy rioted. For several years Humphreys had proclaimed his anti-secessionist views to the citizens of Mississippi. In his view, secession would only end in economic disaster for Mississippi and could involve it in a war that could not be won.

In Woodville, Mississippi, planter, Carnot Posey and retired army general, William Lindsay Brandon took Humphreys' cue and prepared for the worst. Like Humphreys, though, the sixty-year-old Brandon was less than happy with the idea of secession.

As South Carolina inched perilously closer to the fateful step, all eyes, particularly Mississippi's, were fixed on her. If South Carolina seceded, the fate of Mississippi would be sealed; to maintain its stature as a preeminent Southern state, Mississippi would have to secede as well. The idea of secession angered many Southern men who owned neither property or slaves.

Many of them were hardworking farmers who didn't believe in slavery or found its costs prohibitive. (The cost of a prime field hand had risen to two thousand dollars.) The resentment that these poor farmers felt toward the wealthy plantation owners was widespread, and the prospect of going to war to preserve the right of the wealthy to own slaves didn't sit well with the have-nots. However, most of the non-slaveholding farmers realized that if the United States Army marched into the Natchez District it wouldn't bother to distinguish one farmer from the next; all would feel the wrath of the Federal government.

The Natchez District encompassed three Louisiana parishes and five Mississippi counties from Vicksburg to Woodville. It produced about one-tenth (400,000 bales per year) of all the cotton grown in the United States. Even an armchair general could see that if the growing crisis deteriorated into war the Federal government would attempt to destroy King Cotton.

Throughout the South, the scene was much the same. Men who had not joined the militias were arming themselves and making arrangements to hide their livestock and valuables in case of an invasion. Rumors circulated and allegiances were challenged as the tension increased. To blame for all this anxiety was, of course, Lincoln. But Lincoln had his own troubles. He and his wife, Mary, were Southerners by birth, and her half-brothers made it clear that if war came they would take up arms against the United States.

Though national events were careening wildly, daily life in Mississippi and Rhode Island went on fairly normally. Few thought that the country would actually go to war within itself. There would be name-calling and threats and possibly even a skirmish or two, but cooler heads certainly would prevail.

Rhode Island's dashing young governor, William Sprague, had a different view of things. He was ready for the big show offering the services of a regiment of Rhode Island Militia to President Buchanan. Struggling to defuse the situation, Buchanan declined. Sprague felt that war was unavoidable, and he stepped up the manufacturing of war-related materials; should war break out, not only would his diminutive state be ready but it would have a surplus of ordnance. Although claiming to be an ardent Unionist, however, Sprague would use a warship he had personally outfitted to illegally trade arms for cotton during the coming war.

The Greenes watched national events with keen interest, but no one in the family watched as closely as seventeen-year-old Francis (known as Frank). His older brothers were not likely to enter the military, and John wasn't fit for service. The responsibility of carrying on the Greene military legacy was left to Frank.

Caught in the middle of the crisis were Frank's brothers William and twenty-two-year-old George. They had spent five years in the South establishing a successful business, and they were determined that the W. R. Greene Company would weather the coming storm.

At Westmoreland, the story was much the same. Twenty-six-year-old Sam was indispensable to the overseeing of the plantation. Brother Will, a mere fifteen, was neither old enough for the military nor mature enough to assume Sam's duties should he be called away. Their father, William, at fifty, was hardly in a position to join the army; he had a wife and seven daughters to look out for. But in spite of the hardship it meant for the family, both brothers were willing to serve if necessary.

Even as late as November, before Lincoln's inauguration, there seemed plenty of time for a diplomatic solution. Although patriotism suffused men North and South, the prospect of actual war was more a romantic notion than a reality. The prevailing belief in the South was that the North certainly wasn't willing to sacrifice her sons to preserve the Union; conversely, Northerners were convinced that the South wouldn't dare stand up to Northern industry as it turned out weapons of war. Sam, Will, and Frank pondered their futures; but like millions of other

Americans, the events of the next three months would go well beyond anything they could imagine.

The Spark

Like Jefferson Davis and Abraham Lincoln, Major Robert Anderson of the United States Army was a Kentuckian by birth. But unlike Davis and Lincoln, Anderson had never left his native state. Although Anderson owned slaves and loved the South, his loyalty to the United States was above question. Ironically, his father had been a military man who had commanded Fort Moultrie in Charleston Harbor, South Carolina, in the late 1790s. He had unsuccessfully defended Fort Moultrie against the British in 1779, becoming a prisoner of war.

Major Anderson embodied the nation's frustration as it wrestled with its loyalties. Fate would have it that he would inherit the same command as his father; he, too, would not relinquish it without a fight. Until the recent turmoil, Fort Moultrie had been a wonderful assignment. The locals were friendly, and Charleston had the best the South could offer. Restaurants, theaters, and parties provided plenty of social life for Anderson's seventy officers and men. The atmosphere was so pleasant, in fact, that many of the men had brought their families to Charleston.

The men of Fort Moultrie could peer over its walls toward the harbor and the open ocean in search of a hostile navy that didn't exist. The most important of Anderson's duties was to inspect and report on the construction work under way on an abandoned fort in the center of the harbor. Once an imposing presence, Fort Sumter had never been completed; it endured years of neglect because Fort Moultrie could efficiently defend Charleston from a naval attack. If Moultrie was attacked by land, however, the situation would be different altogether; several structures provided high ground for sharpshooters to pick off the men defending inside. Anderson knew that Fort Moultrie could not be held if an attack came from Charleston itself.

Until Lincoln's election, the fort's vulnerability hadn't been a major concern to Anderson. But during the early part of December, Anderson's relationship with the people of Charleston began to deteriorate. Anderson's second-in-command, Captain Abner Doubleday, experienced the change in attitude when he was treated rudely on a visit to the Charleston Hotel, where he frequently dined. It was decided that the Federal troops should remain within the relatively safe confines of the fort until the political climate settled.

Federal soldiers throughout the South faced similar hostility. Soldiers who had enlisted from Southern states were considering resignation and the defense of their home states. With Christmas of 1860 less than a week away, Anderson continued to gaze at Sumter.

It wasn't until late afternoon or evening of 20 December that most people received the news being telegraphed around the country. Governor Pickens and the people of South Carolina had declared themselves an independent nation and ordered all United States forces to withdraw or surrender to the government in South Carolina. Like a death following a prolonged illness, the news was not entirely unexpected; yet it was a shock to most of the country.

Of particular annoyance to South Carolina was the presence of Anderson's men in Charleston. A United States military presence there made secession something of a farce. Anderson and his men would be requested to leave or face forceful eviction. Either way, they would have to go.

America prepared for the holiday anxiously. For the first time, the possibility of war seemed real. Although it was presumed that any conflict would be brief, if war came there would be casualties, and for many families the Christmas of 1861 might be very different.

The prospect of South Carolina's standing alone against the United States was unlikely. Should a number of states secede they would have to form a coalition government, at least temporarily, to facilitate a common defense. In Vicksburg, Mississippi, United States Senator Jefferson Davis had much on his mind. Davis was a hero of the Mexican War and a statesman who was universally respected. The possibility loomed that the unenviable task of presiding over a "nation of necessity" would fall to him.

William Barksdale had been busy. An outspoken advocate of secession and publisher of a pro-slavery newspaper prior to his service in the Mexican War, Barksdale was representing Mississippi in the United States House of Representatives as a Democrat. A war of rebellion seemed inevitable to him, and the only question was when or where it would start. Barksdale was convinced that Mississippi and the South would be victorious if they were willing to sacrifice everything.

Major Anderson and his men prepared for a siege, though it was obvious that they could put up little more than token resistance from Fort Moultrie. Anderson awaited instructions from Washington; Buchanan, hoping to ride out the last few weeks of his presidency, remained passive, though it was clear that the nation was coming apart at its seams.

Journalists around the world wrote about Anderson and his men with morbid fascination. Some portrayed Anderson as a tragic hero of Shakespearean proportions. With only a couple of days remaining before Christmas, the men of Moultrie were living a fishbowl-like existence. Although not everyone in Charleston was an enemy (some, in fact, were friends and feared for the garrison's safety), most agreed that Anderson and his men should simply go home.

On Christmas night, while Charlestonians celebrated and partook of their holiday feasts, a collection of boats assembled at Fort Moultrie's pier. Under the cover of darkness, Anderson's men and their families boarded. When all had been accounted for, the boats began a silent journey to Fort Sumter in the center of Charleston Harbor.

At Sumter, the men and their families prayed and celebrated as the flag of the United States was run up the flagpole. At dawn, the people of Charleston were shocked and horrified at Anderson's perceived treachery. Although Sumter was surrounded by water and there were no means to provision it without exposing supply ships to crippling, even fatal, fire from the shore, South Carolina viewed Anderson's move as an act of aggression. Even President Buchanan was outraged by Anderson's move; he felt that his hand was being forced. The South Carolina Militia swiftly seized Moultrie and its arsenal of twenty thousand rifles. Louisiana, Texas, Georgia, Alabama, Florida, and Mississippi made preparations for secession and war. Frank Greene and Sam and Will Postlethwaite followed events through their local newspapers, the Providence Journal and the Woodville Republican.

The government of Mississippi convened in an emergency session during the first week of 1861. On 9 January, Mississippi seceded from the United States; William Barksdale was named quartermaster general of the Army of the State of Mississippi. Florida seceded the next day. On 11 January, Alabama left the Union. Georgia, Louisiana, and Texas soon joined the parade of states declaring their independence from the United States.

CHAPTER THREE

Rush to Glory

At the Boston Public Library, I obtained a list of every newspaper in Mississippi. I composed another form letter and spent a rainy April afternoon sitting on my living room floor, stuffing envelopes. Having had no experience in dealing with the media, I doubted that my letter would actually appear in any of these papers. To my surprise, the majority did print my letter, and I began to receive phone calls and letters from places completely foreign to me: Hattiesburg, Natchez, and Jackson, Mississippi, and others. Some newspapers had put their own title over the letter: "Do You Know Soldier Sam?"; "Who Is Sam Postlethwaite?"; "Seeking Descendants of Sam Postlethwaite." Mississippi's biggest newspaper, the Jackson Clarion-Ledger, *carried my query in its "Ask Jack Sunn" column, which ended with the message, "Good Luck."*

As I began hearing Mississippi accents over my telephone, it dawned on me that I was venturing into a world that I knew little about. One thing was clear: the people who called or wrote to me were passionate about their heritage. For the first time, I was asked what I was doing and, more importantly, "Why?"

The correspondence my efforts had spawned was confusing initially. I listened to and read family histories unrelated to my subject; nearly everyone I spoke with was adamant about the correct pronunciation of "Postlethwaite," and the variations seemed endless. Only much later would I realize how much I had learned about Mississippi life in general from these exchanges.

Word of my research spread throughout Mississippi and even spilled over into Louisiana. My "shots in the dark" paid off when one afternoon I found a large manila envelope stuffed into my mailbox. Alexander Lathrop Postlethwaite, an eighty-year-old resident of Baton Rouge, had heard of my efforts from a friend in Mississippi. Alex's envelope contained a Postlethwaite family genealogy titled "The Postlethwaites In America."

Alex had been stunned when he'd learned the identity of this lost soldier, and he was determined to help. Alex is Sam's cousin, the last surviving male of their branch of the family tree. "I know exactly who he was," he later told a reporter. "He was the grandson of Samuel and Anne Dunbar. I never knew what happened to him. I thought he may have been lost out on the battlefield somewhere." Alex had been recently widowed, and Sam's plight would become a diversion for him. Through our letters, an ongoing friendship began to evolve. Although I was cheered to have an ally, Alex was soon to be as frustrated as I was in trying to resolve the issue of this forgotten grave.

Another friendship was born on a cold, dreary Saturday afternoon when temptation got the better of me. I contacted the National Archives where personal service records of Civil War soldiers are available. By doing so, I received Sam's military records and was struck by two items. The first was that Sam was shot "through the lungs" at a place called Malvern Hill, Virginia. The second was a mention of another place: Woodville, Mississippi, population 1,200. It was in this small town, relatively unchanged in 130 years, that Sam had joined the Confederate forces.

Dialing directory assistance for Mississippi, I asked for the number of the Woodville Town Hall. A pleasant voice greeted me from the town hall, and I nervously asked if there was anyone there with whom I could talk about the Civil War. I was politely informed that the war was more appropriately referred to as "The War of Northern Aggression," and that there was indeed someone I should talk to.

I called Mrs. James Gross at her home and told her about Sam, then I asked a series of naive questions. I was impressed by the amount of time "Honey," as friends and family call her, spent with me as she began walking me through Mississippi military history. Her enthusiasm cheered me, and we began corresponding on a regular basis; she would eventually spend countless hours researching for me. Everyone involved with Mississippi history knew Honey, and her modesty belied her tenacity. Proving the power of one, she has challenged developers, brought about the relocation of cemeteries, marked dozens of Civil War graves, and as a member of The United Daughters of the Confederacy, impressed upon countless audiences the importance of historic preservation.

After my initial conversation with Honey, I wrote the first of what became a series of letters to the owner of Greenwood Cemetery. In it I explained the historical significance of a Confederate soldier's burial there and asked if he would bring this matter to the attention of the present owner of Sam's lot. I didn't receive a reply.

ANDERSON AND HIS MEN FOUND THEIR NEW HOME TO BE comfortable and stocked with an adequate supply of food and ordnance. Unsure of their loyalties, Anderson sent the construction workers away; he also established written communication with Charleston. His primary concern was to negotiate the safe passage of his men's families out of the area.

Negotiating sessions with the dignitaries of Charleston were surprisingly cordial. At one meeting, the Charlestonians noticed that Anderson's supply of cigars was almost depleted. On their next visit, they presented Anderson with boxes of cigars and several cases of claret. Even the daily mail went uninterrupted. The wives and children were allowed to leave for the safety of the North. Despite this good will, however, Anderson wouldn't leave his post.

In command of the growing military presence in Charleston was West Point graduate Pierre Beauregard. Beauregard and Anderson had much in common. Both had been wounded in the Mexican War, and they knew each other well from West Point, where Beauregard had been Anderson's most gifted artillery student.

President Buchanan finally took some action, deciding to reinforce the fort and send provisions. General Scott convinced the president that the increased firepower on the shoreline would make it difficult to safely send a warship into the harbor. It was agreed that a civilian vessel would sail unprotected into Charleston Harbor and land two hundred fresh troops at Fort Sumter. The ship chosen for this mission was the *Star of the West*, a side-wheeler that would be impossible to mistake for a warship.

On 9 January, the *Star of the West* tentatively entered the harbor and was promptly greeted by Beauregard's artillery. She was struck twice but managed to stay out of range of most of the guns. After several failed attempts to reach Sumter, the *Star of the West* turned back for the safety of the Atlantic. Anderson and his men could only watch as their relief faded into the distance. Doubleday was distraught with Anderson because he hadn't fired on Beauregard to defend a civilian ship flying the flag of the United States.

Not only had Buchanan's plan failed, but his action galvanized the South. Leaders of the seceded states agreed to meet in Montgomery, Alabama, to form a provisional government representing a confederation of Southern states. On 18 February, Jefferson Davis was selected as the first president of the Confederate States of America.

By mid-February, Anderson was forced to reduce his men's rations as they anxiously awaited another attempt at resupply. Wanting action, Doubleday became increasingly impatient and incensed over Anderson's non-confrontational attitude; the fact that Anderson was a Southerner hurt their relationship further. Doubleday felt that, once hostilities commenced, warships of the United States Navy would force their way into the harbor and reinforce the fort. If Sumter fired on Charleston, the navy would have to come to the garrison's aid. As for Anderson, he was determined not to start a civil war. Meanwhile, the people of both the North and South became increasingly obsessed with the men of Sumter, following their plight daily in the newspapers.

On 4 March, under threat of assassination, Abraham Lincoln was sworn in as president of the United States. One of Lincoln's first acts was to order Anderson to hold the fort. As March began, anti-secessionists in the South vainly pleaded their case. In Virginia, an editorial in the *Christian Banner* went so far as to question the validity of Jefferson Davis' presidency:

> Who elected Davis? Was the popular vote of the six seceding states taken? Look at it. And now we are urged to fly for refuge to this newly created confederacy of six states, without having any voice in our representation, either in Congress or as to the President! Thank God, all freemen are not sold yet (Swanberg, 1957).

In Mississippi, the *Corinth Advisor* warned of military defeat should war break out and accused the new government of having "so exasperated the already burdened tax-payers as to only require a leader to induce them to resist the collection of the tax."

An editorial in the *Charleston Mercury* urged the population of the city:

> . . . keep cool and bide your time. The honor of this state is no further involved in this matter. It has been transferred to the shoulders of the government of The Confederate States of America, whether wisely or not, it is too late to discuss. War six weeks ago might have placed Virginia now by our side. War would have been in the name of the State of South Carolina. The glory, prestige, and historical fame would have been hers. It is no longer so. The blood will be hers; but little of the profit (Swanberg, 1957).

Those favoring secession used Lincoln's inaugural address in their argument and proclaimed the decision to withdraw from the Union irreversible. In the address, Lincoln warned "no state, upon its own mere notion, can lawfully get out of the Union . . . . The power confided in me will be used to hold, occupy and possess the property and places belonging to the government." A Tennessee newspaper claimed that "no man can read the inaugural without coming to the conclusion that it is a declaration of war against the seceding states, and in less than thirty days, if its avowals are carried out, we shall have the clangor of resounding arms, with all its concomitants of death, carnage and woe."

The *Charleston Courier*, for its part, was through debating the issue. "Let the argument proceed to the next logical and necessary steps, an appeal to arms. We are ready!" Newspapers sold like never before, and the opportunity to capitalize on the crisis was not lost on merchants, whose advertisements appeared as mock news stories about Sumter. This advertisement appeared in the *Providence Journal* in early March 1861:

FORT SUMTER NOT TAKEN!
neither is
Cunningham's Emporium!
Furniture, Feathers,
Carpeting, Oil Cloth,
Crockery and China
108, 110 and 112 Broad St.

Lincoln and Davis were lampooned to such a degree in their own nations' newspapers that often they were treated only slightly worse in opposition editorials. Lincoln, with his homely features, was an easy target and routinely got the worst of it.

England followed the newspaper accounts of the collapse of the United States intently; war, after all, could bring her an opportunity to re-establish herself as a power in North America. Great Britain, the greatest naval power in the world, might do for the Confederacy what the Confederacy could not do for itself: provide safe trading passages with Europe and the rest of the world. Of course, there were dangers in such alliances with former foes—particularly for the fledgling Confederate states. But mere recognition of the Confederacy as a sovereign nation by Britain (or France) might cripple the North's attempt to punish the South.

The state of Virginia was caught in a dilemma. Virginia was large, wealthy, and powerful but divided on the issue of secession. The home of many of the United States' founding fathers and the site of many of the first colonial settlements, Virginia had a proud heritage. Although the lifestyle in Virginia was decidedly Southern, with slavery and the plantation economy well established, its geographical position spawned many loyalties to the North. The possibility of Virginia becoming a battleground should it secede was not overlooked by its populace. The Confederacy was no military match for the United States, and the eventual outcome of any conflict seemed obvious. But would Virginians take part in the pummeling of their Southern neighbors?

If Virginia seceded, on the other hand, by taking her industry, militia, and ports, not only would the balance of power be dramatically tipped, but the Potomac River would be all that stood between the Confederate States of America and the White House. Virginia's importance was extolled by one of her congressmen, the bellicose Roger Pryor, who used the streets of Charleston as a stage from which he entertained the locals with promises of his native state's Southern allegiance. Pryor urged the commencement of hostilities, contending that Virginia was only waiting for the seceded states to take the fateful step. A commitment to independence could only be demonstrated through violence. Pryor urged, " . . . if you want Virginia to join you, you must strike a blow!"

Lincoln and Anderson were both facing problems. Several members of Lincoln's cabinet urged the president to surrender the fort in order to preserve the loyalty of Virginia and other border states. Lincoln saw such an action as recognition of the Confederate states and wouldn't hear of it. Anderson suffered the suspicions of his men, who couldn't comprehend his dilemma. Although privately he was in favor of evacuating the fort, he would obey his orders to hold Sumter while at the same time attempting to maintain a delicate peace.

Anderson instructed his men, who were weary and subsisting mainly on potatoes, to man only the guns that were protected by casemates. The biggest guns were on the top tier of the fort, but Anderson considered their positions to be too dangerous for his gunners. He also stressed to his gunners that if the fort came under attack they must demonstrate their prowess by destroying Charleston's gun positions without inflicting civilian casualties. Despite their situation, the morale of Anderson's men was surprisingly high, and they were eager to get on with the fight they expected to begin any day.

As Anderson was preparing his men for a fight, so too was Lincoln. On 6 April, Lincoln dispatched a messenger to the governor of South Carolina:

I am directed by the President of the United States to notify you to expect an attempt will be made to supply Fort Sumter with provisions only, and that if such attempt be not resisted, no effort to throw in men, arms or ammunition, will be made, without further notice, or in case of an attack upon the fort (Swanberg, 1957).

This wouldn't be another *Star of The West* episode. The mood inside the fort was jubilant. But the message altered the crisis and put the Confederacy on the defensive. The United States had made it clear that it would not fire the first shot.

The same day, at Westmoreland, Sam Postlethwaite turned twenty-eight years old.

The Confederate government responded to Lincoln's message by completely isolating Fort Sumter. No mail or supplies of any kind were to be sent to Anderson. Outside the harbor, warships of the U.S. Navy began to gather.

President Davis was aware that, even under the strictest rationing, there was barely enough food in the fort to last three or four days. Anderson certainly wouldn't let his men starve; if not resupplied, he would be forced to surrender the fort within a week. What gave Davis pause was the prospect of Lincoln's navy storming into Charleston Harbor, reinforcing the fort, and demolishing Beauregard's artillery. Such a humiliating defeat could crush the spirit of the new nation and bring it to its knees.

Davis decided that his only option was to strike first. His secretary of state, Robert Toombs, however, was nearly hysterical in his opposition to an attack on Fort Sumter:

Mr. President, at this time it is suicide, murder, and will lose us every friend at the North. You will wantonly strike a hornet's nest which extends from mountain to ocean, and legions now quiet will swarm out and sting us to death. It is unnecessary. It puts us in the wrong. It is fatal (Ward, 1990).

Unconvinced, Davis notified Beauregard of his decision. Shortly after midnight on 12 April, Beauregard sent Roger Pryor and a delegation of dignitaries out to the fort. The mood on both sides was somber. Anderson was politely informed that he had until 4 A.M. to surrender the fort. Anderson displayed compassion for his former friends, but to their disappointment he declined and graciously wished them well as they returned to their boats. "If we never meet again in this world may we meet again in a better one," Anderson consoled. With no sign of the U.S. Navy coming to his aid, Anderson resigned himself to waiting for the American Civil War to begin. Events were now controlling the men who had created them.

As desperate as the situation seemed, Lincoln had shrewdly created the scenario he had hoped for. "You can have no conflict without being yourself the aggressor," he had promised the South. As the plight of Sumter's men was played up in newspapers throughout the North, Lincoln needn't have worried about raising the troops he would need to wage war.

At 4:30 A.M., on 12 April 1861, Roger Pryor was offered the honor of firing the first shot at Fort Sumter. But Pryor couldn't bring himself to do the work that for weeks he had been urging others to do. The honor instead went to an elderly secessionist, Edmund Ruffin. One of the first rounds fired at the fort smashed into its five-foot-thick walls only a few feet from where Doubleday was sleeping. As Anderson had given his men strict orders to remain in their quarters until reveille, Doubleday contemptuously ignored the blast.

To many observers, the early spring morning resembled a Fourth of July celebration, as batteries from several points along the shoreline poured shot and shell into the small target in the harbor's center. One shell burst over the fort, creating an image of the palmetto tree, symbol of South Carolina, against the dark sky. For the next two hours, Sumter would sit mute and defenseless.

As the sun emerged, the firing intensified. Amid the din of steady bombardment, reveille was sounded at 6 A.M.

With remarkable cool, the men breakfasted on the last rations of meat, which Anderson had saved for such a moment, and water. Beauregard's batteries continued to hammer the silent fort. Spectators lining the shore and rooftops of the city were beginning to wonder if Sumter would put up a fight at all. Rumors spoke of Sumter's imminent surrender and a failed mutiny by Doubleday. Word of Anderson's resignation spread throughout Charleston. However, Beauregard knew Anderson too well not to expect a fight, and a good one.

At 7:30 A.M., any lingering doubts about their commander evaporated when the men of Sumter were ordered to their posts. Their feelings of anxiety and helplessness were swept away by a rush of excitement. As if to make a point, Anderson asked Doubleday if he would accept the honor of firing the first shot in defense of the United States. Fort Sumter rumbled and its first shell screeched across the harbor. Many in the crowd in Charleston cheered. The American Civil War had begun.

Both teacher and prize pupil were at their best, and their artillery demonstration continued throughout the morning and afternoon. Anderson's men destroyed several Confederate batteries, but Beauregard's guns began reducing Fort Sumter to rubble, setting it ablaze. Within the fort, men were as busy fighting fires as they were working their guns. A fire burned near the fort's main magazine, where dozens of barrels of powder were stored. Disobeying orders, one of Anderson's men manned one of the bigger guns on the exposed parapet. There was no sign of the U.S. Navy.

At one point, Sumter's flagpole was shot away, and Beauregard sent a delegation to the fort under a flag of truce to accept a surrender. Anderson explained that there had been a misunderstanding, and the Stars and Stripes were promptly run up another pole. Unsatisfied, the Southerners departed and the battle resumed.

Although Sumter's gunners carefully selected their targets, Doubleday settled a personal grievance by sending a ball through the roof of the Charleston Hotel

(Moultrie House). There were no injuries. Anderson's men fought in three shifts; their supply of enthusiasm, however, exceeded that of their powder. By dusk, Sumter had fallen silent. Beauregard's firing became sporadic, but through the night his batteries continued to punish the burning target in the harbor.

At dawn, the crowds on the shore could still see Anderson's flag flying through the thick black smoke billowing from the fort. The Confederate gunners had hoped to see a white flag. The performance of Anderson's men brought quiet admiration from their opponents. What was the scene within the fort? How many casualties would have to be inflicted before Anderson gave up? The answer came as Sumter awoke from its slumber to fire a fusillade of iron across the harbor. Civilians, and even some Confederate gunners, cheered.

The navy's attempt to aid Anderson was hampered by rough seas that prevented warships from entering the harbor. The situation inside Sumter was becoming apocalyptic. Thick black smoke hovered a few feet above the floor, forcing the men to operate the guns on their hands and knees. Doubleday recalled the situation:

> One fifth of the fort was on fire, and the wind drove the smoke in dense masses into the angle where we had all taken refuge. It seemed impossible to escape suffocation. Some lay down close to the ground with handkerchiefs over their mouths, and others posted themselves near the embrasures where the smoke was somewhat lessened by the draught of air . . . . Had not a slight change of wind taken place, the result might have been fatal to most of us. Our firing having ceased and the enemy being very jubilant, I thought it would be well to show them that we were not all dead yet, and ordered the gunners to fire a few rounds more. The scene at this time was really terrific. The roaring and crackling of the flames, the dense mass of

whirling smoke, the bursting of the enemy's shells
and our own which were exploding in the burning
rooms, the crashing of the shot, and the sound of
masonry falling in every direction, made the fort a
pandemonium (Swanberg, 1957).

Fort Sumter had been struck more than three thousand
times. Still, within the fort there was no panic. By noon,
however, Sumter was spent, making only token responses
to the onslaught, then falling into silence. With every shot
fired by the men of Sumter, the crowds in Charleston let
out a cheer as they watched the fort struggle for life.

There was no honor in battering a defenseless adversary,
and one man could no longer stand the mismatch. Without
authorization, former Texas senator and ardent secessionist
Louis Wigfall rowed out to the fort under the cover of smoke
and entered carrying a white flag. Wigfall found Anderson
exhausted, covered with dirt and soot, but with pride
intact. "Let us quit this!" Wigfall pleaded. In surrendering
the fort, Anderson sought two conditions: the safe passage
of his men out of Charleston and the honor of taking down
the flag of the United States.

Both sides were astonished to learn that neither side had
suffered a single serious casualty. Anderson complimented
some of Beauregard's gunners on their work. There were
some hard feelings regarding Doubleday's firing on the
Moultrie House, and an explanation was demanded.
Doubleday took responsibility for the incident; his reasoning
was deemed acceptable and the matter was dropped.

Newspapermen began arriving at the fort, and by
Sunday afternoon the harbor was filled with sightseeing
boats. A reporter from the *Providence Journal*
telegraphed:

All the officers and the men look hearty, appear
to be well fed, and to have plenty of provisions.
Anderson said he expected help from the
Carolinians in putting out his fire. This he said was

nothing more than usual in civilized warfare. He was likewise surprised that there was no evidence of bloodshed—best evidence of skill (1861-1865).

On Sunday, 14 April, at half past one in the afternoon, Anderson and his men gathered at the center of Fort Sumter to lower their flag. A ship bound for New York waited for them at Sumter's dock. As they slowly lowered the flag, Sumter's gunners fired a fifty-gun salute. In the cruelest of ironies, one of the guns exploded. One man, according to the *Providence Journal*, was "tossed into the air, and came down a mass of mangled humanity." Another man was taken to a hospital in Charleston, where he died a few hours later. With the fort's flag in his possession, Anderson boarded the vessel that would take his command safely out of Charleston Harbor. The men watched as the smoking ruin in the harbor slowly faded into the distance.

From Woodville to Warwick, news of the battle rocked America like no other single event in its young history. The fates of Frank Greene and Sam and Will Postlethwaite were sealed. Men throughout both nations began to put their personal affairs in order.

Why Don't They Come?

On 15 April, President Lincoln called for seventy-five thousand volunteers for a three-month enlistment to suppress the "insurrection." General Scott, too old for a field command, tendered his resignation. President Lincoln offered the command of the entire United States Army to Robert E. Lee, a Virginian. Although Lee opposed secession, he informed Lincoln that he would accept the command only if Virginia stayed loyal to the Union. But within days of Lincoln's call for troops, Arkansas, Tennessee, North Carolina, and Virginia seceded from the United States. In a meeting with

Lincoln's secretary of war, Simon Cameron, Lee resigned from the U.S. Army; he left the meeting in tears.

When a young girl from a Northern state wrote to Lee requesting a photograph, Lee eerily echoed the prophecy of John Brown in his reply: "I should like, above all things, that our difficulties might be peaceably arranged . . . I foresee that the country will have to pass through a terrible ordeal, a necessary expiation perhaps for our national sins." Lee accepted a command with his home state, assuming the responsibility of organizing the Virginia State Militia.

Upon the secession of Virginia, a western portion of the state, Kanawha, seceded from Virginia, entering U.S. statehood as West Virginia. At last, all allegiances were decided. As John Brown had predicted before his execution, the crimes of the nation were about to be "purged away but with blood."

Although it was one of the chief proponents of secession, Mississippi found itself ill-prepared for conflict; twenty thousand volunteers were denied entry into military service because there weren't enough rifles. This was not the case in Rhode Island. Governor Sprague had responded promptly to Lincoln's call for volunteers, and on Thursday, 18 April, a battery of artillery from the Rhode Island 1st Regiment left Providence on the steamer *Empire State*, bound for Jersey City. The scene of departure was quite a spectacle as thousands of Rhode Islanders crammed the shores of Narragansett Bay to glimpse their fathers, brothers, and sons going off to war. The men aboard the transport waved as bands played and cannon boomed across the water. Over the next few days ten companies of infantry made the same voyage.

Sprague ordered the state treasurer to raise $500,000 to outfit Rhode Island troops. Determined to make Rhode Island's representation in the coming conflict an impressive one, he even spent part of his personal fortune on uniforms and materials.

The command of the 1st Rhode Island Regiment was awarded to thirty-seven-year-old Ambrose Burnside.

Colonel Burnside had graduated from West Point in 1847 and had seen action in the West, where he had been wounded in a battle with Apaches. After leaving the military, Burnside had become involved in the manufacture of firearms, and when the war began he was employed by the Illinois Central Railroad. When summoned to Rhode Island to take command, he and Governor Sprague quickly selected officers from an impressive list of Rhode Island's most distinguished gentlemen. Among those chosen were attorney Sullivan Ballou of Smithfield (a political ally of Simon Henry Greene) and Mexican War veteran John Slocum. After disembarking in New Jersey, the 1st Rhode Island traveled by train to Baltimore, where it would begin its march to a nervous Washington, D.C.; Confederate artillery was already in position along the Potomac River. Maryland was officially a Union state, but there was a tremendous outpouring of Confederate sympathy in Baltimore. On 19 April, a regiment from Massachusetts was attacked by an angry mob when it arrived in the city. Rocks were thrown and shots fired, and when the melee was over several rioters and four soldiers lay dead. The telegraph line that ran from Washington through Maryland to the North was cut, effectively isolating Washington from the rest of the Union. Staring through a White House window, Lincoln wondered aloud if any of the troops he had called for were on their way: "Why don't they come?" he muttered.

The men of the 1st Rhode Island marched along the same route where the Massachusetts men had been attacked; they were showered with obscenities and threats. But the trek turned out to be largely uneventful, and during the first week of May the regiment entered Washington. Regiments from throughout the North had been pouring into the city daily, and accommodations varied from awkward to nonexistent. The Rhode Island men encamped in the most unusual of places, the U.S. Patent Office. The men passed empty hours perusing the exhibits and took particular delight whenever an invention that had originated in Rhode Island was found. After a few days at the Patent Office, the 1st Rhode Island secured a field on which it could set up camp. Burnside dubbed the field "Camp Sprague." For the next few months, this grass field was home to one thousand Rhode Island men.

One of the first regiments to arrive in Washington was the 11th New York under the command of Elmer Ellsworth. Ellsworth was one of America's most promising young men. Born in poverty, he had achieved much in his twenty-four years; for a time, he had worked as an apprentice attorney in Abraham Lincoln's law office in Illinois, and a father-son relationship had developed.

Upon his arrival in the city, Ellsworth noticed a Confederate flag flying over a hotel called the Marshall House. The young colonel personally removed the flag from the roof of the building. As he descended a staircase, still holding the flag, Ellsworth was shot to death by the building's owner. When the news of the murder reached the White House, Lincoln wept openly, and Confederate and Union flags alike were flown at half-mast.

Having been successful in enlisting seventy-five thousand men for three months of service, on 3 May, Lincoln called for yet more troops. The period of service required from this next group of volunteers would be a full three years. Governor Sprague commissioned Major John Slocum, surgeon Frank Wheaton, and Major Sullivan Ballou to organize another regiment, the 2nd Rhode Island. Some of the officers of the 1st Rhode Island resigned their positions to join the 2nd.

During the following week, hundreds of would-be volunteers stood before Slocum and Wheaton. On 5 June, a fair-skinned, blue-eyed young man filled out an enlistment form for Slocum's approval. He stood five feet seven inches tall and had brown hair. When asked his occupation, the enlistee explained that he worked as a clerk in his father's business. Two weeks shy of his nineteenth birthday, Frank Greene became Private Greene of the 2nd Rhode Island Regiment.

Courtesy of Rosalind Colley of Barrington, R.I.

*Believed to be Frank Greene, brother
of William Rogers Greene.*

By 8 June, the 2nd Rhode Island had been formed and outfitted. Private Greene was assigned to Company H (consisting of thirty to one hundred men), which was commanded by Captain Charles Greene (no relation to Frank); it was made up mostly of men from the East Greenwich area. The regiment camped on a field in Providence dubbed "Camp Burnside" by now-Colonel Slocum. The men attended services at the First Baptist Church, at the base of College Hill, on 9 June. That same week the regiment met at Exchange Place to pay tribute to Stephen Douglas, who had died a few days earlier.

Many citizens of Rhode Island presented gifts to local military units they had adopted. The gifts came in the form of cash and material goods, such as the rubber overcoats the men of Frank's company received. One of the more stirring moments of the 2nd Rhode Island's encampment in Providence came on the evening of 12 June, when the mayor of Providence, Jabez Knight, presented the regimental colors to Colonel Slocum. In his presentation, Mayor Knight declared that the regimental flag was a gift from the ladies of Providence and:

in receiving them, you pledge yourselves to be firm and true to every duty, and by them to live, and for them, if necessary, to die . . . . Wave them in triumph and in defense of the right, and bring them back with you, though they may be tattered and torn in the heat and strife of conflict. May God bless and protect you! (Woodbury, 1875).

In his acceptance, Colonel Slocum remarked that he did not intend to make a speech but would rather wait until the 2nd returned victorious from the field of battle. On 16 June, the entire regiment attended a deeply moving service performed by Bishop Clark, the Episcopal Bishop of Rhode Island, at Grace Church. This Mass held greater meaning than usual because the regiment was to break camp and depart for Washington within three days.

What More Should a Man Desire?

As in the North, the sons of poor and wealthy families alike offered up their sons for the cause of the Confederacy. At Westmoreland, William Postlethwaite had amassed a fortune equivalent to nearly 3 million in today's dollars. His eldest son, Sam, had a personal worth of twenty-five thousand dollars. William's sons were eager to enlist in the local volunteer regiments that were forming in Woodville and St. Francisville. All families in West Feliciana Parish felt it their duty to offer their sons in defense of the new nation. The debate over secession had passed; several of the Postlethwaites had moved to the North when Mississippi and Louisiana seceded. But whether the remaining Postlethwaites were privately anti-secession no longer mattered, as Lincoln would soon bring the war directly to them.

On 21 May, young Will Postlethwaite made the eight-mile trek from Westmoreland to Woodville and joined Carnot Posey's Wilkinson (county) Rifles. On his application, Will claimed his height to be five feet nine inches, and he lied about his age. Posey, well over six feet tall and handsome, looked the part of a soldier. At forty-two, he was a successful lawyer and planter. Like so many of his contemporaries he was a veteran of the Mexican War, having served under Jefferson Davis in the Mississippi 1st Regiment. As a young lieutenant, Posey had been wounded during the battle of Buena Vista. After the war, he served as United States district attorney for the Southern District of Mississippi. When the Confederacy was formed, he had been retained in the same position by Jefferson Davis.

Shortly after the organization of the Wilkinson Rifles, the men of the company elected Posey captain. Three days later, as if not to be upstaged by his little brother (who had probably defied his father's wishes), Sam left Westmoreland for Woodville, where William Lindsay Brandon was forming a company. At sixty years of age, Brandon was still an intimidating figure. Cut from the hardiest of Mississippi stock, Brandon's demeanor was purely military. Joined by men of Warren and Claiborne counties, Sam became one of Brandon's Jefferson Davis Guards. He declared his residence to be Woodville, his marital status single, and his occupation that of a planter. At twenty-six, with no dependents, he had the background to make an ideal soldier.

As May turned to June, Will and Sam's days passed like those of Frank Greene in Rhode Island. Men who had never used a firearm were taught their intricacies. The simple arts of cooking and sewing were pursued, with mixed results. Learning how to march and construct shelters was as difficult for some as doing laundry was for others. A common distaste for the bayonet was acquired by soldiers North and South, who sometimes reduced it to a serviceable cooking utensil.

There were benefits to being a soldier. Gifts were plentiful, usually consisting of food, clothing, and equipment. And, of course, there were the girls. The attention bestowed upon these local "Johnnies" and "Billies" by young girls and women made soldiering rather bearable.

The men fortunate enough to have acquired or been issued some sort of uniform were particularly admired.

The more modest soldiers didn't quite know what to make of their new status. One man of the 2nd Rhode Island was granted a pass before departing for Washington. While enjoying time off in Rhode Island, he was under orders to stay in uniform and to wear his belt and cartridge box at all times. The humble soldier described this predicament as one he "did not like." For most men, the biggest frustration was, quite simply, discipline—being told what to do and when to do it. Many of them had never been away from home for an extended period of time and were homesick. To be just a few miles from home and not allowed to leave camp tested their commitment.

As with the men of the 2nd Rhode Island, Brandon's Jefferson Davis Guards and Posey's Wilkinson Rifles soon found the novelty of soldiering wearing thin. Their biggest nemesis was boredom. While the Rhode Islanders' spirits were raised by orders to set off to Washington, the men of Brandon's Jeff Davis Guards were still waiting for something to do in mid-June.

About the time of the 2nd Rhode Island's departure for Washington, Will Postlethwaite and the rest of Carnot Posey's men were transported by steamer to New Orleans. The *New Orleans Picayune* reported the company's arrival:

> Gallant Old Wilkinson. We are glad to welcome the arrival of the Wilkinson Rifles, from Woodville, Miss., under the command of Capt. Carnot Posey. This is a picked company of Mississippians, numbering 100 men rank and file, arrived here on the steamer 'J. A. Cotton', and left by the Jackson Railroad to rendezvous at Corinth. Every man eager for the Fray (Posey Family Scrapbook.)

Arriving in Corinth, Mississippi, the Wilkinson Rifles and ten other companies were incorporated into state service as a regiment, the 16th Mississippi Infantry. As part of the 16th, the Wilkinson Rifles were more commonly referred to by their designation as Company K. At Corinth, two honors were bestowed upon Posey: first was his promotion to colonel in overall command of the regiment; the second was the naming of the regiment's camp as "Camp Posey." On 27 May, the 16th Mississippi Infantry was mustered into the service of the Confederate States of America. The fate of Will Postlethwaite was now in the hands of President Jefferson Davis. Sam and Will wouldn't cross paths again for several months.

The Jefferson Davis Guards were about to be mustered into state service as well, although they remained in the Woodville area. Sam's company was absorbed into the 21st Mississippi Infantry Regiment commanded by Colonel Benjamin Humphreys. The Jefferson Davis Guards were now to be known simply as Company D.

Richmond, Virginia, was now officially the Confederate capital, and like its counterpart to the north it bustled with activity. Thousands of troops and trainloads of supplies poured into the city daily. The suddenly bulging populations of the two capitals created many problems, the most serious being lack of sanitation. The Potomac and James rivers, the main sources of water, were becoming sewers. The most efficient killer of the Civil War, disease, began claiming victims in both armies.

In both cities, the presence of armies attracted the unsavory elements of society. Thieves, prostitutes, and hustlers of all types seized the opportunity to apply their trades. They took advantage of the young recruits, many of whom had never been away from home before. A private earning thirteen dollars per month had to watch his money closely.

Unable to lure Robert E. Lee, Lincoln appointed Major General Irvin McDowell commander of the Army of the Potomac, as the mob of volunteers was called. McDowell was a man of good character, but he had never commanded a division in the field before. Lincoln intended the North's conduct of the war to be outlined by Winfield

Scott, who was now his top military advisor, and executed by McDowell. As McDowell organized the defenses around Washington, he warned Lincoln that the assorted regiments of volunteers from around the North were by no means an army. But Lincoln, eager to avenge Fort Sumter, would tolerate no delay in bringing war to the South. He told McDowell that the Southern army was "green also."

McDowell's Confederate counterpart was General Joseph Johnston. Johnston was a fighter. Having served in the Mexican and Seminole wars, he'd been wounded so many times that he joked about it. Johnston led a force of approximately ten thousand men into the Shenandoah Valley west of Washington. He ordered General Beauregard to position a force of more than twenty thousand along a stream south of the Union capital. This stream, called Bull Run, was within a day's march of Washington. Although these two armies posed no immediate threat to Washington, their strategy forced McDowell to divide his army, thus reducing his numerical advantage. Union General Robert Patterson and twenty thousand Union troops were sent west to keep General Johnston at bay.

The dawn of Wednesday, 19 June, revealed two steamships docked at Fox Point in Providence Harbor. These vessels, the *Kill Von Kull* and the *State of Maine*, awaited the arrival of Frank Greene and the 2nd Rhode Island Regiment. Bishop Clark addressed the soldiers at Exchange Place (today's Kennedy Plaza) and wished them success in the coming campaign. For the first time, the regiment marched in full gear, the men's heavy knapsacks loaded with provisions; they struggled down South Main Street to the wharf. Governor Sprague and Bishop Clark accompanied the regiment on its journey to Washington. Once aboard the steamships, the men received a ration of fatty corned beef, which some promptly threw overboard.

At Elizabeth, New Jersey, the regiment boarded a train bound for Baltimore. A great deal of anxiety preceded the regiment's march through the streets of Baltimore. The mood became grim when the men were issued ammunition before entering the city. Having left weeping and cheering loved ones a mere twenty-four hours before, the Rhode Island men were welcomed by a strikingly different scene in Maryland. The march took the 2nd through what seemed an endless series of neighborhoods, each filled with angry residents shouting obscenities from sidewalks and buildings that lined the route. But apart from the verbal abuse the men had to endure, the march through Baltimore was without incident. On Saturday morning, under cloudy skies, Frank Greene, who had been promoted to corporal on 19 June 1861, entered the nation's capital with his weary comrades.

With a little more than one month remaining in their three-month enlistment, the men of Burnside's 1st Rhode Island cheered the arrival of their Rhode Island friends and welcomed them into Camp Sprague. The men of the 1st sought friends for gifts from home or news of Rhode Island. On an adjacent field, Frank Greene and the 2nd Rhode Island went to work setting up "Camp Clark." The initial excitement of their arrival in Washington was short-lived; it soon became evident that the army was in no hurry to meet the enemy. Instead of fighting, the men were faced with the task of turning Camp Clark into a town of one thousand residents. Engineers began constructing streets, woodsmen chopped down trees, and carpenters began building small living quarters.

Soon the camp had its own economy as men bartered and sold personal belongings and rations. Many of the men spent their private hours reading or writing letters. Others gathered in groups to pray, or, as often was the case, to gamble. Soldiers who obtained passes to visit the city could frequent the libraries, museums, and houses of worship that lined the mud-filled streets. The city life of Washington was a startling change for a soldier from Warwick, Rhode Island, which was a collection of villages with a total population of less than ten thousand. For some soldiers, their sojourn in Washington was an opportunity to patronize the many saloons and brothels not far from the White House.

The 2nd Rhode Island, as was the case with the 16th and 21st Mississippi, consisted to a great extent of decent, honorable men, and disciplinary problems were not as prevalent as in many other regiments. Later in the war, homesickness, supply shortages, fear, and disease would cause discipline and morale problems in all regiments, but in June 1861, a soldier's life was an ideal one. Many of the men were thrilled at the opportunity to travel, and the poor man enjoyed better food and clothing than he had in civilian life. One man from Posey's 16th Mississippi wrote, tongue in cheek:

> It is a queer life we lead here, yet not unpleasant. We have become accustomed to our tents, and often wonder why houses were invented. The multiplication of conveniences and luxuries has multiplied human wants and tastes without materially increasing human comforts. A man never realizes this fact until he has been a soldier a few months, and found within the walls of a tent ten feet square a camp kettle, a knapsack, a frying pan, and a blanket, all the necessities of life. The tent shelters from sun and rain, a blanket and knapsack on the ground make as comfortable a bed as one ever slept soundly upon; the camp kettle makes our coffee, and the frying pan cooks our bacon and bread. The fresh air hardens our constitutions, prevents cold, and gives us health, while the pure mountain streams supply water, cool and delicious. What more should man desire? (Dobbins, 1988).

For Sam, Will, and Frank, the monotonous routine of camp life was made bearable by the anticipation of what all expected to be the first and final battle of the "Second War of Independence" or the "War of the Rebellion." Yet when and where this battle would take place no one knew.

CHAPTER FOUR

Second to None

Nineteen ninety-two was for me a year of research. At every opportunity, I studied the Civil War, plantation life, and the Postlethwaites and Greenes. I was amazed at how much material had survived the years. I spent scores of bleary-eyed hours looking at microfilm, searching for death notices or as-it-happened reports of battles in various newspapers from around the country. Almost daily, my mailbox contained information or advice from researchers whose paths I had crossed. Occasionally, I was able to provide insight to those who were studying their own ancestors' Civil War experiences.

The Virginia Historical Society has the entire collection of the Confederate Veteran *magazine dating back to the late nineteenth century. Scanning the index for any reference to the 21st and 16th Mississippi infantry regiments or their commanding officers, I copied each pertinent article. The anecdotes and remembrances in the magazine were revealing accounts of soldiering, from the mundane to the heroic.*

I located a Postlethwaite family file that contained hundreds of pages at the Department of Archives and History in Jackson, Mississippi. Several inches thick, this file contained pages from the family Bible that were filled with family information. To my amazement, it even contained a letter written in the 1950s from William Greene's daughter Lenore, who lived in California, to her "cousin," Mary Postlethwaite of Natchez, Mississippi. The letter was quite lengthy, and as I sat reading it in the spring afternoon sun my heart raced when I read Lenore's stories of her parents' "civil war romance" and how they had buried "Uncle Sam" in "our lot in Greenwood Cemetery."

Most interesting was a letter to Lenore from a previous owner of Greenwood Cemetery. In the letter, Lee Spencer agreed to take possession of three of the Greene lots in exchange for perpetual care of the grave of Lenore's father. Mr. Spencer went on to mention that Lot 43 contained the remains of a Helen Simmons (Sam's half-sister); he also noted that "there are slight signs of other graves." Mr. Spencer promised that any remains encountered during future burials "would of course be moved to the other [her father's] lot." It was this letter that presented a major dilemma. I wondered how, in the age of "political correctness," news of a Confederate soldier buried in a private cemetery lot would be received by its owner.

The summer of 1993 found me walking in Sam's footsteps in the hills of Maryland and the swamps of Virginia. Williamsburg, Seven Pines, Savage's Station, and Malvern Hill each had its own story to tell. As I drove through Berlin Heights (now Brunswick), Maryland, I felt an eerie sensation. Malvern Hill, with its quiet, open space, haunted me. Even a casual visitor cannot look across that field without sensing tragedy. A fruitless day spent at the Virginia Historical Society trying to find Sam on a list of wounded at Chimborazo Hospital had me

*resigned to the fact that after "The Seven Days" battles
Richmond itself was a hospital.*

*Returning from Virginia, I sought another avenue for
approaching the situation at the cemetery. I wrote to the
American Legion, the Disabled American Veterans, the
Veterans of Foreign Wars, and the Department of Veterans
Affairs, seeking their intervention. Each of these organi-
zations congratulated me for my efforts but could offer
only encouragement. The Department of Veterans Affairs
did, however, offer to issue a bronze grave marker for
Sam, which I gratefully accepted. I'll never forget driving
home one afternoon as "Murph," our mailman, flagged
me down a few houses from my home. "UPS dropped this
package for you at the wrong house. It's real heavy. What
is it?" he asked. Laughing, I could only tell him, "You'll
never believe it!" The marker was stored in my office for
the next two years, often a topic of conversation.*

T HE DIFFERENCES BETWEEN THE UNION AND CONFEDERATE
camps emerged as throngs of troops began to swell
the two capitals. In Camp Clark, there seemed to be an
abundance of everything. The Rhode Islanders received
daily shipments of food, clothing, and a most precious
commodity, ice, from home. In the evening, there were
dress parades and band concerts; the 2nd Rhode Island's
band consisted of twenty-three musicians. These were
grand affairs with national luminaries often in attendance.
In their striking uniforms, the Rhode Islanders were among
the greatest attractions at these ceremonies.

By contrast, most of the Confederate camps were disorganized, poorly equipped, and short on supplies. Many
regiments weren't fully uniformed or had none at all;
others' uniforms closely resembled those of Union regiments. Many Confederate uniforms had buttons of wood
as opposed to the shiny brass of the Northern outfits. The
vegetable dye used in coloring the Confederate uniforms

changed from grey to "butternut" after exposure to spring rains and summer sun. Shortages of shoes and other basic supplies were alarmingly frequent.

The drills of the Army of the Potomac were exercises in excess; there were endless displays of firepower. While daily lessons in the use of arms were often conducted under the supervision of officers who had little military experience, at least there was plenty of ammunition to practice with. These pyrotechnic exhibitions had limited value to the volunteers because correct procedures were rarely followed, and the men's enthusiasm failed to compensate for their lack of experience. Men who had never handled firearms before were a danger to themselves and to those around them. The loading and discharging of artillery and rifles was slow and often executed carelessly. During drills, men became distracted or bored. Even marching proved to be a challenge; a scheduled three-hour march could take hours longer.

In many of the Confederate camps, the soldiers who had been issued guns drilled in much the same manner as Union men; the difference was that they were not issued ammunition, which was already in limited supply. Those without guns marched and labored as they waited for weapons. The initial shortage of firearms wasn't as serious a handicap as it might have been, however; the Confederate volunteers, unlike their Northern counterparts, were mostly outdoorsmen who were well acquainted with firearms. Some even brought their own weapons from home.

The looming conflict coincided with the advent of photography. By the thousands, young men rushed to have their "likenesses" made, parting with a good portion of their pay to have photographs made of them in full uniform, often as they held swords or firearms.

The camps were teeming with newspapermen. To ensure their places in history and to impress their constituents, politicians and celebrities visited camps frequently, promoting themselves in the newspapers back home.

On 24 June, Frank Greene's regiment was reviewed by President Lincoln as it passed the White House. Under Slocum, the volunteers were being transformed into a competent fighting force. The 2nd Rhode Island's soldiers carried a strong sense of pride. Colonel Slocum was liked and respected by his men, who he had promised would be "second to none." Reverend Augustus Woodbury of the 1st Rhode Island remembered, "the future distinction of the 2nd Rhode Island regiment was undoubtedly due to the soldierly character of its first colonel." The men were filled with "pure and conscientious patriotism."

As June came to a close, there was no indication, aside from rumor, that the Army of the Potomac was going anywhere. Lincoln had erred in thinking that his seventy-five thousand three-month volunteers would be ready for action before their term of service had expired. As July began, time was running out and the men were feeling the strain; inactivity was beginning to take its toll in some camps. An explosion in Camp Clark killed two men, devastating the 2nd Rhode Island's morale.

On 4 July, the men of the 2nd celebrated Independence Day as their fates hung undecided. Appropriately, they were entertained by a tightrope walker from Frank's company. Brightening the festivities was news of promotions. Lieutenant Beriah Brown was promoted to captain of Company H, and Frank was named company clerk.

William Rogers Greene and his two brothers were still in St. Louis. Although Missouri and Kentucky struggled to stay out of the looming conflict, the Confederacy and the United States were actively recruiting young men in those states. As the Greenes traveled around the city, they witnessed the bizarre sights of the Wide Awakes and the Minute Men drilling. The Wide Awakes were pro-Union and mostly made up of German immigrants; the Minute Men were pro-secessionists who felt betrayed when Missourians chose not to secede.

After the fall of Fort Sumter, the Illinois Militia, under orders from Lincoln, raided and seized an arsenal of weapons in nearby Kansas City. This intrusion on Missouri soil on behalf of the Federal government swiftly changed the loyalties of thousands who had been pro-Union or undecided. Missouri was one of the few states where instances of brother fighting brother actually occurred.

President Lincoln's growing impatience with Irvin McDowell increased as trainloads of Southern men arrived daily on the south side of the Potomac. Although unlikely, a bold strike by the Confederates against Washington couldn't be ruled out. Aside from a victory over a small Confederate force at Rich Mountain in western Virginia (by General George Brinton McClellan, a rising star), the people of the North had little to cheer about.

The continuing buildup of Beauregard's forces along Bull Run Creek had reached an intolerable level. Lincoln finally ordered McDowell to march into Virginia to sever the Orange & Alexandria Railroad lines at Manassas Junction. At Manassas, one railroad line ran south, deep into the Confederacy; another line branched west into the rich Shenandoah Valley. Although the rank and file of the Army of the Potomac knew nothing of this order, rumors of an impending march circulated daily. A visit to Camp Clark by the president on 11 July only added to the speculation that something was afoot.

While Frank Greene could only speculate on his marching orders, Confederate General Beauregard didn't have to. A young Southern girl gave him a coded message, concealed in her hair, from a Confederate spy detailing the intentions of the Union army. Mrs. Rose Greenhow was part of the Washington social elite and was privy to conversation at the highest level.

Beauregard formed his army in a line along ten miles of Bull Run Creek and awaited orders for the "surprise" attack. Joe Johnston's army began a series of diversionary moves to keep Union General Patterson preoccupied. Patterson, who was in his late sixties, was convinced that

Johnston's army of twelve thousand actually consisted of forty thousand men or more and didn't want to tangle with it. The Confederate plan called for Johnston's army to join Beauregard's just as McDowell attacked. Patterson would be left searching for Johnston; McDowell wouldn't know what had hit him. But the timing needed to be perfect. If Johnston moved to join Beauregard prematurely, Patterson would also have time to reach Bull Run, assuring a Union victory and endangering the Southern cause.

Morale soared at Camp Clark as a sudden bustle of activity indicated that the army was indeed about to move. The time of drilling and parading was over; soon everyone would have his taste of glory.

At Camp Posey in Mississippi, the scene was much the same as Will Postlethwaite and the 16th Mississippi received their marching orders. The 16th was to travel by rail to Lynchburg, Virginia, becoming part of Isaac Trimble's brigade. On the morning of 16 July 1861, the first major offensive of the American Civil War was finally under way.

Struggling under the weight of their knapsacks, the men of the 2nd Rhode Island Regiment assembled on Pennsylvania Avenue, where during the course of the afternoon they formed a brigade with the 2nd New Hampshire, 71st New York, and 1st Rhode Island. The brigade was designated the "Second Brigade" of the "Second Division," which was commanded by Colonel David Hunter of the United States Army. Command of the brigade was bestowed upon Colonel Burnside. The 2nd Rhode Island contributed a battery of artillery to the brigade. Colonel Slocum and the 2nd led four brigades in the march across the Long Bridge over the Potomac. McDowell's force of five divisions totaled thirty-five thousand men.

Hundreds of excited Washingtonians, some shouting "On to Richmond" or "Whip the Rebs," accompanied McDowell's army into Virginia toward Annandale, where it camped. Along the ten-mile march, many soldiers were caught up in the festive atmosphere, mingling with civilians and flirting with young girls. The day turned hot and some soldiers straggled, picking berries or wandering into the woods in search of water. McDowell's grand march deteriorated into a traffic jam, his soldiers far ahead of their supply wagons.

General Patterson's responsibility to keep Johnston out of McDowell's way was making him nervous. As McDowell marched toward Beauregard, Patterson "demonstrated" (exposing his strength and numbers) toward Johnston near Winchester. Troubling Patterson was a series of vague, often contradictory, orders from General Scott in Washington. Convinced of Johnston's superior numbers and paralyzed by Scott's vagueness, Patterson reversed his march and withdrew to Charlestown. A full day of marching now separated Patterson from Johnston, and the Confederate general eagerly awaited orders to slip away.

Convinced that McDowell's attack was imminent and that he was greatly outnumbered, Beauregard sent an urgent message to General Johnston: "If you will help me, now is the time!" The trap had been set. Johnston's response was to send a cavalry unit commanded by one of his most talented officers, Colonel J. E. B. (Jeb) Stuart, north to harass Patterson. Patterson froze into a defensive position, convinced that he was about to be attacked by Johnston's entire army. The bulk of Johnston's army was, in fact, already heading east to join Beauregard.

The brigade of Virginians that led the way from the Shenandoah Valley to Manassas was commanded by thirty-seven-year-old Brigadier General Thomas Jonathan Jackson, a fearless eccentric who thrived in the heat of battle. During the Mexican War he had once been in a particularly trying position, enemy artillery pouring iron into his position. But focused on his orders, he had remained oblivious to the fire. A native Virginian, Jackson marched his troops on the double-quick out of the Shenandoah Valley toward Bull Run Creek.

Regiment after regiment streamed out of the valley to join Beauregard along Bull Run. More reinforcements would soon be arriving by train at Manassas Junction. For the time being, Johnston left a third of his army in the Shenandoah to entertain Patterson. From all regions of the Confederacy, troops were being rushed to Manassas; among them was Posey's 16th Mississippi Infantry. Mississippi regiments already in the field along Bull Run were the 2nd, 11th, 12th, 18th, and the 13th, which was commanded by Colonel William Barksdale.

Before daylight on the morning of the 17th, the Army of the Potomac resumed its march toward Manassas Junction. Once again, logistics and errors derailed the march. Maps, even the finest available, were grossly inaccurate regarding the locations of streams and secondary roads, and once again supply wagons ground to a halt. It was the first time an American army had endeavored to move such large quantities of men and materials, and the operation fell miserably behind schedule.

As the Army of the Potomac advanced into the town of Fairfax Court House, McDowell became concerned that Beauregard might take the offensive and attack his leading columns before the supply wagons arrived. Fairfax Court House had been evacuated only hours before; Confederate flags were still flying over its government buildings when McDowell's men entered. The thrill of hauling down the "Stars and Bars" deteriorated into the looting and plundering of private residences, and McDowell struggled to regain control of his men. Amid the confusion, McDowell received word that his 3rd Division was encountering light resistance from enemy pickets, and he halted his army.

Frank Greene spent the next two days at Fairfax Court House. As McDowell sat, the Confederate forces along Bull Run swelled until they nearly matched the Union numbers. Out of boredom and from lack of rations, Union soldiers foraged freely, stealing anything that could be carried or consumed. Occasionally, a house or barn was set ablaze, and there was sporadic gunfire in the cow pastures. The men of the 2nd Rhode Island bedded down on the evenings of the 18th and 19th with the aroma of broiled beef wafting in the night air.

On the 18th, McDowell ordered his 1st Division, under General Daniel Tyler, on a reconnaissance mission to determine Confederate positions and secure a suitable point for his army to cross Bull Run. Tyler was under strict orders not to engage the enemy. As his division approached Bull Run, a brigade under Colonel Israel Richardson was ordered to the edge of the creek. Two excellent crossings were discovered at this position: Mitchell's Ford and, about a mile east, Blackburn's Ford. Unfortunately for Richardson, Beauregard agreed with this appraisal, having discovered the crossings weeks before. Beauregard had set up his strongest defenses there.

From across the stream the crackle of gunfire split the air. Within seconds it increased in intensity as Richardson's men vainly tried to return fire against an invisible enemy. Confederate infantrymen cheered as the panic-stricken soldiers in blue struggled up a slope to the safety of woods. Tyler's men came under severe artillery fire; Union Colonel William Tecumseh Sherman later recalled that he had seen men actually struck down by cannonballs. The first test of the two armies, although brief, ended in humiliation for the Union.

The confrontation at Mitchell's Ford exemplified two of the Confederacy's biggest advantages. Unlike the Union forces, whose officers were appointed without consideration of their military experience, Davis, for the most part, selected his officers solely on their military credentials. On the Union side was the legendary General Scott, a genuine American hero. Although devoted to his nation, he could not provide what was needed most at this critical hour: a field commander. General Patterson had served his country well in the War of 1812, however, that fact alone meant that his time had also passed. General McDowell's only qualification was his study of military tactics in Europe.

Last of all was General Benjamin Butler, who had received his appointment for political reasons and had no military experience at all.

On the Confederate side was the brilliant Joseph Johnston, who had already displayed his talents by jolting and eluding Patterson in the Shenandoah Valley. Pierre Beauregard, the hero of Fort Sumter, was proving to be as masterful with infantry as he was with artillery. And there was iron-willed William Barksdale, whose Mississippians would follow him anywhere; young Thomas Jackson with his "foot cavalry"; and Jeb Stuart, with all of his flair and bravado. These characters the Union army was not prepared for.

The other glaring Confederate advantage came with the nature of the war itself. If the Union army wanted a fight it would have to come looking for one. With the advent of the rifled musket, deadly at a range of several hundred yards, the entrenched Confederates could lie in waiting for the arrival of their adversaries, unleashing deadly volleys into an enemy that was using obsolete tactics, as happened at Mitchell's Ford.

The 2nd Rhode Island broke camp at Fairfax Court House on Saturday morning, the 20th. Rested and refreshed, the men looked forward to resuming the march. Over the clanking and rumbling of Colonel Slocum's advancing column, gunfire could be heard in the distance. Less than a half-dozen miles from Bull Run the 2nd Rhode Island arrived at the outskirts of Centreville. The atmosphere was charged on both sides of the creek. Worried about his lagging supply wagons, McDowell ordered his army to halt. He intended to resume the march at 6 P.M., but again chose to delay.

Confused and disappointed, the men of the 2nd went to work building shelters and began to worry that they might be attacked themselves. Their camp was aptly dubbed "Camp Bush." Amid the sounds of distant skirmishing, the men of the 2nd wrote letters and tried to sleep as darkness closed upon them.

Arriving at Bull Run, Johnston asserted his rank over Beauregard and took command of the combined armies. The two generals agreed that the element of surprise now belonged to them, and they planned an attack on McDowell's left flank for the morning. Ironically, McDowell's supply wagons had finally arrived, and he also intended to strike the enemy's left flank the next morning.

McDowell's plan was to attack in two phases. The 2nd and 3rd divisions, spearheaded by the 2nd Rhode Island, would march north about two miles east of Bull Run, crossing at Sudley Springs Ford. Tyler's 1st Division would have a chance to redeem itself by marching out of Centreville down the Warrenton Turnpike and fighting its way over Bull Run at Stone Bridge, two miles south of the other force. Once across Bull Run, the 2nd Rhode Island would drive into the unsuspecting Confederate left as it attempted to hold Stone Bridge. The 2nd would then lead the effort to cut the railroad line that led to the Shenandoah Valley.

Just after midnight, Frank and the rest of the 2nd packed their gear. By 2 A.M., they were marching through the thick woods around Centreville and would eventually arrive at the Warrenton Turnpike. Strict silence was enforced along the march, and the stillness of the night was broken only by the squeaking wheels of wagons and artillery. Thousands of new blue uniforms with gleaming buttons and bayonets moving through the night created what must have been a surreal scene as hundreds of civilians tagged along. About to meet the enemy at last, the marchers were filled with apprehension.

Having fulfilled their enlistment obligation, entire companies of ninety-day volunteers dropped out of the advance and began walking back to Washington. The 2nd Rhode Island, however, and the bulk of the Army of the Potomac pressed on to Bull Run.

Upon reaching the Warrenton Turnpike, the column encountered several fallen trees, prompting another traffic jam. To make matters worse, Tyler's division blocked the

Fatigued, Burnside and his troops rest after a shocking victory at Bull Run.

road for hours in clumsy confusion. The glory of soldiering was steadily losing its luster. McDowell's army plodded along like "a bristling monster lifting himself by a slow, wavy motion up the laborious ascent."

Why Are They Doing This?

At first light, units of the Union 1st and 5th divisions began a disorganized assault upon Stone Bridge. Beauregard was breakfasting at the home of Wilmer McLean, where he was making final preparations to attack McDowell's left near Blackburn's Ford. After breaking McDowell's left flank, the Confederates would push on toward Centreville, cutting the Union supply lines. Beauregard's scheme was changed in an instant when a cannonball tore through the kitchen of the McLean house.

Johnston was unaware of the movements of the 2nd Rhode Island and the two divisions following it; the fighting at Stone Bridge appeared to him to be McDowell's main thrust. But before the 2nd could get into action it had to contend with the obstacle of Bull Run Creek.

Tyler's assault was going poorly. The general had failed to launch a coordinated attack; he sent brigades into action piecemeal, but they were driven back. The planned Confederate drive toward Centreville was scuttled when reports of a huge dust cloud in the vicinity of Sudley Springs Ford reached Johnston and Beauregard. The Confederate generals quickly opted for defense rather than offense. This decision was a master stroke of luck, or genius, for in dealing with the attack at Stone Bridge, the Confederate army was concentrated at its center rather than spread out, as McDowell had hoped it would be.

Unsure of McDowell's intentions and successfully stopping Tyler at Stone Bridge, Beauregard and Johnston ordered a division north to Sudley Springs, along with the brigades of Jackson, General Barnard Bee, and Colonel Francis Bartow.

Two miles to the north, Frank Greene was among the first troops to begin fording the cool waters of Bull Run. As the bulk of the Confederate force raced to meet them, the men of the 2nd Rhode Island rested in the shade and filled canteens. The several delays had fatigued many of McDowell's men, who were growing hungry and tired and were now more interested in picking berries than engaging the enemy.

As the Army of the Potomac dragged itself across the creek, any possibility of surprising the Confederates was gone. Colonels Burnside and Slocum ordered the 2nd Rhode Island out of its repose, and once again the regiment marched toward the sound of battle. Hearts raced, and the sight of Governor Sprague, armed and on horseback, lifted the morale of the Rhode Island men. Scared, hungry, and in a foul mood, the 2nd Rhode Island was ready for a fight. Although it was not yet 10 A.M., this Sunday morning was already quite warm.

Burnside's brigade continued south as the sound of gun-fire grew louder. Confederate Colonel Nathan "Shanks" Evans' troops rushed two six-pound howitzers into the path of the oncoming 2nd Rhode Island, and infantry scattered into the surrounding woods. Burnside chose not to send out pickets to locate the enemy, instead placing the eyes and ears of his brigade on his left and right flanks.

With a flash of light and a thunderous roar, the Confederate artillery announced its presence. A burst of rifle fire from the woods intensified into an endless crackle as cannonballs tore up the earth; the morning air rapidly filled with smoke and confusion. Instinctively, the men of the 2nd Rhode Island hit the ground as iron and lead flew in every direction. In a vain attempt to return fire, the Rhode Islanders aimed too high, their Minié balls sailing over their targets. Looking behind them, Slocum's men realized that they were alone on the field.

Clutching the ground in terror, Frank Greene witnessed a moment no one in the regiment would ever forget. Amid a hail of bullets, Colonel Slocum astonished his young volunteers by ordering the regiment to its feet. Crossing the field, the 2nd's battery of artillery came up on the right and began delivering effective fire into the enemy ranks. The Rhode Island artillery disheartened Confederate Colonel Evans, whose line was beginning to break. To their credit, Evans' men valiantly tried to hold their position until help arrived.

Gradually, the 2nd Rhode Island began to turn the enemy's right and left flanks. Sensing victory, Slocum pushed his troops forward. Turning to encourage the regiment, he was struck by a Minié ball that crushed the top of his skull. He was carried from the field to a nearby house that was rapidly turning into a hospital. Men were falling every-where, even at the well outside the house, as doctors Harris and Rivers struggled to keep up with the influx of wounded. Alert but unable to speak, Colonel Slocum was carried into the house as his life ebbed away.

Major Ballou was struck in the ankle by a cannonball and crawled to a wooden fence where he sat upright, in shock, as the battle raged around him. His leg grotesquely shattered, he was carried to the field hospital, where he and Colonel Slocum died.

The 2nd Rhode Island had been alone on the field for about thirty minutes. On 23 July 1861, a reporter for the *Providence Journal* gave this account of the action:

> We made a circuit of five or six miles through the woods, coming out about ten o'clock upon open ground, around which was grouped the enemy's batteries, of whose strength and number we knew nothing.
>
> As we did so, we saw the R.I. Second drawn up to the right of a piece of woods, with their battery, and immediately formed in line with the New York 71st on our left.
>
> Meanwhile the enemy had opened on our 2nd with shot, shell and musketry, which was returned with great spirit by them and Capt. Reynolds' battery, causing them to retreat from the brow of the hill. The 1st and 71st were now advanced into the grove, and told to wait for orders. Meanwhile the enemy had altered their range, so that the shot and shell which had been bursting harmlessly over our heads, began to fall thick and fast among us. This was the most trying time of all; this forced inaction, while our men were dropping here and there, mangled and dying, was dreadful. This was the moment which, more than any after, no matter how furious the conflict, puts a man's nerves to the test. The sight of the first dead man, especially if he be one of your own, causes a sickening feeling, not experienced afterwards on the field covered with the wrecks of war. Yet not a man flinched that I saw. Presently came Col. Burnside, God bless him! riding into the woods, and gave the order: "Forward, First Rhode Island!" We moved out of the woods to the brow of the hill, the 71st in our front, passing

on the way the dead body of Capt. Tower of our 2nd, and many others. Then came the order, "Lie down 71st, and let Rhode Island pass to the front!"

They did so unwillingly, and we marched through and over them with a front almost as straight and steady as on dress parade. Arrived at the edge of the hill we were greeted by a storm of musket balls from a large body of men, Alabama troops, drawn up in a corn field in front, which whistled past our ears, every minute dropping one of our brave fellows, for about a half an hour. We returned it with interest, every man advancing to the front, firing and falling back to load as quick as possible. The 71st were now brought forward and fought well and bravely by our side. Presently someone cried, "Hold, we are firing on our own men!" This slackened our fire for a moment, when the Colonel rode up and told us to keep up the fire. At the same moment out Adjutant ordered our standard (flag) advanced. A tremendous fire was at once concentrated upon it and Sergeant Becherer who bore it fell, shot through the arm; another man seized it instantly and waved it defiantly to the foe three or four times, when he, too, was led off with a shattered arm. The flag fell for a moment, but a third man sprang forward, raised it without letting go of his musket, and continued to bear it through the action. It seems pretty certain that our crafty adversaries raised a United States (flag) at one time which started the report that we were firing on our friends, and caused us to slacken our fire.

With the rest of its brigade on the field, the 2nd Rhode Island continued to lead the pursuit of the retreating Confederates. Crossing a field where the late Elmer Ellsworth's regiment had been fighting, Corporal Frank Greene witnessed a gruesome scene—dead and dying men piled three and four deep.

Governor Sprague stayed at the front with Colonel Burnside; at one point his horse was shot out from under him. The enemy had been driven back and the day seemed to be won. A large force of men in blue approached on the left, and the men of the 2nd wondered if they were friend or foe. After a few anxious moments, it became clear that this was Sherman's brigade coming to their support.

In a life-shattering second, Frank Greene was knocked to the ground as a Minié ball smashed into his left leg just above the ankle. In excruciating pain and in the early stages of shock, he lay helpless as the 2nd kept up a steady fire. Friends carried Frank to a haystack.

As Frank lay motionless, covered with hay, the Army of the Potomac continued to punish the Confederates. The brigades of Bartow, Bee, and Evans, whose brigade had been badly cut up, were pushed across a small stream and fell back over the Warrenton Turnpike. Upon his arrival, General Jackson coolly took stock of the situation and ordered the broken brigades to position themselves on high ground near the Henry house.

In the heat of early afternoon, McDowell could taste victory, and he ordered a final assault against the heavily outnumbered Confederates. But while McDowell and his staff braved the dangers of the front lines with their troops, Johnston and Beauregard skillfully orchestrated the movements of the Confederate army as a whole. Beauregard maintained a coordinated defensive line with Jackson while Johnston stayed in the rear sending reinforcements, which were arriving by train from the valley, to the front.

With victory seemingly assured, the 2nd Rhode Island, badly mauled and almost out of ammunition, had done more than its share of the day's work. The *Providence Journal* reporter's account continued:

> I cannot particularize instances of personal coolness and bravery, but I will say with perfect truth that I did not see one Rhode Island man quit, though of course many were too excited to take

deliberate aim, often endangering their comrades fighting beside and in front of them, and throwing away a vast amount of lead. The coolest thing I heard was from an officer of the 1st, who walked quietly along the front of his company, remarking, 'Boys, it takes 700 pounds of lead to kill one of you, so go in, and give them one for me!' meaning, no doubt, 700 rounds, but the mistake was excusable. The enemy fought with determined courage, but our fire grew too hot for them at last—the rattling storm of Minié balls fell less thickly among us, and they began to retire. At this moment, Governor Sprague seized a musket and offered to lead a charge. But Col. Burnside would not permit it, a column of regulars (U.S. Army) was brought up, who drove the retreating back to their batteries. Thus was the attempt to outflank us on the left frustrated, and so far as the Rhode Island 1st and 2nd and the 71st (New York) was concerned it was a complete victory. We were withdrawn in perfect order to the grove, except our gallant battery (of the 2nd), which continued to keep up a hot fire upon the masked batteries on the hill.

As the men of the 2nd fell back toward Sudley Springs, they searched among the dead and wounded for their comrades. Frank's friends returned to the haystack where they had left him hours before. Dazed, suffering from loss of blood, and with two fractured bones in his leg, he was carried to the field hospital.

The bodies of the dead were already lined up in rows outside the field hospital when Frank was brought in. His wound was dressed by Dr. Rivers, who continued to treat scores of wounded men. Some men refused treatment and begged to be returned to the field. Some of the dying asked the doctors to help the men who might be saved. Among these men were several Confederates, who received the same care as the Union men. As screams and moans filled the house, news of the Union victory was reaching the capitals of Richmond and Washington.

Union artillery fire grew so hot that it seemed the Confederates on Henry Hill could no longer hold their position. Ignoring a wound to his finger, Jackson rode up and down the line reassuring his men: "Steady boys! All is well!" General Bee, worried that his men might break under the strain, rode over to Jackson seeking advice. Bee begged Jackson to see how frightfully near they were to being overrun by the Federals. With an icy stare, Jackson replied, "Then sir, we shall give them the bayonet!" Bee returned to his brigade and pointed to Jackson's position, saying, "Look, there is Jackson's brigade standing like a stone wall!" At that moment, General Bee was killed.

Despite the situation on the hill, McDowell couldn't dislodge the Confederate brigades holding it. Once again, confusion entered the fight. The blue-clad Virginia 33rd Regiment, mistaken as friendly by two Union batteries, was allowed to position itself close to the Union guns. In a gallant charge the Virginians overwhelmed the two batteries, killing many of the gunners. But the 33rd was soon driven back, and the captured artillery sat unmanned between the two armies as Jeb Stuart chased Ellsworth's regiment down the slope of the hill. Beauregard and Johnston had won what they needed most: time. By late afternoon, the remainder of Johnston's army was in position, depriving McDowell of the numerical advantage he had enjoyed throughout the day.

By mid-afternoon, McDowell's infantry began making steady progress up the hill, and once again a Union victory seemed imminent. Confederate brigades began to fall back as Union soldiers approached the crest of the hill, and a sense of panic set in among Confederate officers and infantry alike.

Jackson's men nervously awaited orders as the determined Union army approached their position. In a firm voice, Jackson ordered his men to hold their fire, fix bayonets, and keep low. They were told to wait until the heads of the enemy became visible over the crest of the hill. Then, jumping to their feet, the Virginians fired a volley into the faces of the enemy and followed Jackson's order to "give them the bayonet; and when you charge, yell like furies!"

The Union men reaching the brow of the hill had been confident that the honor of securing the final victory was theirs. It appeared to them that the enemy had evacuated the hill when Jackson's brigade suddenly leapt into their faces and, with a shrill howl, slammed into their ranks. Wielding daggers, the wild-eyed Louisiana Tigers plunged into the blue line. Only a handful of veterans who had fought Indians in the West had ever experienced anything so terrifying.

As the stunned Union men fell back in panic, Johnston unleashed the full weight of his army on McDowell. Union officers frantically tried to prevent the scramble down the hill from deteriorating into full panic. McDowell tried to get Burnside to bring his men back onto the field, but the brigade was spent. The men of the 2nd spent the afternoon in a shaded grove burying their dead and taking care of the wounded. The cost of the day's "victory" had been high. The captains of six companies had been killed or wounded. In all, the regiment had lost 104 men dead, missing, or wounded.

In light of what he had seen on the battlefield, Burnside found it difficult to commit his men again to a battle they thought they had won. Before he could organize the 2nd to re-enter the fight, terrified soldiers began streaming through the grove. Burnside received a message indicating that McDowell had ordered a full retreat. This news was greeted by the men of the 2nd with astonishment. One soldier later wrote that he was "flabbergasted." Meanwhile, President Davis had arrived from Richmond to personally witness the humiliation of Lincoln's army, while Lincoln stared out of a White House window wondering how things had gone so wrong.

Having staggered McDowell's army, Johnston now had the opportunity to destroy it. Across Stone Bridge and along the Warrenton Turnpike, the defeated mob stampeded in fear of a final assault by the Confederates. Civilians and soldiers alike fled for Washington.

Unfortunately for Johnston, his army had taken a serious beating and was not up to the task of delivering a final blow. Many regiments had become intermingled and many officers had been lost, disrupting the chain of command. Although Davis was disappointed, he and Johnston would have to be satisfied with the day's ending. No ground had been won or lost by either side.

A thinking man's warrior, Jackson concluded that McDowell's defeat would ultimately hurt the Confederate cause. He felt that the North would now commit itself to fighting a real war—not merely a war of dress parades and picnics. Never again would the Union forces underestimate the strength and courage of their Southern brethren.

The doctors continued to treat Frank and the others who were unable to flee from the approaching Confederates. No one knew how prisoners of war would be treated; some feared that they would simply be shot.

In the late afternoon, sun lay the remnants of the day's battle. Broken and abandoned gun carriages sat amid a sea of knapsacks, rifles, and other articles of war. The smoking battlefield was filled with the sounds of wounded and dying men and horses. In all, around three thousand dead and wounded men were strewn about the field. In terms of human life, the battle had been a draw.

As Confederate officers entered the makeshift hospital, they must have been impressed by the sight of Confederates being treated by Union doctors. Frank Greene, the rest of the wounded, and the doctors were taken by horse-drawn ambulances to Manassas Junction, where they were put on rail cars bound for Richmond.

Although there is no evidence of mistreatment of prisoners by their Confederate captors, there was at least one heinous incident. In a display of contempt for the 2nd Rhode Island, a group of Confederates decapitated the remains of Major Ballou and burned the body. Ballou's charred remains were later sent to Camp Clark and shipped to Rhode Island for burial at Swan Point Cemetery in Providence.

The brutality of the war's first battle shocked America, both North and South. Casualty lists appeared in newspapers throughout both nations, and the two capitals saw what war looked like as trainloads of wounded arrived in Richmond and weary, beaten soldiers straggled into Washington. Union soldiers arrived in small groups or alone as "The Great Skedaddle" continued for days. Most of the men had discarded their knapsacks and weapons in their haste to escape.

The shock of the defeat was probably summed up best by two soldiers from the 2nd Rhode Island. They had clambered up the slope along Bull Run, making no attempt to return fire, when Confederate artillery began firing on the two scared Rhode Island boys. Hysterical, one soldier thought aloud, "What are they trying to do?" Realizing the absurdity of the question, the second soldier responded, "They're trying to kill every damned one of us, that's what they're trying to do!"

On 22 July, the following report appeared on the front page of the *Providence Journal*:

> Francis C. Greene, of Company H, was wounded, shot in the leg below the knee, and carefully taken to the hospital. Surgeon James Harris was also at the hospital and remained there to attend to the wounded. Both are probably in the hands of the enemy.

At the bottom of the same page was this quote from the *New Orleans Delta* describing the successes of a young Union general in western Virginia: "Whatever may be the result of General George McClellan's movement in Western Virginia, it is one of great boldness." If Lincoln needed some positive news for Northerners, he found it in the brash young general. McClellan was summoned to Washington to be offered field command of the Army of the Potomac.

Southern patriotism swelled to bursting as the news of the "victory" swept the Confederacy. Newspapers were sold in record numbers, and no one was about to let facts get in the way of a good story. One newspaper got a little carried away with the story; the *New Orleans Picayune* on 24 July gleefully reported:

GLORIOUS VICTORY

THE ENEMY 80,000 STRONG!

Their loss 10,000 to 15,000!
Gallant Conduct of The Louisiana Boys!

Many Prisoners Captured!

Slaughter of the Enemy Dreadful!

The New York Herald offered a somber report of the action on 22 July:

> The retreat was nothing more or less than a stampede. The defeat is attributed in a great measure to Patterson's tardiness. Gov. Sprague's bravery brought some degree of order out of the chaos. McDowell displayed great bravery, but his efforts to arrest the panic were unavailing. The New York 71st, 14th and 27th, and Maine regiments were mowed down like grass. The list of killed and wounded embraces a large number of officers.

On 26 July, as Frank Greene's military career was coming to a close and General McClellan was meeting with Lincoln, a train carrying Will Postlethwaite and the 16th Mississippi arrived in Richmond. Having missed the battle because of an outbreak of measles, Posey's men were immediately sent to Manassas Junction.

The war was three months old. The North had suffered the indignity of Fort Sumter and the humiliation of Bull Run. Lincoln's seventy-five thousand three-month volunteers were going home. Many Northerners, particularly those whose families had suffered casualties, questioned the very purpose of the war. Lincoln's popularity plunged. The North was desperate for good news, however little, and the responsibility of bringing this good news was bestowed upon George Brinton McClellan.

CHAPTER FIVE

A Good Taw

Although I was stymied by the situation at the cemetery, information about my subject seemed to be everywhere. Census records and death certificates were available at state archives. I found burial records at a church near Greenwood Cemetery. The Bureau of Labor Statistics translated the net worth of the Greenes and Postlethwaites into current values. From records held by The Church of Jesus Christ of Latter-day Saints to the Department of the Army, I intended to turn over every stone.

Daily, my mailbox held as many as half a dozen pieces of "Sam's mail." The kindness and generosity of people responding to my queries was remarkable, and my file cabinet filled to overflowing. People from around the country were spending hours in libraries and sending me photocopies of their discoveries. Seemingly useless bits of information often became vital months later as Sam's story came together like a puzzle. In some cases, I exchanged so many letters with "Sam's friends" that their content was more of a personal nature than historical. For the first time, I thought that if Sam's grave was ever marked, there should be an opportunity for everyone involved to meet.

As my research continued, information often came through unlikely sources. A lumberyard stands on property that once was the Clyde Print Works; its owner gave me an original blueprint of the mill complex. A most unusual find came from Port Gibson, Mississippi. After reading an article I wrote, a woman asked her father, who collected civil war envelopes, to check his collection for the name Postlethwaite. To the amazement of all parties, I was soon in possession of a photocopy of an envelope addressed to "Private Will Postlethwaite, 9th Louisiana Cavalry, Prisoner of War, Fort Delaware Prison." I had earlier concluded that Will's military career must have ended with his discharge from the 16th Mississippi Infantry after the battle at Antietam.

Contacting a Fort Delaware State Park historian, I discovered that there had been no record of Will's incarceration there until this envelope surfaced. With this new information I checked the National Archives to learn if Will had a file as a member of the 9th Louisiana Cavalry. Not only was there a file, but within it was a letter to President Lincoln written by a relative seeking a pardon for Will.

I made the most exciting discovery of all at the Rhode Island Historical Society Library. How often I had wished I could turn back time and walk into Greenwood Cemetery a hundred years ago to see Sam's marble marker. I settled for the next best thing. In 1904, James Newell Arnold was commissioned by the government of Rhode Island to transcribe the inscriptions on gravestones throughout the state. Unfortunately, Arnold had no apparent system for indexing his work; the researcher is forced to flip through page after page of Arnold's notes to find a particular inscription.

With aching eyes I scanned Arnold's guide to Greenwood Cemetery until I found "William Rogers Greene, In Whom There Was No Guile." On the same page was Christopher, William's four-year-old son. I was disappointed that I could find no reference to Samuel Postlethwaite. Doubt about Sam's interment at Greenwood crept into my mind. Discouraged, I spent the rest of the afternoon researching the Greene family. Before calling it a day, I decided to make a photocopy of Arnold's transcription of William Greene's headstone. Once again turning to page 213, I noticed something I had somehow missed the first time. At the bottom of the page, following entries for William and Christopher Greene, were the words "marble block, 'S.P.'" Sam was there. Unable to stop smiling, I made my copies and went home.

Sam's initials are found at the bottom of this transcription of inscriptions on gravestones throughout Rhode Island.

IN THE DAYS IMMEDIATELY FOLLOWING THE BATTLE AT MANASSAS, Washington and Richmond were both visited by the grim reality of warfare. Never before had such carnage been inflicted upon Americans in a single day's combat.

President Davis had sent an urgent request for troops to the governor of Tennessee; it was noticed by the governor of Mississippi, who telegraphed Davis, "I have had a conference with Governor Harris as to your call for six regiments. He says he can spare only five. As your call is pressing, I send you the 16th Mississippi from Corinth."

The Confederate capital that greeted Will Postlethwaite and the 16th Mississippi as they stepped off their train was hardly what they had imagined. Richmond was overcrowded, filthy, and permeated by death. Regiments from various Southern states were arriving and departing for the front continuously. The once-peaceful port city now served as a massive camp, prison, and hospital. As in Washington, no one had anticipated the need to care for and shelter the thousands of wounded and prisoners of war. Saloons, schools, municipal buildings, and private residences were transformed into hospitals. When no beds were available, doors were removed from their hinges and used instead. Most of the wounded were treated on floors.

The Confederate government scrambled to come up with a solution to the problem of housing the prisoners. Many were guarded in groups in the open air; others were held in empty buildings around the city. The largest of these buildings was a 150- by 100-foot three-story brick warehouse at the corner of Cary and 20th streets. This building had been leased since 1854 as a tobacco warehouse. At its rear was a canal that provided easy access to the ocean. Above the doors of this building were large signs announcing "L. Libby & Son, Ship Chandlers." No one ever bothered to remove the signs, and "Libby" became the prison's name. Across the street from Libby stood its twin, a barrel factory. This building was also seized by the Confederate government for the purpose of housing prisoners. It was dubbed "Castle Thunder."

The cobblestone basement of Libby Prison was used as a kitchen. The first floor served as offices and a storage area. The second floor was completely open except for two rows of wooden support posts running through the room. Although the third floor was similar to the second, the second floor was used as the main prison. This stark, inhospitable room would be shared by hundreds of men for the foreseeable future.

Thanks to the prompt attention of Dr. Harris at Manassas and the work of doctors at Libby, Frank didn't lose his leg. His tibia shattered, suffering from necrosis of the leg, Frank would never walk normally again; his career as a soldier was over. The terrible sights of the battlefield, a gruesome wounding, and falling into the hands of the enemy had produced severe trauma in Frank. Harsh, empty days at Libby would only weaken his mental state.

Most of the prisoners at Libby and Castle Thunder were quick to adjust to their new surroundings and prison fare, as well as rude treatment by some of the guards. Brusque treatment was to be expected, but there was one indignity that Frank and his comrades did not suffer gladly. The men were terrorized by a large black bloodhound that belonged to the assistant provost marshal at Castle Thunder. This canine had the run of the prisons and barked viciously at the men, earning their unanimous hatred. Only letters and packages from home made daily life with "Hero" bearable.

Soon after the prisons were established, a petite, blue-eyed, fortyish woman became a common sight at Libby. Elizabeth Van Lew was a wealthy, pro-Union resident of Richmond whose mansion was located near the prisons. Her stature in Richmond allowed her regular visits to the men. She often brought food from her home and copies of *Atlantic Monthly* and *Harpers* magazines, and she sometimes joined the men in Bible readings. The prisoners, many of whom had fallen into depression, were cheered by "Miss Lizzie's" words of encouragement. Her presence was a pleasant diversion from the never-ending games of chess and whist that filled many of the men's days.

The boredom sometimes became unbearable. Some prisoners with mechanical skills requested to be allowed to work on a new furnace that was being installed. The proposal was approved; working on the project would allow the men to do something productive and assure that there would be some heat in the drafty building. The Confederate government was so pleased with the results that it paid the prisoners the same wages an outside contractor would have commanded. But even with the new furnace the massive structure was often bitterly cold during the winter months.

The number of prisoners at Libby would eventually swell to about one thousand (more than the population of most American towns in 1860). It was so crowded that the men were forced to sleep on their sides. During the course of a night, a signal would indicate that it was time for every prisoner to roll over and sleep on his other side. The prison became increasingly difficult to maintain; forty black servants were brought in to cook, clean, and wash mountains of laundry. Eighteen servants continuously washed Libby's floors.

As thirty-four-year-old George Brinton McClellan stepped off his train on 26 July, he witnessed the hysteria that gripped Washington. Evidence of defeat was everywhere, and rumors of an impending Confederate attack on the city dominated conversation. There was even talk of the government evacuating Washington. Civilians hid their valuables and were prepared to flee at a moment's notice. McClellan was shocked by the lack of military preparedness and security around the city.

If the capital's deplorable state surprised the young general, the reaction to his arrival amazed him. Everywhere he went he was gawked at and whispered about. Although only five feet eight inches tall, McClellan, with his bold features and broad chest, was an imposing figure. As intelligent as he was handsome, he was adored by women and admired by men. He was the Union's darling during the dark days of the young war, garnering the nicknames "Little Mac" and "Young Napoleon."

Having graduated second in his class at West Point, McClellan went on to serve with distinction in the Mexican War. Upon retiring from the military, he took an administrative position with the Illinois Central Railroad. There he met Abraham Lincoln, who was employed by the railroad as a lawyer. When Fort Sumter fell, McClellan was appointed a major general in command of the volunteer forces of Illinois, Ohio, and Indiana. In early June, McClellan moved his forces into western Virginia to support pro-Union sentiment there. His successes led directly to West Virginia becoming a Union state. He also sent detailed suggestions to President Lincoln and General Scott on how to defeat the Confederacy.

After the Bull Run debacle, the choice of who should lead the Union army was never in question. On 26 July, after consulting with Secretary of War Cameron and General Scott, Lincoln offered field command of the Army of the Potomac to McClellan.

McClellan went to work immediately, reorganizing Washington's defenses. To his wife, Ellen, he complained, "I found no army to command, a mere collection of regiments cowering on the banks of the Potomac, some perfectly raw, others dispirited by the recent defeat." He also expressed bewilderment about his appointment:

> I find myself in a new and strange position here: President, Cabinet, General Scott, and all deferring to me. By some strange operation of magic, I seem to have become the power of the land. Oh! —how sincerely I pray to God that I may be endowed with the wisdom and courage necessary to accomplish the work (McClellan, 1887).

McClellan restructured the chain of command and enforced a strict code of discipline. The high morale of the volunteers that had preceded Bull Run had deteriorated dangerously. Gambling, thievery, and drunkenness was rampant in many camps.

McClellan was faced with the task of forming unfocused, discouraged volunteers into a fighting machine, and he knew that turning these troops around was going to take time. Until the men were properly trained and their confidence restored, their chances for success on the field of battle were slim; no longer would marching and parading make a man into soldier. For the first time, qualified officers, not political appointees, began instructing the men. Proper conduct under fire was taught and re-taught. Little Mac was seen everywhere, usually mounted on his black charger, Dan Webster. His presence thrilled the volunteers, who jumped at the chance to demonstrate their improving skills. Steadily the Army of the Potomac recovered from the debacle of 21 July. While he was encouraged, McClellan knew that his men were not ready to tangle with the likes of Beauregard, Johnston, and Jackson.

Lincoln had promised full cooperation to McClellan as he rebuilt the army. McClellan viewed the North's vast resources as his most important asset. To fight the Confederates on their own terms, piecemeal and in limited engagements, would only end in failure. The population of the North was 22 million compared with 9 million for the South; the manufacturing and industrial strength of the Union dwarfed that of the Confederacy.

There was no doubt that, in time, the Union could build an army so powerful that it would crush the Confederate army no matter how valiantly it resisted. Despite the certainty of heavy casualties, McClellan felt that this strategy would result in a quicker end to the conflict; the resulting casualties would be considerably fewer than those incurred in a protracted war that could last for years. In military circles, this strategy made perfect sense; time was on the side of the Union. The South was being weakened daily by a U.S. Navy blockade. Shortages of food and other products would soon be felt by Confederate civilians, and it was hoped that their support for the war would wane. If Lincoln, Cameron, and the Northern population could be patient, the outcome was inevitable.

Will Postlethwaite's stay in Richmond was brief. The 16th Mississippi was once again put on a train, arriving in Lynchburg on Monday, 29 July. The men camped between Staunton and Lynchburg, awaiting orders.

By August, McClellan's army outnumbered Joseph Johnston's sixty-five thousand to forty thousand. Insisting on a preponderance of power, McClellan requested 200,000 more men. He hired his own intelligence men led by Allen Pinkerton, who remained gainfully employed by feeding the general exaggerated information. McClellan was falsely informed that Johnston's army had as many as 100,000 men.

McClellan soon became frustrated at having to defer to General Scott, who was desperate to resurrect his glorious past. Further annoyances were the constant suggestions and opinions of Lincoln and Secretary of War Cameron, neither of whom had any military experience. In letters to his wife, McClellan began referring to the president as "the original gorilla," mocking his backwoods humor and story-telling.

Less than three weeks after Bull Run, as McClellan was rebuilding his army, Lincoln ordered a Union offensive in Missouri. On 10 August, General Nathaniel Lyon attacked the Confederates at Wilson's Creek. The results were disastrous. The Union defeat was as sweeping as that at Manassas, and General Lyon was killed. The North was outraged and the newspapers had a field day with Lincoln. In Maryland, on 14 August, the *Baltimore Republican* proclaimed:

ANOTHER DEFEAT OF THE TYRANTS
Our paper today will bear abroad the tidings of another defeat of the Federal forces and the death of the commanding general. It is hoped that a few more battles of similar character may teach the infatuated despots at Washington the madness of their attempt to enslave the freemen of the South. We would only remind our readers that the present

account is from Federal authority, and therefore will be satisfactory so far as the acknowledgment of another total defeat and rout is concerned. No doubt the real facts are much more disastrous to the Federal arms than is reported.

Two days before the battle at Wilson's Creek, the 16th Mississippi was ordered to Manassas, where it joined Johnston's army. The *Lynchburg Virginian* lauded the regiment on 5 August:

The 16th Mississippi Regiment, (under) Colonel Carnot Posey, paraded our streets yesterday, preceded by their brass band. This is a noble body of men, admirably equipped, one of the companies having the improved rifles, with sword bayonets. The regiment will leave here for Manassas next Tuesday. They will do good service anywhere.

Lincoln desperately needed a victory. There was no question that he would demand an offensive from McClellan before winter brought military operations to a halt. The general deemed his men unready for battle and refused to betray the volunteers who had placed their faith in him. The army would continue to train, build confidence, and grow.

McClellan's frustration with the administration deepened as Indian Summer turned into fall. While his relationship with the president soured, the young general went to war with General Scott. Scott was becoming uncomfortable with McClellan's tremendous popularity among soldiers and civilians alike, and it appeared to the old general that this "Young Napoleon" had no interest in fighting anyone except the president.

Since Bull Run, the Confederate states had exuded confidence, and the stunning victory at Wilson's Creek only added to the euphoria. European intervention on the side of the South seemed to be only a few victories away.

Although shortages of goods were a hardship, it seemed certain to Southern leaders that a quick end to the war would make these tough times worth bearing.

Some, though—among them General Jackson—were not filled with optimism. Jackson worried about McClellan's inactivity. As the heavy industry of the Northern states churned out artillery and other ordnance, Jackson saw any hope of victory slipping away with each passing day. He wanted President Davis to attack the North immediately. Deeply troubled, he confided in General Gustavus Smith, hoping Smith could use his influence in the Southern hierarchy. Jackson begged Smith to hear him out:

> McClellan, with his army of recruits, will not attempt to come out against us this autumn. If we remain inactive they will have greatly the advantage over us next spring. Their raw recruits will have then become an organized army, vastly superior in numbers to our own. We are ready at the present moment for active operations in the field, while they are not. We ought to invade their country now, and not wait for them to make the necessary preparations to invade ours.
>
> If the president would reinforce this army by taking troops from other points not threatened, and let us make an active campaign of invasion before winter sets in, McClellan's raw recruits could not stand against us in the field. Crossing the Upper Potomac, occupying Baltimore, and taking possession of Maryland, we could cut off communications of Washington, force the Federal Government to abandon the capital, beat McClellan's army if it came out against us in the open country, destroy industrial establishments wherever we found them, break up the lines of interior commercial intercourse, close the coal mines, seize and, if necessary, destroy the manufactories

and commerce of Philadelphia, and of any other large cities within our reach; subsist mainly on the country we traverse, and making unrelenting war amidst their homes, force the people of the North to understand what it will cost them to hold the South in the Union at the bayonet's point (Henderson, 1988).

Smith found himself in an awkward situation. Jackson's observations were most likely correct; in time the superior numbers of the Northern armies would force the Confederacy to fight a defensive war over a thousand-mile front. But for the moment there was no viable Union threat anywhere. Never again would the Confederate army be in a better position to invade the North.

Smith's response crushed the hero of Manassas. He revealed that there had been a meeting of Davis, Johnston, and Beauregard at Fairfax Court House during the first week of October. At this meeting, a military strategy had been decided upon. The South would fight a defensive war, forcing the Union army to fight on unfamiliar ground; there would be no invasion of the North. Jackson was distraught. A few days later he was ordered away from the front and into the Shenandoah Valley.

An attack by the Union army before winter wasn't likely, but it was possible. Will Postlethwaite's days were busy as he helped build earthworks and bombproofs (cave-like shelters constructed of logs and dirt) along the Potomac and took his turn at picket duty. A soldier's life has been described as consisting of extended periods of boredom interrupted by brief moments of high excitement, and life in the 16th Mississippi's camp was precisely that. Rumors of imminent attack by McClellan's army created some anxiety, but Will's days continued to be peaceful.

As October began, Will's life was exciting compared

with that of his brother Sam, who was still in Mississippi. Sam's daily regimen blurred one day into the next: 5 A.M., reveille; roll call and breakfast at 7 A.M.; surgeon's call at 8 A.M.; guard duty, if assigned, at 9 A.M.; drilling in the manual of arms until 10 A.M.; company drill at 11 A.M.; lunch and time off from 12 to 2 P.M.; regimental drilling from 2 P.M. to 4 or 5 P.M.; dress parade at 6 P.M.; evening meal at 7 P.M.; and taps at 9 P.M.

Recreation at Sam's camp was typical. There was reading and letter-writing, and games of all kinds became increasingly popular. The sight of men playing checkers, chess, and card games in front of their tents was common. Even the children's game of marbles was rediscovered by many of the Southern soldiers, the innocent game becoming a vehicle for gambling. Marbles was quickly established as the most popular game in the camps, and the more talented players with a "good taw" could add considerably to their eleven-dollar-per-month army pay by hustling their hapless comrades.

Also popular was a game called "base." Since the Mexican War, the baseball craze had swept the country, and the minor inconvenience of a civil war was not about to derail its popularity. There were several incidents in which soldiers from both sides sneaked through enemy lines to peer into the opposing army's camp, not to spy but to watch the games.

Music was also a popular diversion. Regimental bands held regular concerts, and small groups of soldiers sang or played instruments in front of glowing campfires. Just as their comrades were sharpening their skills at checkers, chess, or marbles, many of these musicians became quite good.

Once the men were deployed in the field, the diet of the Confederate soldier changed dramatically. Aside from any foods received from home or occasional wild game, Will and Sam's diet consisted of standard Confederate rations. The daily ration per soldier in 1861 was three-quarters of a pound of pork, one-quarter pound of salted beef, and eighteen ounces of hardbread or one and one-quarter pounds of cornmeal. The government also provided rations per one hundred men: ten pounds of rice, six pounds of coffee, twelve pounds of sugar, four quarts of vinegar, and two quarts of salt.

Even in these heady days of the Confederacy, logistical problems and shortages often prevented issue of the standard rations. In any case, this sparse fare would soon be remembered almost as fondly as home-cooked meals. By the following spring, the Confederate government would order that the rations be reduced; they often existed on paper only. The absence of fresh fruit contributed to health problems in both armies, and diseases like scurvy began to appear in the camps.

It was unusual when soldiers received even their basic rations with any regularity. This situation prompted the demand for independent vendors, or sutlers, who provided food and various goods. These enterprising businessmen soon appeared in all camps, sharing the dangers of army life with the rest of the men. Many soldiers spent a good portion of their pay on the sutler's wares.

During August and September, a total of seven companies from the 21st Mississippi had been ordered to Virginia. By late September, two more companies left Mississippi for Virginia. On 11 September, Colonel Benjamin Humphreys took command of the 21st Mississippi. Sam's company captain, William Lindsay Brandon, was promoted to lieutenant colonel. Taking Brandon's place as captain of Company D was John Sims.

The regiment was reorganized and in early October transferred north to Manassas, where it would be brigaded. The second week of October was unusually cold and rainy as what became known as "battle summer" drew to a close. On Friday, 10 October, Sam Postlethwaite was officially mustered into the army of the Confederate States of America. It is possible that Sam and Will were reunited at Manassas; a pass to visit a family member in another camp was easily obtainable. They had not seen each other for five months.

On the evening preceding Sam's arrival at Manassas,

Will's regiment had its first brush with the enemy. An account of this event by an unknown member of the regiment was published in *The Mississippian* on 19 October:

> On the evening of the 9th we were notified to prepare for an early start on the morrow. We marched at shouldered arms, our colors flying and band playing past General Johnston's headquarters and through the town. We afterwards learned that our regiment was considered as the largest and finest in the Confederate Service, that is the General said so, and the Richmond papers reported it. Centreville is filled with Confederate soldiers, and among all these, the 16th Mississippi Regiment stands preeminently one of the first in size, conduct and drill. Our company, 'A', also known as the Summit Rifles from Pike County, was posted along the Accotink Creek, about a mile and a half from Annandale. On Saturday Major Stockdale heard that our Cavalry pickets had been fired upon, and that a company of Yankees were at an old church on the road to Alexandria. He took our company, Lieutenant Antly's company and half of Captain Davis' company from Crystal Springs. Major Stockdale deserves a great deal of credit, and our officers behaved with remarkable bravery, and the boys fought like veterans (Posey Family Scrapbook).

Though this skirmish was hardly worth mentioning when compared with Wilson's Creek or Manassas, Will now had a war story to tell his big brother.

I Can Do It All!

By late August, Scott was adamant that McClellan take action against the Confederate positions around

Washington. One such position was more an insult than a threat. Only a few miles from Washington stood Munson's Hill, from which the U.S. capitol building was clearly visible. At its peak loomed a large, ominous-looking Confederate cannon. The fact that Johnston had the audacity to place this monster so close to Washington only aggravated the already touchy relationship between McClellan and his superiors. Scott assured the president that the numbers of Confederates manning positions across the Potomac were not nearly what McClellan was insisting.

McClellan tried to ignore the constant "interference" from Scott, but he could no longer conceal his annoyance. McClellan began to treat the old general rudely and often displayed his contempt by snubbing him at public appearances. McClellan wrote to his wife, Ellen:

He understands nothing, appreciates nothing. General Scott is the great obstacle. He will not comprehend the danger. I have to fight my way against him. General Scott is the most dangerous antagonist I have. The people call upon me to save the country. I must save it, and I cannot respect anything that is in the way. I was called to it; my previous life seems to have been unwittingly directed to this great end (McClellan, 1887).

Scott was feeling unappreciated, and he began to question whether he had indeed outgrown his usefulness. After so many years of service to his country, he had no intention of tolerating McClellan's disrespect. He offered his resignation to Lincoln, who urged him to reconsider. In agreeing to remain in his position, Scott found it impossible to contain his bitterness toward McClellan. He leveled McClellan during a War Department meeting when he bluntly reminded him, "You were called here by my advice. The times require vigilance and activity. I am not active and never shall be again. When I proposed that you should come here to aid, not supersede me, you had my friendship and confidence. You still have my confidence." Both men knew the outcome of their contest was inevitable, but Scott was determined to maintain his pride.

After a brief Union assault upon Munson's Hill in which a New Jersey regiment was turned back, General Johnston decided that the position wasn't worth the cost of holding it. At the end of September, Johnston withdrew, leaving behind the black-painted log that Washington had been so preoccupied with. The revelation of the "Quaker gun" was yet another humiliation for the Union.

For Will and Sam, life in camp dragged on. Soon after Sam's arrival at Manassas, fall weather set in. Trees displayed their multicolored foliage and the air turned crisp. Men on both sides of the Potomac huddled around evening campfires. The men of the Mississippi regiments weren't looking forward to spending the coming winter in such an unfriendly climate.

With weather conditions becoming increasingly unsuitable for large-scale military operations, Lincoln grew more desperate. The possibility of securing a major victory before winter was remote, for Johnston's army was firmly entrenched and McClellan's army still had a long way to go before it would be ready to move south. As Union General George Meade observed, "Soldiers they are not in any sense of the word." If he couldn't have a victory to ward off his critics over the long winter, Lincoln had to have something—anything—to keep public support for the war from disappearing entirely.

In mid-October, a deserter from William Barksdale's 13th Mississippi told Union interrogators of a withdrawal of Confederate troops from a bluff overlooking the Potomac, near Leesburg. This unexpected development gave McClellan an opportunity to "demonstrate" his Army of the Potomac. If Union troops could be moved into the vacated Confederate position quickly enough, it would appear that McClellan had chased the enemy out.

The plan pleased everybody. For Lincoln, it was a

chance to bolster his sinking popularity, and Scott would be pleased because the army, or a least a portion of it, was finally moving. McClellan, for the time being, would have both of them off of his back.

Edward Baker and Abraham Lincoln had been such good friends that Lincoln had named his second son for the senator from Oregon. When the war broke out, Baker had been given command of the 71st Pennsylvania. But even though Baker had served in the Mexican War, he had no experience in leading men, having achieved the rank of colonel through purely political means. Baker hated the Confederacy and berated the seceded states on the Senate floor several times while in full uniform, sometimes wearing a sword. A lover of poetry, he had the irritating habit of inserting verse into everyday conversation. Baker was determined to play an important role in this ruse of an operation.

As the operation got under way, General Charles Stone feared that the withdrawing Confederates would fall back to the safety of General Johnston's main line before he could engage them, so he hurried two regiments aboard three small boats. This process was painfully slow, as the boats could only accommodate twenty-five men at a time. But by the morning of 21 October, most of Stone's men had reached the Virginia side of the Potomac at the base of a one hundred-foot bank called Ball's Bluff.

The only access to the field atop the bluff was a long, winding cow path. Stone was so concerned with reaching the field that he neglected to probe the enemy position with a small force. The first regiment to reach the top was the 20th Massachusetts, whose men promptly hung their heavy, scarlet-lined overcoats, which were recent gifts from the ladies back home, on tree branches as the morning sun warmed the fall air. There was no sign of Confederates, and the field appeared secured as Colonel Baker was arriving with his 71st Pennsylvania and two cannons. Getting the two field pieces to the top of the bluff was no small accomplishment. As the men wrestled them up the cow path, they heard the sound of gunfire from above.

Forming a line of battle only a few feet from the edge of the bluff, Stone and his men were startled by a brief burst of gunfire from the wooded area across the field. The Massachusetts men discovered that their overcoats had been shot to pieces.

Baker was thrilled to be on the field; he barked orders and encouraged his men while spouting poetry. Believing he was facing a small force, perhaps only a handful of pickets, Baker couldn't contain his excitement over a battle won.

Another volley of gunfire burst from the woods, this time closer and thicker. The sickening thud of lead striking flesh and bone was heard throughout Baker's line. Men began to fall, and others glanced warily at the edge of the bluff only a few steps behind them. Baker's two cannons got into the fight, taking down trees at the edge of the woods. Confederate sharpshooters returned fire, silencing the artillery.

When a colonel from a New York regiment reached the top of the bluff, he couldn't believe what he was seeing. Some of Baker's men courageously tried to get the cannons back into the fight but were killed. Something had gone dreadfully wrong; the enemy in the woods was not about to withdraw and was in a fighting mood. As the Confederates advanced out of the woods, revealing their numbers, Baker realized the full extent of the ambush. It was the last thing he saw as a Minié ball passed through his brain.

Having gotten wind of Lincoln's plan to make a "slight demonstration" against the Confederates holding Ball's Bluff, General Johnston had ordered several regiments under the command of General Nathan Evans to greet Baker. Along with some Virginia regiments, the 13th Mississippi under Barksdale and the 17th under the command of a former lawyer and Indian fighter, Winfield Scott Featherston, had quick-marched to meet Baker.

The confident Mississippians charged out of the woods and across the field as Baker's men desperately tried to hold their ground. Groups of Union men began to flee down the cow path. The Mississippians picked them off as men scrambled over the bodies of their friends in panic. But many stoically withstood the Confederate onslaught until they were struck down or taken prisoner. One Confederate remembered: "A kind of shiver ran through the huddled mass upon the brow of the cliff, it gave way; rushed a few steps; then, in one wild, panic-stricken herd, rolled, leaped, tumbled over the precipice."

Many of the Mississippians didn't know how to react to this rout of the enemy. New to battle, many of the Southern men simply went wild. As Union men clumsily descended the slope, volley upon volley was poured into them. Some of the Mississippians even went to the extent of climbing trees, which overlooked the bluff, to get a better angle on their targets, most of whom were no longer carrying weapons. Featherston led a charge of his 17th into the ranks of some remaining Union men. As the men of the 17th slammed into the Union line, they physically pushed many of the Northerners over the edge.

The men lucky enough to reach the boats at the bottom of the bluff were overwhelmed with fright and overloaded the boats. As one boat moved away from the Virginia shore, some of its passengers were shot, and it capsized. Approximately thirty men drowned in the murky waters of the Potomac. Some of the stronger swimmers made it safely to an island, and a few managed to find a shallow crossing.

As Evans' men counted their thirty-three dead, they were appalled by the carnage around them. Among the dead was the son of the governor of Mississippi. Also killed was a Colonel Burt of the 18th. On the field high above the Potomac, on the slope of the bluff, and in the river were two hundred dead and wounded men in blue. Another seven hundred stood nervously at gunpoint, prisoners of war. Those lucky enough to survive would always recall the slippery, bloody slopes of Ball's Bluff.

Physically shaken, with tears streaming down his face, Lincoln paced the White House, trying to make sense of the events of 21 October. His aides could only watch, unable to console the president. Lincoln took his vengeance on General Stone, who, although never charged with an offense, was imprisoned for six months.

Four days after Ball's Bluff, McClellan wrote to Ellen, "How weary I am of all this business! Care after care, blunder after blunder, trick upon trick." Scott had also had enough. On 1 November, he once again offered his resignation to the president; this time it was accepted.

The sterling military career of General Winfield Scott came to a close at a Washington train station—not in a blaze of glory but with a mere whimper as the general sat surrounded by a few dignitaries. Reporters noted that he rose from his chair with great difficulty as he received the good wishes of several visitors. As Scott sat waiting for his train, he looked every bit like a soldier whose time had passed. It was an awkward scene for the hero of two wars, who once boasted that he was "a year older than the Constitution."

Minutes before Scott's train arrived, the general was surprised by the sudden appearance of his successor and nemesis. Two days earlier, Lincoln had named General McClellan general-in-chief. It was four o'clock in the morning and rain was falling as Scott's train arrived. Out of respect for Scott, McClellan wore a sparkling uniform and showered the old general with platitudes and an outpouring of admiration. The departing Scott seemed sincerely touched by McClellan's gesture and extended kind wishes to his wife and new baby.

The scene was markedly different from that of 1 November, when Lincoln had accepted Scott's resignation at the White House. Scott had urged Lincoln to appoint General Henry Halleck as his successor. While offering the command to McClellan, Lincoln expressed concern that the job might be too much for the thirty-four-year-old general. McClellan cockily responded, "I can do it all!" When told of Lincoln's decision, Scott grumbled, "Wherever I spend the little remainder of my life, my frequent and latest prayer will be God save the Union!"

McClellan confessed to Ellen that his handling of Scott's departure was "a little rhetorical" but that it seemed "to have accomplished the object." But it was evident that he was also moved by the episode:

> The old man said that his sensations were very peculiar in leaving Washington and active life. I can easily understand them; and it may be that some distant day I, too, shall totter away from Washington, a worn-out soldier, with naught to do but make my peace with God. The sight of this morning was a lesson to me which I hope not soon to forget (McClellan, 1887).

With Scott out of the way and Lincoln seemingly willing to cooperate with him, Little Mac was looking forward to demonstrating his talent for building and directing an army. However, McClellan suffered a personal setback, which would hamper his progress in readying his army for a spring offensive. Although the living quarters of officers were vastly superior to those of the average foot soldier, no one was safe from the diseases that spread as a result of tainted water and unsanitary conditions. Within weeks of his appointment as general-in-chief, McClellan contracted typhoid fever. By mid-December, he was bedridden with fever and internal bleeding.

Although he received surprisingly little blame after the Ball's Bluff debacle, as Scott's resignation and Stone's arrest captured public attention, McClellan's star dimmed during the last two months of 1861. In the North, the adjectives "timid" and "cautious" were commonly attached to the his name. In Confederate camps, he was disparagingly referred to as "George." However, his inter-action with his own troops only increased their loyalty. He took a fatherly approach to his men and displayed genuine concern for their well-being.

Five days after Scott's departure, Great Britain and the

United States nearly went to war over the blockade of the Confederacy. Two Confederate agents had been arrested when they were discovered aboard the H.M.S. *Trent.* Lincoln threatened to hang the men as pirates. The two countries postured threateningly and the situation grew warlike. President Davis made it clear that if either of the men was hanged, he would authorize the hanging of prisoners at Libby Prison, where Frank Greene was incarcerated. The "Trent Affair" blew over.

As presidents Davis and Lincoln sparred, the military hierarchy in Richmond reorganized Joe Johnston's army. On a cloudy and cold Monday, 2 December, the 21st Mississippi was ordered to move to Yorktown. Before this order could be executed, however, it was rescinded. The voracity with which the Mississippi regiments had devoured Union troops at Ball's Bluff had been so impressive that it was decided to organize a brigade of Mississippians. On 3 December, Joe Johnston received the following order:

> The President directs the immediate assignment of the Mississippi regiments to brigades as follows; To 1st Brigade, under W.H.C. Whiting, the regiments under Colonels W.C. Faulkner, W.H. Moore, William Barksdale (13th), W.S. Featherston (17th) and T.M. Griffin. To 2nd Brigade, under Richard Griffith, the regiments under Colonels H. Hughes, Carnot Posey (16th), C.H. Mott, and B.G. Humphreys (21st) (U.S. War Dept., 1880–1901).

After six months of soldiering, Will and Sam could share each other's company. The brigade positioned itself on the Potomac near Leesburg as 1861 drew to a close. The Postlethwaite brothers' brigade commander was Richard Griffith, a former Mississippi state treasurer. When the war began, he had resigned his position and organized the 12th Mississippi Infantry, of which he was elected colonel. On 2 November, he had been promoted to brigadier general.

The command of the combined Confederate forces around Leesburg was in the hands of a former mathematics teacher and Mexican War veteran named Daniel "Harvey" Hill. In marrying the daughter of a North Carolina clergyman, Hill bore the unenviable burden of being compared to his brother-in-law, Stonewall Jackson.

In the first nine months of the conflict, the Union army had been defeated at Fort Sumter, Manassas, Wilson's Creek, and Ball's Bluff. President Lincoln had mourned the death of two close friends. Will and Sam Postlethwaite were camped on the Southern side of the Potomac, the 2nd Rhode Island resided within the confines of Washington, and Frank Greene languished in Libby Prison. No one spoke of "a short war" any longer.

McClellan wrote to his wife, "It now begins to look as if we are condemned to a winter of inactivity. If it is so the fault will be not mine."

CHAPTER SIX

He'll Be Heard From

Sam's death notice in the Providence Journal *announced that his funeral would originate at the "residence of William R. Greene, WOODSIDE." Since this would certainly have been a large estate, I began studying nineteenth-century maps, hoping to determine its location, and hoping that it still existed. Was Woodside the name of the residence, hence the name of the street directly in front of the cemetery gate? Or had the house simply been situated on Woodside Avenue? Some of the local historians pointed out several "Greene" houses in the area; two were on Woodside Avenue. Although they are beautifully restored, I thought they would have been much too small to house the growing Greene/ Postlethwaite clan.*

Many local residents remembered the largest of the Greene houses, Henry Lehre Greene's. This mansion house had been razed in the 1970s to make way for a senior citizen high-rise known as Clyde Tower. On a wall in Clyde Tower's recreation room hang the ceramic tiles from the fireplace of Henry Lehre Greene's estate; they are the only surviving artifacts of a once-proud structure.

The mystery of Woodside continued to gnaw at me. Even the grantor/grantee indexes in the city archives yielded little information. In 1912, the area in question had seceded from Warwick and been incorporated as the Town of West Warwick; real estate records had been shared, divided, and lost. I did discover that William had a summer cottage on Greenwich Bay in a section of Warwick known as the Button Woods, now commonly known as Buttonwoods. Several people I spoke with remembered one more house but couldn't recall who had owned it. It was an imposing white house that stood at the corner of Woodside and Fairview avenues directly across the street from the graves of William and Sam. It then occurred to me that, unlike the other graves at Greenwood, which faced away from the front of the cemetery, William's stone faced the street, directly toward where this house once stood.

Seeking information about the house, I decided to write a letter to the Pawtuxet Valley Historical Society. I was later told that the house became quite a topic of discussion at the society's next meeting, as members searched their memories trying to recall who had owned the house more than twenty years before. The day after the meeting, the society called to tell me that a woman by the name of Ruth Cardin was certain the house had belonged to a Tom Quinn, who now lived in Warwick. Mrs. Cardin, the unknowing owner of Sam's gravesite who had purchased the lot in the 1970s, was suddenly helping me with my research. (From the inscription on Lionel Pete Cardin's gravestone, who is buried on Sam's lot, I was able to determine the date of his death. I then looked up his obituary on microfilm at a local library. Ruth's name is also inscribed in the stone.)

I sent a letter to Tom Quinn, assuming that I would get no response. To my delight, he called the next day and was very eager to speak with me. A retired attorney in his eighties, he asked if I would like to spend a few hours with him visiting the site and learning of its history. Before I hung up, I asked Tom a question: "What street did it face?" He answered, "Corotoman Farm, as it was called, main entrance was on Woodside Avenue. There was a circular carriageway that featured a large granite stepping stone on which to exit a stage coach or buggy. The first thing my father did when he bought the house was grind off the previous owner's initials and inscribe his own." Tom had no recollection of the person from whom his father had purchased the farm, but he always remembered the inscription his father had ground off of the stone: "W. R. G." (Tom's father had worked for Simon Henry Greene as a boy. Simon Greene was born in 1799.)

Tom and I spent an enjoyable Saturday driving around the subdivision that had once been his estate. He showed me where the tennis courts had been and where the trout stream had run. "Now I'll tell you a funny story," he beamed. "You see those walls? Notice anything unusual about them?" All that remains of Corotoman Farm today are several beautiful New England dry walls that at one time surrounded the property. Upon inspection, I noticed that a long section of wall along Woodside Avenue had been cemented. Tom told me that although his was a family of teetotalers, they loved to make jellies and preserves, so the property was covered in grapevines. Once, while spending several months abroad, the Quinns had left Corotoman Farm in the hands of two trusted caretakers from Portugal. While the family was away, the caretakers had taken the liberty of making two huge casks of red wine, consuming one and most of the other during the course of the summer. Under the influence of the grape, the two well-meaning men had decided to "spruce the place up" and "finish those walls." Of course the Quinns were horrified when they returned *to find the cemented walls, but all was soon forgiven. Never again, however, would wine be made at Corotoman Farm. Sadly, no one in Tom's family ever thought to take a photograph of the house before they sold it. Tom had assumed it would always be there. Still, to this day he laughs when he drives past the cemented "dry walls" on Woodside Avenue.*

Courtesy of Tom Quinn

Tom Quinn at Corotoman Farm. His father,
Patrick, worked for Simon Henry Greene as a
boy and later purchased the Greene home.

THE ARMY OF THE POTOMAC WAS QUITE SETTLED IN AT its "temporary" quarters in Washington as winter brought 1861 to a close. "One day is much like another," wrote a soldier in the 2nd Rhode Island.

Sam and Will were stationed at Woodyards Ford, six miles from their original camp, Camp Pickens, at Manassas Junction. There they spent November and December waiting for McClellan's army to cross the Potomac. In mid-December, the 21st got into a skirmish with Union pickets near Berlin Heights, Maryland. Although there is little record of this clash, it was Sam's first engagement with the enemy.

In late December, an ill General McClellan returned to his headquarters to be told that President Lincoln was waiting for him in the parlor. McClellan refused to meet the president and instead went to bed. Insulted and annoyed, President Lincoln left to seek the advice of General McDowell, complaining that he had no one in the army to talk to. Lincoln, his cabinet, and General McDowell held a series of meetings beginning on 10 January. Simon Cameron was embroiled in scandal, and the administration was effectively without a secretary of war. At one point, when neither Cameron nor McClellan was present, McDowell seized an opportunity to regain stature and proposed to Lincoln that the Army of the Potomac should again attempt to attack Richmond by way of Manassas. Again on the 11th, McDowell, being the only true military mind present aside from General William Franklin, held court with Lincoln and his cabinet. Lincoln remarked that if McClellan did not intend to use the army then he "would like to borrow it for a time."

The next day, feeling somewhat better, McClellan rose from his sick bed and joined Lincoln's council. In a foul mood, he quickly made his presence felt, glaring at a nervous McDowell. The atmosphere was tense. Secretary of State Seward demanded that the Army of the Potomac get moving. Secretary of the Treasury Salmon Chase accused McClellan of not having a plan for an offensive against the enemy and dared him to present one. McClellan politely insisted that he did indeed have a sound plan. When Chase voiced doubt about McClellan's statements, the general-in-chief stung the cabinet by icily informing the president that, because of the high number of security leaks from the White House, he felt that he could not trust the group with such privileged information. Their patriotism challenged, the distinguished group sat in stunned disbelief when Lincoln agreed with McClellan.

In early January, Sam and Will's regiments set up camp near Leesburg, Virginia. Exclusively a camp of Mississippians, it was aptly named Camp Mississippi. The women of Richmond presented a hand-stitched silk battle flag for the 16th Mississippi; it displayed twelve cotton stars on red and blue wool bunting. At the center of the flag was the handwritten inscription, "Through God We Shall Do Valiantly, For He Is That Shall Tread Down Our Enemies." Moved by this gesture, the men of Will's regiment voted to donate one day's ration per week to the needy people of Richmond.

Frank Greene survived the threat of being hanged by his captors at Libby Prison, but he was in terrible physical shape. He was suffering from traumatic stress disorder, or "shock" as it was known in the 1860s. He certainly posed no threat to the Confederacy. Struggling to provide food and medical supplies to fighting men, Davis' government could ill afford to provide for the needs of wounded prisoners.

On 17 January 1862, a sunny, warm, spring-like day, Frank was taken to a site on the James River and released in an exchange of prisoners. At Camp Brightwood, he was examined by army doctors and diagnosed as suffering from trauma, pulmonary disorder, and necrosis of the tibia in the left leg. He was deemed "probably permanently disabled." Corporal Frank Greene was ordered discharged on 25 January. He was nineteen years old.

Returning to his father's home in Riverpoint, Frank was a disheartening sight. A friend of the Greene family remembered, "He returned to his home, hoping by care and repose to regain his health, but exposure and suffering had shattered his constitution and planted the seed of fatal disease in his system."

14 January was cold and snowy as Will and Sam's regiments received orders from Richmond. The two had been brigaded together for six quiet weeks, but their reunion was over. Although they would both remain in the Leesburg area, they would no longer be part of the same brigade; thus began two distinctly different military careers.

Sam's 21st was now brigaded with the 13th, 17th, and 18th Mississippi, remaining under the command of General Richard Griffith. Will's 16th was brigaded with the 15th Alabama, 21st Georgia, 21st North Carolina, and a battery of artillery from Virginia. This brigade was commanded by General Isaac Trimble. Although in his sixties, Trimble was fiery and quick-witted; he demonstrated his aggressiveness by burning several bridges in Northern Baltimore immediately after the fall of Fort Sumter. Trimble had spent the balance of 1861 supervising the construction of Confederate defenses along the Potomac River.

For the next several weeks, both armies endured the cold and snow as winter gripped the mid-Atlantic states. Lincoln gave McClellan an ultimatum, ordering the general to strike the enemy by 22 February. McClellan insisted that an attack on the Confederate defenses along the Potomac would be a disaster and placated the president by unveiling his "plan."

Not only was McClellan's stratagem brilliant, it was the biggest, grandest mobilization of men and materials in the history of the world. McClellan understood that defeating an entrenched enemy, even if he held a numerical advantage of two to one, was extremely unlikely. So instead of advancing on Manassas overland, the Army of the Potomac would be transported by ships down the Potomac into the Chesapeake Bay, landing at the small town of Urbanna at the mouth of the Rappahannock River. McClellan's army would then begin a sixty-mile march behind Johnston's lines, against little resistance, east to Richmond. Catching Joe Johnston's Confederate army off balance, the Union army would capture Richmond in a matter of days. If McClellan's march went according to plan, any units of

Johnston's army that made it back to Richmond would be too disorganized to put up an effective resistance.

McClellan explained to Lincoln that aside from thousands of artillery pieces and horses and miles of supply trains, he would require at least 150,000 men to guarantee victory. Satisfied that the Army of the Potomac was to move at last, Lincoln accepted McClellan's plan and urged him to carry it through. McClellan would get his 150,000 troops.

The end of winter brought with it an air of uncertainty. There was no doubt that the Army of the Potomac was ready for a spring offensive. No longer a collection of green volunteers, the army was finally razor sharp. Still, there were doubts, and Lincoln and his new secretary of war, Edwin Stanton, continued to meddle in McClellan's work. Lincoln had been shattered by the death of his eleven-year-old son, Willie, on 20 February; a White House employee remarked, "I never saw a man so bowed down in grief." Unable to come to grips with the loss of Willie, Lincoln was acting erratically.

Preparations for McClellan's great expedition were progressing steadily. The 2nd Rhode Island Regiment was "packed up and ready to move." Only a snowstorm on 2 March delayed the beginning of the operation.

Without the firing of a shot, Saturday, 8 March, turned out to be one of the most eventful days of the war. Early that morning, as McClellan was riding to the White House, he noticed an ominous black cloud hanging over the Confederate side of the Potomac.

Sensing a move by McClellan, General Johnston had ordered an organized withdrawal to the Southern side of the Rappahannock River. Early that morning Sam and Will were ordered to burn anything they couldn't carry. The fire was spectacular. Anything that could be of use to McClellan's army was torched, including a million pounds of bacon. Johnston's move would force McClellan to alter everything he had planned for the past seven months.

Knowing that Lincoln wouldn't tolerate another delay, McClellan decided that his amphibious operation would have to go forward, however, a new landing place would have to be selected. The practical choice was the Union-held Fortress Monroe at the southeastern tip of the peninsula that lay between the James and York rivers. Landing at Fortress Monroe would force the Army of the Potomac to march twice the distance originally planned, through unfamiliar territory. Worse, Johnston's army now was closer to Richmond; once McClellan began his long march from Fortress Monroe the Confederate army would have more time to set up adequate defenses in front of the capital. But McClellan saw no other options. Further troubling the general was word from Lincoln that vicious rumors questioning McClellan's loyalty were swirling through the highest echelons of the government. Though Lincoln said he didn't believe the rumors, McClellan's relationship with him reached a new low. At this time, the *Monitor* and the *Merrimac* (re-named C.S.S. *Virginia*), the first ironclad warships, had their historic confrontation, making naval warfare as it had been known obsolete.

Three days after expressing his confidence in McClellan, Lincoln removed him as general-in-chief. Lincoln and Stanton, amateurs in military affairs, decided to take personal control of all the armed forces, leaving McClellan in command of the Army of the Potomac only. While he felt betrayed, McClellan didn't resign; instead he continued making preparations for the amphibious landing on the York-James peninsula.

Worried that Johnston's withdrawal was a ploy to lure the Army of the Potomac into a trap, McClellan ordered a cautious probing of what remained of the Confederate defenses. Accompanied by the press, a foray discovered that although Johnston's defenses had been formidable, they were hardly of the size and scope that McClellan had claimed over the last seven months. Cleverly, Johnston had left wooden "Quaker guns" in place. Northern politicians and newspapers had a field day, calling for the "timid" general to resign. Senator Fessenden of Maine declared that an incompetent president was responsible for putting McClellan in charge of the army. He wrote to his family, "You will have heard of the wooden guns at Centreville. It is no longer doubtful that General McClellan is utterly unfit for his position. And yet the president will keep him in command . . . . Well, it cannot be helped. We went for a rail-splitter, and we have got one."

Despite the growing criticism, the Army of the Potomac continued to mobilize for the coming campaign. On 17 March, six days after being removed as general-in-chief, McClellan spoke to his men:

> I will bring you now face to face with the rebels. . . . I am to watch over you as a parent over his children; and you know that your general loves you from the depths of his heart. It shall be my care to gain success with the least possible loss; but I know that, if it is necessary, you will willingly follow me to your graves for our righteous cause. I shall demand of you great, heroic exertions, rapid and long marches, desperate combats, privations perhaps. We shall share all these together; and when this sad war is over we will return to our homes, and feel that we can ask no higher honor than the proud consciousness that we belonged to the Army of the Potomac (Sears, 1992).

After these words, four hundred ships carrying 121,500 men, 15,000 horses, 1,200 wagons, seventy-five batteries of artillery, tons of supplies, and miles of telegraph wire set sail for Fortress Monroe.

As McClellan's armada began to sail south, the remains of the Union dead who had fallen at Manassas were being exhumed from the battlefield and returned to their home states. When the bodies of Colonel Slocum and Major Sullivan Ballou were brought into the camp of the 2nd Rhode Island, there were feelings of sorrow and anger. Word of Ballou's mutilation spread through camp, and the men of the 2nd vowed vengeance.

The Army of the Potomac sailed down the coast to Fortress Monroe amid cheers of "On to Richmond!" in a scene reminiscent of the army's departure for Manassas the previous summer. Will and Sam Postlethwaite waited in their defensive works on the Rappahannock until Johnston, informed of a great movement of Union troops by water, ordered his army further south along the banks of the Rapidan. Davis, Lee, and Johnston could only wait to see where McClellan intended to strike. But because of his squabbles with Lincoln and the evacuation of the Confederate army around Manassas, McClellan had lost the key element of his plan: surprise.

The Union hierarchy was worried. Jackson's "Army of the Valley" was somewhere in the Shenandoah, which pointed like a dagger at Washington. Wary of Jackson, Lincoln ordered 20,000 men under the command of General Nathaniel Banks to clear Jackson from the valley. With that accomplished Lincoln would feel confident enough to commit McDowell's army, along with other units, to McClellan.

Although convinced that he couldn't take Richmond without the 150,000 men that Lincoln had promised, McClellan didn't argue about the move against Jackson. While the world watched in fascination, events on the peninsula began to unfold; few realized that the campaign's outcome would be decided in the Shenandoah Valley.

In early March, Jackson's army of 4,200 men was encamped at the northern tip of the valley at the town of Winchester, a mere seventy miles from the White House. Humble and deeply religious, Jackson was not amused by his celebrity status; he downplayed his notoriety. He carefully avoided reading newspaper accounts pertaining to himself, and he had little use for the luxuries and adoration afforded to most generals. Orphaned at the age of three, growing up poor and lacking in education, Thomas Jackson had been enrolled at West Point at the age of eighteen. He struggled academically there, but he became more accustomed to the rigors of higher learning and began to excel toward the end of his stay. Many of his classmates were only half-joking when they remarked that Jackson would have graduated first in his class had the course lasted a year longer. He graduated in 1846, served in the Mexican War and was promoted twice for bravery. A widower, Jackson remarried in 1857, becoming the devoted husband of Mary Anna Morrison.

Jackson's eccentric personality was probably described best by one of his West Point classmates soon after John Brown's unsuccessful raid at Harper's Ferry.

> Old Jack is quite a character, genius or just a little crazy. He lives quietly and don't meddle. He's as systematic as a multiplication table and as full of military as an arsenal. Stiff, you see, never laughs, but kind hearted as a woman, and by Jupiter, he teaches a nigger Sunday School. But, mind, if this John Brown business leads to war, he'll be heard from!" (Henderson, 1988).

Jackson smiled often, and when not immersed in the business of war he was known for his kindness. However, when it came to military discipline, his men thought him harsh—even cruel. In December 1861, he ordered a soldier executed after the soldier got into a fight with a captain. Jackson's staff officers pleaded with him to spare the soldier's life, and the general was nearly brought to tears by their appeals, but the soldier was executed.

Jackson was a man of few words; even his closest aides had no way of knowing what he was thinking. He never sought the opinions or advice of his staff officers. He stressed to his men, "If this valley is lost, Virginia is lost!" He shared only a vague notion of his strategy with those around him, saying, "Mystery . . . mystery is the key to success." Few understood what he meant. More popular with the people of the North than most Union generals, this was the legendary figure whom General Banks had been sent to the valley to contend with.

Having served in Congress for several years and later as governor of Massachusetts, Nathaniel Banks was the president of the Illinois Central Railroad when Fort Sumter fell. In May 1861, the forty-four-year-old Banks joined the United States Volunteers. On 9 March 1862, his army was camped at Charlestown, West Virginia, fifteen miles from Jackson's base at Winchester.

While Jackson held the advantage of having battle-tested, eager troops, Banks' men had never been in a fight. The prospect of taking on the hero of Bull Run their first time out didn't promote confidence. Jackson did not want to evacuate Winchester and instead planned to boldly strike Banks' green troops.

Looking for a fight, Banks entered Winchester on 12 March only to discover that Jackson was gone. Jackson held his army just outside the town, waiting to spring his trap. Knowing his sudden disappearance would cause Banks' troops to feel a bit uneasy, he planned to reappear with a chilling bayonet charge just as darkness fell. Banks refused to underestimate Jackson and quickly fortified the town.

Before the battle could commence, Jackson was informed that several of his brigades had wandered as far as ten miles away and wouldn't be available for action. He was livid. His first impulse was to launch the attack anyway, but he thought better of it. Uncharacteristically, he muttered to himself, "No, I must not do it, it may cost the lives of too many brave men. I must retreat and wait for a better time."

While Jackson moved thirty miles south, Banks divided his army, sending a division under General James Shields in pursuit of Jackson. For the next ten days, Federal cavalry scoured the valley for Jackson, concluding that his forces were gone. With the valley seemingly secured, Lincoln ordered the bulk of Banks' army to begin leaving the valley to join McClellan. Jackson's sense of "mystery" would manifest itself in the events that followed.

After a week and a half in hiding, Jackson abruptly ordered his troops on a grueling march of twenty-two miles. Camping near Strasburg on the evening of 22 March, Jackson received a message through one of his sources in Winchester that General Shields' division had withdrawn, leaving behind only a small force to protect its rear flank near the town of Kernstown, five miles south of Winchester.

Early on 23 March, Jackson again ordered his troops on a forced march; many of them collapsed or fell ill. After fourteen miles, he halted the march and ordered his men to rest and make camp, then immediately reversed the order. Realizing that his position was clearly visible to the enemy, he decided to take the offensive at once. It was Sunday.

Jackson's cavalry, under the command of Colonel Turner Ashby, had estimated the strength of Shields' rear guard to be about four thousand. Ashby's reports were trusted; his reports had previously been accurate. On this day, however, Ashby was wrong. Jackson's philosophy was to always attack a smaller, isolated force, but nine thousand Union men were available for a fight near the little town of Kernstown.

Plowing season had begun, and the valley had seen its share of spring rains; Jackson's men found the going slow and rough. Moving up on an entrenched enemy through fields of mud, scores of Jackson's men fell as the attack got under way. Union reinforcements were rapidly brought to the field, and Jackson watched as his Virginians hammered away at Shields' position to no avail. Hundreds of his finest men were killed or wounded, and hundreds more were overwhelmed by the enemy and taken prisoner. Trying to turn the tide, Jackson called for a bayonet charge by two regiments which had been held in reserve. When they did not materialize, Jackson took out his impatience on a young drummer boy who had straggled off the field. The general rode over to the boy, grabbed him by the coat, and dragged him back to the field, ordering him to "Beat the rally!"

Desperate, Jackson went looking for his reinforcements. Instead of advancing against Shields, the two regiments were making an orderly retreat and taking up a rear guard position. On the field, some of Jackson's men were not only holding their ground but were giving the enemy all they could handle. But with no reinforcements in sight, these men were finally forced from the field when they ran out of ammunition.

After two hours of hot fighting, his army in disarray and with darkness coming, Jackson had been thoroughly defeated. The "green" Union troops had refused to flinch. The flag of one Union regiment, the 5th Ohio, had changed hands several times. After the battle, the Ohioans counted forty-eight bullet holes in the flag.

Jackson's battered army straggled south into the valley and set up camp. Jackson, stoic as ever, fell asleep on a makeshift bed. It would only be a day or two before the impact of his decision to attack Banks at Kernstown was felt.

On the peninsula, McClellan's transports arrived daily at Fortress Monroe, turning it into small city. The 2nd Rhode Island departed Alexandria on 26 March aboard the *John Brooks*. The men of the 2nd were thrilled to get a brief glimpse of the ironclad *Monitor* in Hampton Roads. Landing at the summer resort of Hampton, they were stunned to find that only burnt foundations and rubble remained of the town. This was the work of the Confederates, who had refused to let the town fall into Union hands intact.

Throughout the last week of March, McClellan's army assembled at Fortress Monroe. Rough waters made navigation on the crowded bay treacherous, and many of the men were plagued by seasickness. There were a number of logistical problems, and a shortage of transport ships delayed the beginning of the campaign. Allen Pinkerton assured McClellan that there were no fewer than twenty thousand Confederates in and around the historic town of Yorktown, the site of George Washington's greatest victory, and another fifteen thousand under the command of General Huger at nearby Norfolk, home port of the ironclad *Virginia*. These were typical Pinkerton numbers. In fact, the entire Confederate force numbered fewer than five thousand men.

Prince John

In command of this small Confederate force was the colorful General John Magruder. Magruder liked the finer things and was well-known for his lavish lifestyle. When stationed before the war at Fort Adams in Newport, Rhode Island, he was the darling of society, and his parties had been highlights of the social season. He had a particular weakness for the theater and often used his parties as an opportunity to put on small plays.

Born as John Magruder, he wasn't satisfied with such an ordinary moniker and added the worldly sounding "Bankhead" to his name. For all his eccentricities, he was a good soldier. He had earned two promotions during the Indian wars in Florida and had served on the western frontier. A week after Fort Sumter he resigned from the United States Army to serve as a colonel in the Confederate army.

President Davis had been alerted to the situation on the peninsula and the threat it posed to Richmond. Whether this was a feint by McClellan to disguise a major assault against Johnston along the Rapidan, or an operation against Norfolk, neither Davis nor Robert E. Lee could guess. Worried, Johnston began sending reinforcements to Magruder to ward off any Union advance on the peninsula. On Friday, 28 March, the same day the 2nd Rhode Island arrived at Fortress Monroe, the 21st Mississippi began a long march from the Rapidan to Yorktown.

McClellan left for Fortress Monroe on April Fool's Day and arrived in a pouring rain on 2 April. On the 3rd he was informed that the ten thousand men garrisoned at Monroe would not be under his command, as had originally been agreed. In fact, if the fortress came under attack he would have to defer to its commander, General Wool. In addition, the James River had been closed to naval operations because of the presence of the *Virginia*. Essential pieces of McClellan's invasion force were being stripped from him even before the campaign began. The downpours that greeted McClellan upon his arrival intensified during the first week of April, introducing the worst rainy season in twenty years.

Davis and Lee worried about an attack on Richmond, but as action in the Western theater increased they ordered Beauregard to Tennessee, leaving Joe Johnston in sole command of the Confederate army in Virginia.

McClellan's scouts were agitated to discover that the Warwick River did not run parallel to the York and James rivers, as their army maps indicated, but instead ran east to west across the entirety of the peninsula. This essentially placed the Army of the Potomac on an island. River crossings under the most ideal conditions were difficult and slow, but crossing in a cold, wind-driven rain under enemy fire could be disastrous.

Seven miles behind the Confederate line along the Warwick was the town of Williamsburg, where General Magruder had built an imposing fort, naming it for himself. If the Army of the Potomac managed to cross the Warwick it would have to contend with Fort Magruder before making its final push to Richmond. Scattered throughout the peninsula were remnants of earthworks from the revolution of eighty years before. Although these reminders of the American Revolution gave the field a ghostly feel, men on both sides found them to be quite convenient and went to work restoring the entrenchments for their own use.

Bad weather hampered McClellan. The narrow wheels of wagons and artillery cut into muddy roads, sometimes creating mud holes two to three feet deep. What had started as a glorious march steadily turned into a massive traffic jam. Magruder's men were beginning to suffer as well. Most of the men in the Confederate army were from warmer climates and were falling ill from the wet and cold. The incessant rain that inundated the peninsula was inescapable, and the men's small, two-man tents failed to provide adequate shelter. Many of Magruder's men chose to bivouac outside rather than sleep in their damp, moldy tents. Everything was soaked, and a swampy mist hung in the air as spring tried to assert itself against late winter. Men began to grow beards to protect their faces and throats from the elements.

Another major problem confronting Magruder's men was a sudden outbreak of childhood diseases like measles and chicken pox. Having grown up in small towns or farming communities, most of the soldiers were for the first time living in close quarters, unlike their Northern counterparts from the big cities. Whole companies of Southern men fell victim to measles or whooping cough.

Adding to this misery was the lack of rations. In the haste to meet the threat on the peninsula, priority had been given to manpower and weaponry over food and supplies. Another problem was keeping any food that could be obtained fresh in the foul climate. Such was the sad state of Magruder's command, which had grown to eleven thousand men. Their task was to keep 100,000 Union soldiers out of Richmond.

The fact that Prince John Magruder held the responsibility of keeping McClellan at bay was fateful. With his small Army of the Peninsula entrenched, Magruder could inflict terrible casualties upon the Army of the Potomac if an attack came, but ultimately Magruder would be overrun. Magruder's only hope for success was to stall McClellan until Johnston's army arrived from the Rapidan.

Out of genius or desperation, Magruder applied his affinity for the theater to the field of battle. In contrast to his small dinner party productions, he now faced an audience of more than eighty-five thousand. He spread his few artillery pieces along the entire length of the Warwick River and began a random, ineffective bombardment of the Union side of the river. Although it inflicted few casualties, the strategy played upon the psyche of McClellan's frustrated army.

As Pinkerton's detectives peered across the river, Magruder's regiments marched in and out of the woods in full view. A corporal from Alabama wrote, "This morning we were called out on the 'long roll' and have been traveling most of the day, seeming with no other view than to show ourselves to the enemy at as many different points of the line as possible. I am pretty tired." In the evening, regimental bands played as loud and as long as possible.

McClellan wanted more information. Negroes interviewed by McClellan's staff were so eager to provide information to the Union army that they often gave false or exaggerated descriptions of Confederate strength. Union scouts, generals, Pinkerton, and McClellan himself fell for Magruder's elaborate ruse. Prince John couldn't believe his luck.

In the Shenandoah Valley, Jackson had once again disappeared. Although he had been decisively beaten by General Banks on 23 March, Jackson's attack had rattled Lincoln. Jackson certainly wouldn't have attacked at Kernstown without having at least as many men as Banks. Had Jackson's numbers been superior, his attack failing merely due to organizational problems? Or had Shields' men simply fought better than anyone could have expected? Perhaps Jackson had been the victim of faulty intelligence. Banks concluded that the Confederate Army of the Valley was much larger than previously estimated.

Once again, Lincoln feared for the safety of the capital, and even McClellan couldn't argue with him. Not only would McClellan not receive Banks' eighteen thousand men, neither would he get McDowell's force of forty thousand originally promised by Lincoln. Before any troops would be sent to McClellan's aid, Jackson would have to be driven from the Shenandoah Valley. To achieve this, Lincoln divided the seventy thousand-man army around Washington into three groups, each larger than Jackson's army. By dividing his army, Lincoln risked a possible defeat if any one of its parts should be struck by Jackson; but Jackson's position would then be exposed to the other two Union armies, which could then hunt him down.

McClellan complained to the president about having had Wool's ten thousand troops taken away from him, and the president promised that no further reductions would be made in his force. Now, only one day after arriving on the peninsula, Little Mac's army had been reduced by almost seventy thousand men. The original plan to land several thousand troops behind Magruder had to be scrapped. Instead, McClellan was faced with the prospect of launching a headlong assault on the center of Magruder's line. He feared heavy casualties and claimed in a report that he was "shocked" by the president's actions.

McClellan was determined to make the president aware of the impact of the troop reductions on the campaign. His telegram to the president was short and sarcastic:

> I have the honor to state that my entire force for duty amounts to only about 85,000 men. General Wool's command has been taken out of my control. The only use that can be made of his command is to protect my communications in rear of this point. At this time, only 53,000 men have joined me, but they are coming up as rapidly as my means of transportation will permit.

Convinced that Secretary of War Stanton was influencing Lincoln, McClellan ended his message to the president by urging him to show the telegram to Stanton, as if to point out the damage the secretary was doing to the campaign.

Although the telegram clearly expressed his disappointment, it appears to have caused the general to brood. Later in the day he decided to send a second message:

> The whole line of the Warwick, which really heads within a mile of Yorktown, is strongly defended by detached redoubts and other fortifications, armed with heavy and light guns. It will be necessary to resort to the use of heavy guns and some siege operations before we assault.
>
> The prisoners state that General Johnston arrived at Yorktown yesterday with strong reinforcements. It seems clear that I shall have the whole force of the enemy on my hands, probably not less

than 100,000 men, and probably more. In consequence my force is probably less than that of the
enemy, while they have all the advantage of position.

Since my arrangements were made for this campaign at least 50,000 men have been taken from my
command. When my present command all join, I
shall have about 85,000 men for duty, from which a
large force must be taken for guards, scouts; & etc.
With this army I could assault the enemy's works,
and perhaps carry them, but were I in possession of
their entrenchments and assailed by double my
numbers I should have no fear as to the result.

McClellan went on to clearly place the responsibility for
any possible defeat with the president:

Under the circumstances that have developed
since we arrived here, I feel fully impressed with
the conviction that here is to be fought the great
battle that is to decide the existing contest. I shall
of course commence the attack as soon as I can get
up my siege train, and shall do all in my power to
carry the enemy's works; but to do this with a reasonable degree of certainty requires, in my judgement, that I should, if possible, have at least the
whole of the First Corps [McDowell's] to land upon
the Severn River and attack [the enemy] in the
rear. My present strength will not admit of a
detachment sufficient for this purpose.

To remove any doubt that he might be overstating the
enemy's strength, McClellan also sent Stanton a copy of a letter written by General Erasmus Keyes to Senator Ira Harris,
warning of the Army of the Potomac's perilous position.

This army being reduced by 45,000 troops,
some of them among the best in the service, and
without any support from the navy, the plan to

which we are reduced bears scarcely any resemblance to the one I voted for.

[Confederate defenses are protected by] "a stream or succession of ponds, nowhere fordable. What can we do next? The roads are very bad . . . the strength of the enemy's line and the number of his guns prove to be almost immeasurably greater than I had been led to expect. The line in front of us, in the opinion of all the military men who are all competent to judge, is one of the strongest in the world. The great battle will be more horrible than I care to tell you. The plan was good. But with the reduction of force means the plan is entirely changed, and now is a bad plan . . . with means insufficient for success.

Do not look upon this letter as the offspring of despondency, I never despond. I am now working to my utmost. Please show this letter to the President (and Stanton).

General Keyes' letter shows that McClellan was not alone in his estimation of the Confederate strength along the Warwick; Allan Pinkerton's exaggerated estimations certainly clouded the matter further.

Lincoln, meanwhile, was alarmed by Stanton's insistence that McClellan had deliberately left the capital defenseless. If McClellan's telegrams were designed to sway the president away from Stanton, they failed to produce the desired effect. Lincoln responded to the general's communications with an angry tone.

After you left, I ascertained that less than 20,000 unorganized men, without a single battery [were left behind] for the defense of Washington. And allow me to ask, do you really think I should permit the line from Richmond to Manassas Junction to this city to be entirely open except what resistance could be presented by less than

20,000 unorganized troops? I think it is the precise time for you to strike a blow. You will do me the justice to remember I always insisted that going down the bay in search of a field, instead of fighting at or near Manassas, was only shifting and not surmounting a difficulty; that we shall find the same enemy and the same or equal entrenchments at either place. The country will not fail to note, is now noting, that the present hesitation to move upon an entrenched enemy is but the story of Manassas repeated.

I beg to assure you that I have never written to you or spoken to you in greater kindness of feeling than now, nor with a fuller promise to sustain you, so far as, in my most anxious judgement, I consistently can. But you must act (U.S. War Dept., 1880–1901).

In a letter to his wife, McClellan wrote, "The President very coolly telegraphed me . . . that he thought I should break the enemy's lines at once. I was much tempted to reply that he had better come and do it himself." Lincoln's frustration with what he felt was a lack of initiative on McClellan's part was exacerbated by Union successes in the west. In February, little-known General Ulysses Grant earned national fame at Fort Donelson, Tennessee, where he secured the Cumberland River for the Union. In early March, a Union victory at the Battle of Pea Ridge ended Confederate military operations in Missouri, and word of another victory in New Mexico reached Washington just days before McClellan left for the peninsula.

These Union victories caused enthusiasm for the war to wane slightly throughout the South, and enlistments tailed off. The Confederate Congress was forced to pass the first conscription law in American history; it called upon all healthy white men between the ages of eighteen and thirty-five to serve for a three-year period. States' rights had to be put on hold.

The rain continued to turn the peninsula into a bog as McClellan began siege operations against Magruder. Bringing his heavy siege guns into action, McClellan hurled thousands of pounds of shot and shell into Yorktown and along the Warwick line. This twenty-four-hour-a-day pounding of Magruder's men was a maddening experience for Sam and his comrades; the screech and roar of the artillery was deafening.

Magruder's men dug deeper into the earth as Union shells landed randomly among them; no position was safe. Some men dared to light small fires to cook or keep warm, only to become the focal point of the artillery fire. Despite the cold rain, Magruder issued an order forbidding campfires.

CHAPTER SEVEN

Siege

By October 1993, I was both weary and frustrated, as I seemed to be no closer to resolving Sam's plight. One afternoon, on a whim, I called the Jackson Clarion-Ledger down in Mississippi. "Do you want a good story?" I asked the newsroom reporter who picked up the phone. I launched into Sam's story, and the reporter was intrigued enough to interview Alex and me. He titled the resulting article "Rhode Island Yankee's Struggle To Preserve Confederate Grave."

In his article, Lee Howard quoted me: "It just became very sad to me, considering the hardships this poor soldier endured." He also contacted the cemetery owner, who in reference to the deeds I had sent

at first told the *Clarion-Ledger* he did not remember meeting Rolston or having any knowledge of the deeds. He later acknowledged Rolston's visit, but he said he didn't remember the nature of their conversation. "Maybe I did talk to him but it must have been a long time ago. These old deeds are kinda scary because I don't know if they're valid." Rolston said he'd like to place the new marker on Postlethwaite's grave. "But I have no reason to put it there if it's not going to remain in place (19 October 1993).

Howard was just as puzzled by the cemetery owner's evasiveness as I had been.

The article prompted a minor stir in Ole Miss, causing my phone to ring for a couple of days with offerings of burial plots and caskets and some strong doses of anti-Yankee sentiment as well. As I politely listened to the callers, I heard stories of Union soldiers' graves being preserved and marked by Southerners. I knew then that I was on the right course. Sam would not be moved. Somehow I would get both the cemetery and the lot owner to guarantee it.

One of the more interesting, and tempting, telephone offers came from a Jackson businessman who offered to pick up the expenses for exhumation, transportation, and reburial in Mississippi. He told me that a Confederate honor guard would accompany Sam on his train journey home. A similar offer came from Natchez. When I informed Alex, he became excited, and exhumation papers were drawn up for him to sign. However, I began to have second thoughts; an exhumation might upset the lot's owner, Ruth Cardin. If the grave of her husband, Pete, a navy veteran, were to be accidentally disturbed, I would have felt responsible. The offer was withdrawn after a near-fatal accident resulted in the gentleman from Jackson being hospitalized indefinitely.

Although I was now determined that Sam should rest undisturbed, by Memorial Day 1994, I was out of ideas, and frankly my enthusiasm for the project had been dampened by disappointment. It was obvious that few agencies or elected officials, even in the South, were eager to have their names associated with anything "Confederate." Perhaps, I wondered, I had wasted my time and unnecessarily drawn the Postlethwaite family into an emotional and futile cause; maybe it was time to give up.

The parades and solemn ceremonies of Memorial Day depressed me a bit, but the flags lining my neighborhood cemetery jarred loose an idea. At social events, at work, and even at the grocery store I was frequently asked how the "Sam thing" was coming along. Most people I encountered were genuinely fascinated by the story, so I called the state newspaper and spoke with the editor of the Providence Sunday Journal Magazine. *I was thrilled by his interest. He asked me to write Sam's story for an upcoming issue. Although I had never written anything for publication, I jumped at the chance. Unfortunately, at 2,500 words, the article I submitted exceeded the editor's page constraints, and I was forced to cut and cut again; I finally gave the piece to a friend to edit. When the article finally appeared in October 1994, there was no mention of the fact that I was trying to preserve the site. Rather, it somehow gave the impression that the problem had been resolved. (I later learned that Ruth Cardin had posted the article on her refrigerator and had been quite touched by the story.) "Lost Soul: Rhode Island's Forgotten Civil War Soldier" failed to marshal public sentiment as I had intended; however, Sam's story was about to take a fateful turn.*

F OR SAM AND WILL, THE WAR WAS CHANGING. WITH MINOR exceptions like the Ball's Bluff fiasco, the average soldier in the eastern theater had yet to see action of any significance. Homesickness, bad food, cold weather, and boredom combined to make camp life miserable. Men tried to amuse themselves by attending the sermons of the regimental chaplains, writing letters, and poring over newspapers from Richmond.

With the exception of payday, the most anticipated event in camp was mail call. Many soldiers wrote home regularly. Usually their letters contained inquiries about the well-being of relatives and friends, as well as requests for clothing or favorite books to be sent from home. In a touching series of letters, one soldier, Elijah Clarke Mounger, in the 16th Mississippi infantry, expressed concern to his mother about his brother Uriah, who was in another brigade.

> We have just received a dispatch from Col. Shannon to his wife. It is dated July 2nd 1862 killed in Jasper Greys in Richmond Battle 27th June, Overstreet, Shelton, Bruce, Clem Burnes. Badly wounded Capt. Walton, Wm. Davis, Merego; rest all safe, McClellan in full retreat, glorious victory. This is exactly as it came to us. I don't know any one in the company by the name of Merego. I am afraid it is a mistake in the name. I fear that it is Mounger instead of Merego. I hope and pray that it is not Uriah. If you hear anything from him let me know immediately, for I am uneasy and will be until I hear from them again.

> Your son, E.C. Mounger
> (Mounger Collection)

Sadly, within a few days, it was apparent that E.C.'s fears were well-placed.

Some of the men were beginning to realize that they might be in for a long war. Even more depressing were reports of the North's growing war machine. Predictions of glorious victory were gradually replaced by complaints about incompetent surgeons or questions regarding the sincerity of the chaplains. Soldiers almost always closed their letters by asking the receiver to write back; they often scolded those at home who had failed to answer previous letters.

Liquor was plentiful in the camp of the 16th Mississippi; if they didn't drink, many men escaped the empty hours by sleeping them away. Oliver Wendell Holmes, who had been a survivor of Ball's Bluff, described camp life as "organized boredom."

For President Davis, too, these were difficult days. The war was going badly. Confederate forces were in retreat everywhere except along the Rappahannock and Rapidan rivers and on the peninsula, and those forces had yet to be tested. Even the *Virginia* sat idly in Norfolk, reluctant to venture out into Hampton Roads where the *Monitor* waited. General Magruder, in typical army fashion, could not resist putting the knock on the navy by deeming the *Virginia* useless.

Several victories in the west enabled Union gunboats to pass freely along the Tennessee and Cumberland rivers into Tennessee. By the first week of April, 60,000 Union troops under Ulysses Grant were now in the very heart of the Confederacy, at Pittsburgh Landing, Tennessee. Union soldiers, unfamiliar with their surroundings, named the area for Shiloh Church, a prominent landmark.

Sam began April 1862 on the swampy banks of the Rapidan, hungry and cold. The men of the 21st were ordered to be ready to move; there were wild rumors of an impending attack on Philadelphia or Baltimore. Another rumor was of a major battle raging back home, near Corinth, Mississippi. Both of these rumors had some basis in fact; Davis and Lee had briefly considered taking the offensive against a Northern city; they had thought better of it, however, and stayed on the defensive.

Finally, on 29 May 1861, several companies of the 21st, including Sam's Company D, were ordered to board railroad cars from New Orleans, bound for Richmond. Arriving in Richmond almost twenty-four hours later, the men of the regiment were thrilled by the warm greeting given them by their senators and representatives. The high

point of this reception was a lavish breakfast, after which
the 21st marched to a wharf on the James River, where
they boarded a transport that would carry them to the
peninsula and General Magruder. Soaked to the bone by a
chilling rain, the 21st arrived at Yorktown 7 April 1862 to
share the misery. The scene that greeted Sam and the 21st
was bleak. The men spent day after day clinging to the
muddy earthworks they had built along the banks of the
Warwick as bullets whistled above them.

Early in the war, a prominent New York businessman
had come up with a novel alternative to raising a regiment
of local companies. Hiram Berdan created one of the
American military's first elite forces by advertising
throughout the North for the services of the finest marks-
men in the country. After careful scrutiny, candidates were
subjected to rigorous training and strict discipline. Those
who qualified were outfitted with Sharps rifles, arguably
the finest weapons of the day, complete with telescopic
sights. Berdan's 1st U.S. Sharpshooters were among the
most feared, and hated, men of the war.

Berdan's force seemed almost superhuman to the new
Confederate arrivals along the Warwick; one soldier
recalled how a demonstration swiftly convinced the
skeptics:

> The [enemy] rifle pits were well manned by
> sharpshooters, as I found reason to know. And the
> man who showed even his head for an instant
> above our works was sure to attract a bullet, or
> perhaps two or three, and sometimes with fatal
> results. One of the boys in the ditch, in order to
> prove to me that they had not been regaling me
> with a fairy tale of the abilities of those fellows as
> marksmen, put his hat on a short stick and pushed
> the hat up slowly in imitation of one who wanted to
> steal a sly glance. Barely had it appeared above the
> parapet before a bullet tore through it. I was con-
> vinced they could shoot straight. They were

Berdan's Sharpshooters, a semi-independent corps and went when and where they pleased, usually toward the front, however (*Confederate Veteran,* 1893-1994).

The Confederates also employed sharpshooters. These men were universally despised, even on their own side. Unlike the average foot soldiers, who had their own unspoken code of ethics ("never shoot a man answering a call of nature," for example), a sharpshooter would kill a man at any time. They took particular delight in picking off enemy sharpshooters, a practice they callously referred to as "squirrel shooting." Throughout the daylight hours, sharpshooters on both sides kept unblinking eyes focused on the earthworks across the river.

McClellan could only watch as his campaign disintegrated. His army, only a fraction of the 150,000 men he had been promised, was mired in the mud and rain along the roads leading to the Warwick River. The Confederates had built a series of dams across the Warwick to widen it; McClellan's men would have to charge across these dams in single file if they attacked.

Unwilling to suffer any further insinuations about his loyalty, McClellan agreed that some of the troops originally promised him, namely McDowell's corps of 30,000 men, should remain outside Washington until the threat of an attack by Jackson had passed. McDowell's corps was considered to be the best trained and best equipped of the five corps in the eastern theater.

McClellan was committed to a strategy of siege, but this didn't prevent Lincoln from pressing him to engage the enemy. Even though Pinkerton and General Keyes advised him that the Confederate line was heavily fortified, McClellan realized that it must be tested to determine its actual strength. At some point along its nine-mile span, the Warwick River would have to be breached. If this attempt failed, of course, it would prove to Lincoln the need for more troops.

On 4 April, as McClellan continued to deploy his troops along the Warwick River, Sam and the 21st covertly crossed it on a reconnaissance mission. About five miles southeast of Yorktown, the 21st encountered Union troops at Howard's Mill. After a brief skirmish with the enemy, the outnumbered 21st fell back along the Warwick Road toward Yorktown.

The following day, under a steady snowfall occasionally mixed with rain, Confederate troops poured into the Yorktown area. Bracing for a bloodbath, Magruder's men were determined to hold this ground until the bulk of Johnston's army arrived.

Sam spent his twenty-eighth birthday hungry and in the rain. The booming of McClellan's guns and the prospect of an all-out Union assault made sleep difficult, if not impossible. But there would be no attack. McClellan had decided to evict the force from Yorktown by battering the town to pieces with some of the heaviest guns in the world. Only when the weather improved and the Confederates had been sufficiently pounded would McClellan attempt to take the town. If McDowell's corps had been available, it could have swept up the York River landing just north of Yorktown and trapping the Confederate forces.

News of fighting at Shiloh spread along both sides of the Warwick River. Word passed initially among the Confederates that Shiloh had been a great victory. One soldier of Sam's brigade recalled that news of the fighting at Shiloh created "great excitement among the troops." But as more accurate reports arrived, the news was grim. Outnumbered Confederate forces had thrown themselves against Grant's near Shiloh Church, and casualties dwarfed those of previous battles. The fighting at Shiloh was in its second day as the 21st Mississippi endured an artillery bombardment that continued to increase in intensity.

The Confederate defeat at Shiloh severed the railroad connection between the Deep South and Richmond. Worse, the Union navy had secured control of the

Mississippi River, cutting the states in the eastern Confederacy off from those in the west. The war had come to Mississippi.

A sense of worry and betrayal swept through the ranks of the 21st as the men received news of the fighting back home. A quarter of the forty thousand Confederates engaged at Shiloh had been killed or wounded. Confederate General Albert Sidney Johnston, considered one of the finest military minds of the war, was among the dead. And attention, once again, was focused on the brash, cigar-smoking Grant, who was perceived to be as bold as McClellan was timid.

Confederate morale plummeted as men worried about their loved ones back home; desertion was tempting. McClellan's gunners did their best to worsen the mood. Fouling the situation further still was a decision by the Confederate government to allow a conscription defer-ment to any man who was wealthy enough to own twenty slaves. The common Southern man disdainfully referred to this exemption as the "twenty nigger law." The face of the war had changed abruptly in just two days.

The daily lives of the soldiers on each side of the Warwick River were markedly different. As the 2nd Rhode Island ate beef, pork, and sweet potatoes, the Confederates had to settle for rancid, wormy meat and hardtack. Often the men resorted to eating the dried corn intended for horses.

Both sides endured the cold rain that produced some degree of illness in almost everyone. Diarrhea was a com-mon malady, and human excrement was spread through-out the camps because many men were too ill to reach the latrines. Men who prided themselves on impeccable dress and meticulous personal hygiene found themselves living in squalor. Their morning routines often included helping one another remove wood ticks they attracted during the night. The ticks were a minor nuisance compared to the newest epidemic sweeping the camps: lice. Forbidden by Magruder to light fires at the front, men hiked deep into the woods, huddling around campfires as they boiled clothes and blankets in large pots. Delousing was, of course, only a temporary solution. Men would later recall that only firsthand experience can lend appreciation for the extreme humiliation they felt on discovering an infestation of "graybacks" upon their bodies. Mosquitoes were another major annoyance. To the dismay of those dug in along the Warwick on both sides, they relentlessly assaulted the men, who wondered how these bothersome creatures had survived the winter.

One Confederate soldier described his existence on the peninsula in a letter to his sister:

> We have an awful amount of sickness in camp in consequence of having to lie in the open air. Last night and yesterday evening it rained harder than I ever saw it, and all of us were completely drenched. Flux and diarrhea are doing their work among us, especially among new recruits. The company to which I belong numbers ninety-eight privates, and forty-eight are all that reported for duty this morning (*Confederate Veteran*, 1893-1994).

Like McClellan, Magruder had a deep concern for his men. As spirits sank, Magruder worried that morale might break entirely. In a message to his troops, he tried to offer what little encouragement he could, predicting better times to come if only the men would hold on. He promised them that McClellan would fail because the North's objective in the war was merely financial rather than moral. He predicted that the sick and hungry Confederate army would one day rise up and invade the North. "From St. Louis to Washington and from Washington to New Orleans the command is: 'Onward to the destruction of the South!' Let us, therefore, stand ready to welcome these strangers to 'hospitable graves.'"

While Magruder kept to himself the sadness he felt for his men, he recalled years later:

This army served without relief in the trenches. Many companies of artillery were never relieved during this long period. It rained almost incessantly, the trenches were filled with water, the weather was exceedingly cold, no fires could be allowed. The artillery of the enemy played upon our men almost continuously day and night. The army subsisted on flour and salt meat, and that in reduced quantities, and yet no murmurs were heard. Patriotism made them indifferent to suffering, disease, danger, and death (*Confederate Veteran*, 1893-1994).

Harvey Hill shared a similar recollection of the soldiers dug in along the Warwick when he recalled, "Notwithstanding the rain, mud, cold, hunger, watching, and fatigue, I never heard a murmur or witnessed a single act of insubordination."

And like McClellan, Magruder felt it important to mingle with his men. On one occasion, Magruder dropped in at the table of a worn-out private who was devouring his first meal in days; Prince John was hoping to boost morale with this visit. Enjoying his good fortune, the soldier couldn't be bothered to take note of someone else's presence at the table. Somewhat flustered by his failure to inspire the young man, Magruder blurted, "Sir, do you know with whom you are eating?" Without looking up or missing a bite the soldier mumbled, "No I don't; and since I went into the army I ain't particular who I eat with if the vittles is clean."

On 9 April, President Davis ordered Johnston and his army to Richmond to prepare for an impending attack by McClellan. Three days later, Johnston arrived at Yorktown to meet with Magruder. Inspecting the defenses along the Warwick River, Johnston was dumbfounded, stating "no one but McClellan could have hesitated to attack." Johnston returned to Richmond immediately to alert President Davis to the dire situation on the peninsula.

In consultation with Davis, Robert E. Lee, and General James Longstreet, Johnston argued for pulling Confederate troops from the peninsula as well as from other critical lines of defense in order to form a massive army in front of Richmond. Upon McClellan's arrival at Richmond, he would find himself the hunted rather than the hunter, insisted Johnston. Lee disagreed, stating that protecting Richmond while leaving the bulk of the Confederacy defenseless would be pointless. Besides, Lee pointed out, the abysmal conditions on the peninsula were ideal for a smaller, entrenched army to defeat a lumbering giant of an army that had probably already seen enough of Virginia.

The argument continued early into the next morning, and Lee eventually won out. During these discussions Davis insisted that McClellan, whom he held in high regard, be referred to only in the most respectful terms. Johnston returned to Yorktown to take command of Magruder's forces.

While Johnston pleaded his case in Richmond, a steady stream of regiments, bayonets gleaming and battle flags waving, had passed through the capital on the way to the peninsula. Though Confederate numbers were still nowhere near what Pinkerton and McClellan believed, with each passing day the Union's numerical advantage diminished slightly.

As new regiments from both sides arrived daily on the banks of the Warwick, they eagerly announced their presence to the enemy. The men of the 2nd Rhode Island were surprised, but not amused, by the sight of familiar-looking equipment being hoisted and waved over entrenchments across the river. This equipment, emblazoned "2nd Rhode Island," had been captured at Bull Run. On some occasions men who had known each other before the war shouted inquiries across the river as to their friends' whereabouts.

On 11 April, the *Philadelphia Inquirer* ran an account of the situation on the peninsula:

The weather still continues to be unfavorable for military operations. It has been raining for two days. The creeks are much swollen, and the low ground covered with water, making the road almost impassable for empty wagons.

Information received shows that the Rebels have a force of sixty thousand, which is rapidly being added to by troops from the neighborhood of Richmond, which is one day from Yorktown by railroad and river. They have four steamers and transports in use, and by the time the roads are in condition for the Union army to move, the Rebels may be able to meet them with one hundred thousand men, the flower of their army, with their best arms. Besides, they are in a strongly entrenched position.

Information obtained through deserters, contrabands and other sources, show that the enemy have nearly five hundred guns, some of them of the largest caliber.

The Rebel General, JOHNSTON, with some of his forces, has arrived and taken command in person, showing that they intend making a desperate resistance to the advance of our troops at every point. The entrenchments extend entirely across the peninsula from James to York river.

The storm still continued, but had somewhat abated last evening. Accounts from the Peninsula report our troops meeting the storm with characteristic ingenuity in the way of improvised shelters. Their enthusiasm and confidence in General McCLELLAN is unabated.

Though the storm at this time is unfortunate, the time has not been lost, and the retreat of Rebel MAGRUDER and his forces, or their defeat, is about as certain as any possible future event. The prospect of a clear-up in the weather is looked for with great anxiety, from a belief that the sunshine and the Merrimac (C.S.S. *Virginia*) will come together. All seem confident that she will be captured or sunk if she comes out.

McClellan's despair over the weather only compounded his problems. He had come to the peninsula to fight, not to sit mired in the mud. Nevertheless, he was convinced that, due to the reductions Lincoln had made in the size of his army, a strategy of siege was the only course. In a report, he explained:

> I feel confident, if he (Lincoln) could have made a personal inspection of the enemy's defenses he would have forbidden me risking the safety of the army and the possible successes of the campaign on a sanguinary assault of an advantageous and formidable position, which, even if successful, could not have been followed up to any other or better result than would have been reached by the regular operations of a siege. Still less could I forego the conclusions of my most instructed judgement for the mere sake of avoiding the personal consequences intimated in the President's dispatch (McClellan, 1887).

Except for a brief and inconsequential skirmish near Lee's Mill, both armies continued to sit. About a mile upstream, toward Yorktown, Magruder continued fortifying a position that McClellan's scouts had reported to be a weak link in the Confederate line. If this was a hole in Magruder's defenses, McClellan could use it to thrust his army across the river. It was at this point along the Confederate line that Magruder had his men construct Dam No. 1, the first of three dams used to control the depth and flow of the Warwick. These dams allowed Magruder to flood portions of the shallowest points along the Warwick, making it difficult and dangerous for McClellan to attempt a crossing.

At three o'clock on the afternoon of Thursday, 16 April, artillery of the 3rd New York opened up on the Confederate fortifications near Dam No. 1. Under the cover of this fire, two hundred men of the 3rd Vermont entered the cold waters of the Warwick. Holding their guns and cartridge boxes over their heads, they began wading across. After anxiously anticipating McClellan's attack for weeks, the men in the Confederate trenches were convinced that this was the beginning of a major thrust.

As the "Green Mountain Boys" felt their way through the waist-deep waters, they drew fire from the Confederate rifle pits. Vermonters began to fall, and the Warwick became dotted with floating dead. The Confederate fire, most of it delivered by the 15th North Carolina, commanded by Colonel William McKinney, grew increasingly deadly as the first of the Green Mountain Boys reached the river's edge and charged into the enemy trenches. On the Union side of the river, men cheered as the Vermonters drove the outnumbered Carolinians from their works. Inexplicably, however, no other units were ordered to cross the river to reinforce their comrades.

McKinney's regiment began to fall apart as an order to fall back spread through the Carolinians' ranks; no one knew who gave the initial order. Valiantly trying to rally his men, Colonel McKinney was killed by a Vermonter's bullet. Then three regiments from Georgia were brought up and began pouring lead into the attackers. The 2nd Louisiana came on line with the Carolinians, forcing the 3rd Vermont back into the river. In horror and disbelief, the Vermont men looked across the river, hoping to see supporting regiments coming to their aid. Isolated and low on ammunition, the survivors of the 3rd Vermont, who had taken and held the enemy's trenches for almost an hour, were forced to withdraw. As they waded back to the Union side, they took heavy losses. Survivors struggling ashore were greeted by the 4th and 6th Vermont, who were readying to cross the Warwick. With the Confederate position reorganized and the element of surprise lost, these regiments were easily repulsed. The only attempt to move the enemy from its trenches in the peninsula campaign had failed miserably.

The disaster at Dam No. 1 was certainly an indication of the tragedy that might have occurred had 100,000 Union troops attempted to cross it. McClellan couldn't justify, or accept, the likelihood of thousands of killed and wounded that would result from a full-scale assault across the river. He continued to agonize over the absence of McDowell's thirty thousand men.

By 20 April, faced with what he believed to be the possible failure of his campaign, McClellan became agitated and pleaded with Washington to send "all the 20 pound Parrott (guns) you can as soon as you can, I am short of siege guns!" These guns were capable of accurately firing heavy balls over a distance of two miles into Yorktown itself.

In a telegram, McClellan complained that he was facing a force of eighty thousand commanded by Robert E. Lee. This, of course, was untrue. McClellan telegraphed the navy, urgently requesting the services of the powerful gunboat *Galena*. In a thinly veiled attempt to shift blame to the navy should his campaign fail, he pointedly stressed, "I am fast reaching the point where the success of my operations must to a certain point depend upon the fact of her co-operation or the reverse."

While McClellan cautiously guarded his men's wellbeing, he displayed little concern for his own safety. On one occasion, while he was observing enemy positions, Confederate artillery opened fire on his position. While others frantically sought cover, McClellan stood, defiantly puffing on a cigar. Incidents such as this endeared Little Mac to his men.

The siege of Yorktown had begun on 5 April; ironically, it contributed to the crippling of McClellan's campaign. Heavy guns and ordnance trains ruined the already muddy roads outside Yorktown, rendering them impassable. The roads from Fortress Monroe were clogged with wagons, mules, and heavy guns, sometimes partially submerged in a sea of mud, stalling angry mobs of infantrymen who were forced to wait in the rain. Lumberjacks worked continuously, felling trees and laying them across the muddy roads to make them passable.

Soldiers spent weeks subsisting on the sorriest of rations in these Yorktown trenches.

On 23 April William Lindsay Brandon wrote a revealing letter to his son Robert, telling him of the 21st's recent experiences:

> We are here on the Peninsula, near the famous Yorktown. We have been engaged three times with the enemy as a reconnoitering party, there is some uneasiness about the enemy attacking us here, we are ready for it, but fear. They may leave the Peninsula and make their attack at some other point. Yesterday we had quite a sharp affair, killing 8 or 10 of the enemy. I having two of the Fort Adams boys wounded, Isaiah Bell and [unreadable], the former through the leg, the latter seriously through the hand. I was in command of the party. Our boys all behaved well.
>
> A good many letters are received from Wilkinson (County). I think McGehee gets a letter every week, concludes me to fear you do not write

as often as you proposed. You must not think as you have no stirring incidents to chronicle, that your letters will not interest. Trifles about Home are of the greatest interest to us.

We have come down to soldiering in earnest, we had to throw away our tents and leave our baggage. I have worn a shirt 8 days, lived on hard bread 6 days, drank sassafras tea time out a mind. We have some coffee now, enough to last a week, but if the enemy should change his point of attack, and go somewhere else, we will have to leave all behind. I have slept on one blanket, without any covering (on) cold rainy nights after marching for miles and miles through the rain and mud. (We) drink bad water and eat half raw biscuit filled with lard (Brandon Letters, 1862).

Brandon closed his letter by expressing deep concern for the condition of his crops and the rising waters of the Mississippi River.

Escape

As April drew to a close, McClellan's engineers continued constructing siege works for his heavy guns. Some of the guns weighed sixty-four thousand pounds and required teams of one hundred horses to transport. McClellan had hoped to have fourteen of these guns operational by the end of the first week of May. When May began, twelve were in place and ready for use. Each gun was capable of hurling a two hundred-pound ball almost one mile. The balls were commonly known as "nail kegs."

To the dismay of many soldiers and politicians alike, McClellan refused to use the twelve guns. He preferred instead to wait until he could unleash the deadly power of all fourteen at once. With the guns battering Johnston's lines, as well as Yorktown itself, Johnston's determined army would either be forced to retreat to Richmond or be destroyed. The blow was to be total and crushing.

The tiny army with which Prince John had held McClellan had grown to more than fifty thousand men under General Johnston. But even with these reinforcements, McClellan outnumbered Johnston two to one.

On 1 May McClellan intensified the artillery fire directed at Johnston's men, and for the second time in two months Johnston ordered the Confederate army to retreat without a fight. This time, however, there could be no doubt as to McClellan's intentions, and Davis agreed with Johnston's decision. As had been the case in the withdrawal from Manassas, logistical problems hindered Johnston's getaway. As the earth rumbled and bursting shells lit the sky, the Confederate retreat fell into confusion. Regiments straggled out of Yorktown, burning whatever they couldn't carry, and began making their way to Williamsburg. As Johnston evacuated Yorktown, a frustrated Lincoln telegraphed McClellan, asking, "Is anything to be done?"

A soldier in the 2nd Rhode Island, watching the artillery barrage across the river, wrote that "it sounded like the 4th of July." As desperate as conditions were for Sam and his Confederate comrades, it would get worse; McClellan would soon be battering them with a storm of six hundred tons of metal per day.

To ensure his army's escape, Johnston ordered his artillery to hit Union positions across the Warwick at dusk on 3 May. Gunners manning nine-inch cannons were ordered to maintain a slow, steady fire. Hearing the thunder of their own artillery, Sam and his comrades must have felt a sense of satisfaction after weeks of suffering from the elements and McClellan's firestorm. The effect was limited, however, as a Confederate artillerist later recalled: "Whether we did any damage or not we never knew, but it was a grand sight to see the shells, flaming fuses, flying through the clear, starlit night and the flashings of the bursting shells in the direction of the enemy's lines.

Whether anyone else knew it or not, we were throwing away our ammunition."

Before the Confederate artillery barrage, McClellan had written a letter to his wife, Ellen, stating that he was concerned about the "quiet" on Johnston's side of the river. He feared that the enemy might be evacuating and that he would lose his chance to give the "rascals a sound drubbing." Perhaps sensing the reaction in Washington should Johnston slip away, the general expressed his feelings of isolation in stating that "I have not one single friend at the seat of government. Any day may bring an order relieving me of command."

Between ten and eleven o'clock that night, the fire from the Confederate artillery fire grew intense; the earth trembled and shook under the deafening assault. By midnight, the fire slackened and slowly died away. The Union men looked forward to the morning, when, it was hoped, they would at last put an end to the siege.

Johnston had neither enough time nor manpower to evacuate his heavy guns. He was forced to abandon more than fifty pieces of artillery and stockpiles of ammunition, but his cannons blazed away until the last possible moment. After the criticism Johnston had suffered following the withdrawal from Manassas in March, his decision to surrender more equipment to the enemy was a difficult one.

In any successfully executed retreat, there must be organization. Units must await their turns so that avenues of escape are clear of the units that left previously. Obviously, some unit must be the last to leave, a test of both discipline and honor as the enemy's gunfire grows steadily closer. Such a rear guard assignment involves destroying any artillery that has to be left behind, ensuring that the sick or wounded are cared for, and burning supplies, bridges, and sometimes an entire town. The final responsibility is to escape. As McClellan readied his main assault and the main body of Joe Johnston's army slipped out of Yorktown, the 21st Mississippi was designated part of the rear guard. Evacuating Yorktown early on the morning of 4 May, the 21st began a single-file march (carefully avoiding land mines that Johnston had planted) in the direction of Richmond via the historic town of Williamsburg.

Johnston's evacuation seemed to be a success, and he was intent on distancing his army from McClellan's, which would soon be in hot pursuit. While a deserter was rumored to have crossed into Union lines as the last Confederates were leaving Yorktown, informing McClellan of the evacuation, it wasn't until dawn on the 4th that McClellan's treetop observers got a glimpse of the Confederate works across the river and realized that something was drastically different. Crossing the river, Union pickets cautiously approached the Confederate trenches, fearing an ambush. Garbage and debris littered the camps, and broken vehicles and discarded weapons were strewn about the town. Before McClellan had fired a single round from his siege guns, Johnston had simply packed up and left.

In an attempt to put the best face on an embarrassing situation, McClellan wired Lincoln, "The success is brilliant!" He gave Lincoln impressive reports of the elaborate Confederate works and insisted that the strategy of siege had indeed been the correct one.

Although the evacuation of Yorktown was a success, Johnston had little to celebrate. The evacuation necessitated the abandonment of Norfolk, with its navy yard, and the ironclad *Virginia*. As the *Monitor* and the U.S. Navy waited for the *Virginia* to fight her way out, the Confederates, not willing to risk her capture, blew her up.

For the first time since the campaign had begun, McClellan was able to use the navy; it now had free passage along the York and James rivers. Only Confederate shore batteries kept the navy from approaching Richmond itself.

Johnston's retreat was impeded by torrential rain. Another problem was fatigue. After weeks of sitting and subsisting on the sorriest of rations, many of Johnston's men simply were not up for a hard march and straggled or collapsed. Weeks spent in trenches filled with water had taken a toll on both armies; McClellan lost one-fifth of his army to disease during the siege.

McClellan wasted no time in pursuing Johnston; the Confederate general fully expected that his rear guard would be attacked by advancing Union units. To prevent the entire retreating army from being drawn into battle, Johnston ordered his rear guard to make a stand between Yorktown and Williamsburg and deliver to McClellan's advancing columns a strategic punch in the nose. This holding action would ensure the safe arrival of the bulk of Johnston's army in the outskirts of Richmond; the rear guard would be on its own. Selected to command the rear guard was General James Longstreet.

With a long, flowing beard, six-foot frame, and steel-gray eyes, forty-one-year-old Longstreet was an impressive-looking soldier. "Old Pete" was a veteran of the Mexican War and had also served in the West. To some, Longstreet seemed shy, avoiding conversation and giving clipped responses to inquiries. Longstreet, in fact, suffered from a hearing impairment which made it difficult for him to follow conversation in a group. To those who knew him well, he was friendly and outgoing. He had a penchant for card games, particularly poker, and enjoyed an occasional drink.

Longstreet had been married and was the proud father of three children, the oldest being a twelve-year-old son, but in January 1862, his family life was crushed by tragedy. Longstreet was called from the field by a desperate message from his wife in Richmond. In late 1861 and early 1862, scarlet fever had swept the city. Longstreet returned to find his two youngest children wracked by sickness, barely clinging to life. Both children died, and the Longstreets buried them on the same day. A week later their twelve-year-old son was also dead.

He returned to duty a changed man. Hearing impairment or not, Longstreet now was truly withdrawn, and his social activity diminished greatly. In mourning, Longstreet immersed himself in his duties. As it had with Magruder, fate had made an interesting choice in pitting Longstreet against McClellan.

CHAPTER EIGHT

The Next Few Days Are Quite Uncertain

As if of their own accord, events began to align in a series of coincidences during the late summer of 1994. Having achieved nothing tangible with the Sunday Journal Magazine article, I promised myself one last effort. Taking a second look at my original draft of the article, I remembered the passion generated by the piece in the Mississippi newspaper a year earlier. I submitted my original draft to Civil War magazine (as well as Sam's hometown newspaper, the Woodville Republican). The article was given a new subtitle by the magazine's editor: "A Yankee's Fight For A Rebel's Dignity"; it ended not with my address but with the address of the Providence Journal Bulletin. The message was clear: if the people of the South didn't care for one of their fallen sons, Sam would disappear into history. The article was published in October; one month later, it appeared in Confederate Veteran magazine, which also urged readers to contact Rhode Island's largest newspaper with their concerns.

During the first week of November, I received a call from a woman in Uxbridge, Massachusetts. While grocery shopping in Rhode Island some weeks before, Mae Wrona had purchased a Sunday newspaper. She had been struck by the short article about Sam for an unlikely reason. Her son, John, she explained, was involved with a living history group that portrayed the 21st Mississippi Infantry. Of the thousands of Confederate regiments they could have selected, these Massachusetts natives had chosen Sam's for no reason other than the fact that they knew it had been a good one.

John Wrona, by profession a social worker and by avocation a living history enthusiast, called me a couple of days after I'd spoken with his mother. He asked my permission to allow the group to honor its fallen comrade with a brief ceremony and gun salute on the upcoming Monday, Veteran's Day.

Appreciating John's interest, I told him that although I thought it was an appropriate gesture, I had no authority with the cemetery. Undaunted, John assured me that he would obtain all the necessary permits to hold such an event. I agreed to attend as a spectator and perhaps deliver some brief remarks and to place, if only for a few moments, the marker provided by the Department of Veterans Affairs. I wasn't at all prepared for what was to follow.

JOHNSTON'S WEARY ARMY PLODDED TOWARD RICHMOND throughout the morning of 5 May 1862. Rain and fog reduced visibility greatly, and the men cursed the mud that clung to their shoes. Nervousness about McClellan's advancing cavalry pushed Sam and the other men into the vicinity of Fort Magruder on the outskirts of Williamsburg.

Prince John had constructed this earthen fort months before as a safe haven from the Union army. (To this day major features of Fort Magruder remain intact. The earthworks look out of place adjacent to the swimming pool of the elegant Fort Magruder Inn in Williamsburg.) Confederate batteries within the fort would hold off McClellan's advance upon the retreating columns as they struggled to reach their new line of defense.

Johnston's original plan, a stand before Richmond, was being realized. The Chickahominy River originates north of Richmond and passes the city five miles to the east as it meanders southwest toward Williamsburg, where it empties into the James. The two rivers merge five miles west of Williamsburg. Johnston's intention was to march his retreating army thirty miles on the north side of the Chickahominy before crossing and setting up a line of defense five miles south of Richmond.

This strategic scenario had limited chances for success; the formidable Army of the Potomac was still the feline in this game of cat and mouse. Johnston felt he had no other options, but the prospects of a successful defense of Richmond from the banks of the Chickahominy were grim; the chances of Johnston getting his army across the river before being overrun by leading elements of McClellan's army were even worse.

McClellan was keen to cut off Johnston's retreat; at Yorktown he oversaw the newly arrived troops of General William Franklin as they boarded transports on the York River. If these troops could be landed north of Johnston, Richmond might be taken without a fight. The process of moving men and material onto ships in a torrential downpour was a slow one, however, and the chances of catching Johnston by way of the York diminished with each passing hour. Johnston's escape and McClellan's pursuit were both falling behind schedule.

Spearheading the Army of the Potomac's pursuit of Johnston was the corps of Edwin Vose Sumner. Sumner, sixty-five years old, was McClellan's second-in-command.

Although he was known for his fearlessness in the field, Sumner was considered by some to have seen better days. One journalist reported that Sumner projected "an air of stupidity that perfectly expresses his mental state."

For Sam and the other men in Johnston's army, the war for some time had been a series of hardships followed by long marches of retreat. Civilian morale had suffered, too, as Johnston's army retreated first from Manassas to the Rapidan and now from the peninsula. Feeling abandoned and left at the mercy of the Yankees, not all of the civilians in the evacuated areas held their tongues. Many feared that their property would be stolen or destroyed after Johnston's evacuation. The blank stares of the civilians along the march stung the dispirited soldiers, who were cold, wet, tired, and hungry.

It was into this atmosphere of futility that the sound of Fort Magruder's guns intruded. General Joseph Hooker of Massachusetts was leading a division within range of Fort Magruder's batteries at about half past seven in the morning on 4 May when the Confederate guns suddenly belched iron and flame through dense fog. Benjamin Humphreys' 21st Mississippi was ordered to turn and prepare to meet the enemy, and several brigades were ordered to reverse their march. Cheers went up and adrenaline flowed; men were finally about to have a go at McClellan.

A member of the 9th Alabama recalled the moment:

> A shell burst in the air. In an instant, everything was changed. The men wheeled in their tracks, changing the musical strains of their song (Dixie!) to the wild, discordant shout which had already been noised around the world as the "Rebel Yell."
>
> Soon a cry came from the rear, "Clear the way for the artillery!" and the rushing mass drifted to the left as a battery of four field guns, with their caissons drawn by six and four horses respectively, came thundering down the street at a full gallop. A staff officer shouted to the captain of the battery as

the guns swept by: "Drive into the redoubt! Lock wheels with 'em if you must and fight 'em hand to hand until the infantry gets there!" Leaving the road, the battery dashed down the hill in a straight line for the redoubt, over obstructions of briars, bushes, stones, and gullies which it seemed, considering the speed at which they were moving, should have appalled the hearts of any human creature not daft from excitement (*Confederate Veteran*, 1893–1994).

Longstreet approached Williamsburg by marching north from Yorktown along the Hampton Road about midnight, 3 May 1862. In a series of charges and countercharges, Longstreet and Sumner's men clashed over the possession of Fort Magruder. Opposing artillerymen pounded each other as well as opposing infantrymen. Longstreet ordered his men to save their ammunition as rain, fog, and smoke blurred the scene. His men hugged the ground while missiles of both friend and foe flew over their heads. From across the field came a wave of blue that was greeted by the batteries within Fort Magruder. Canister and grapeshot cut swaths into the Union ranks, tearing companies of men into mangled corpses. McClellan's men wavered, closed ranks, and pressed ahead.

The 2nd Rhode Island was so close to the fort that the men could see the artillerymen working their cannons; one soldier recorded how dire his predicament was:

Until dark we could see the Rebel gunners load and fire the cannon from inside the fort, and we had to stand it, for we were ordered for some reason not to fire. All night the shells continued to burst over our heads, and in the mud and discomfort we prayed for daylight (Rhodes, 1985).

As the fatigued 21st Mississippi arrived at the outskirts of Williamsburg, Colonel Humphreys ordered his men to form a line of battle and await the advance of the enemy. For hours Sam and his comrades anxiously listened to the sounds of battle to their left, right, and front. Dawn broke and with it came the eerie sight of an empty field before them. Where was the enemy? As morning turned into early afternoon, Humphreys' men became increasingly unnerved. As they sat in the eye of a human hurricane, men were dying by the hundreds all around them. The afternoon dragged on uneventfully until Colonel Mott and his 19th Mississippi arrived on the field in relief of the 21st. Exhausted, the men of the 21st marched to the rear and out of harm's way—unaware that after their departure the 19th was savagely attacked and suffered heavy casualties, losing its colonel.

The Battle of Williamsburg became a heated contest of will between tired, hungry soldiers. As the Union line advanced upon the cowering Confederates, it broke into a headlong charge. The Confederates were ordered to their feet as officers screamed, "Fire and charge!" Hundreds of rifles went off at once. Longstreet's men lowered bayonets and threw themselves into the blue ranks.

It was war at its cruelest. Cold rain stung the soldiers' faces; they killed staring into their victims' eyes. A Confederate survivor recalled, "The advancing masses of the enemy reel and stagger, a starry banner falls, a gallant officer is unhorsed, military cohesion is lost, friends and foe mingle and struggle for one brief moment, while the iron-throated monarchs of battle are awed into silence!"

A Union soldier also vividly remembered the nightmarish scene:

> We were in the midst of felled timber, and we screened ourselves as much as possible behind the stumps and logs. I got behind a stump about two feet across at the top and settled down to business amid the roar of cannon, the shrieking of solid shot and shells, with the incessant zip, whiz, and whistle of bullets, and at times the ping of the deadly

messenger as it entered the body of a comrade. This, along with dense smoke from the fire of the guns on both sides along with the loud yells from the contestants, made it an indescribable and indelible scene. My comrade, Jack Slater, started to come toward me from behind a log and fell over backwards with a hole in his forehead, the blood fairly covering his face (*Confederate Veteran*, 1893–1994).

Confederate cavalry arrived as the battle continued, neither side gaining a clear advantage. However, the bulk of Johnston's army continued to make its way to the Chickahominy.

News of the fighting reached McClellan in Yorktown; he realized that Franklin wouldn't be able to land his troops in time to catch Johnston. In the afternoon, McClellan mounted his magnificent horse, "Dan Webster," and along with his staff, raced to Williamsburg.

Before Little Mac arrived, another Union division, under the command of General Phil Kearny, entered the fight. Kearny was a true warrior, utterly fearless. He had fought with the French Army in its war with Italy, studying French cavalry techniques. He had lost an arm in the Mexican War, but this did little to diminish his abilities. Kearny's New Jersey boys loved him, and their fearlessness in battle inspired other weary regiments to reform and rally.

These reinforcements were turning the tide of battle in McClellan's favor as he arrived at Williamsburg, and Kearny had the situation under control. As always, the sight of McClellan buoyed his men, and they cheered for him. McClellan was deeply annoyed with Sumner and described his second-in-command's "utter stupidity and worthlessness" in a letter to his wife, Ellen. He credited himself (perhaps too much) by telling his wife that "the men feel that I have saved the day."

As night fell, Longstreet's men continued to hold Fort Magruder. Throughout the evening, until almost midnight, steady artillery fire from the fort announced the Confederate presence. Gradually the fire slackened and ceased. Having been pinned down in the mud for several hours, troops of the 2nd Rhode Island cautiously crawled to the fort. Once again, Johnston had escaped. Sam and the 21st Mississippi, covering the Confederate rear, were among the last of the retreating troops to reach the outskirts of Richmond.

For McClellan, it was Yorktown all over again—but this time there were casualties. The Army of the Potomac counted 456 dead, and more than 1,400 Union men had been seriously wounded. On Longstreet's side approximately seven hundred were killed and another eight hundred wounded. Most of the wounded fell into Union hands. Any chance for McClellan to catch Johnston before he reached Richmond had been lost. For McClellan, Williamsburg was a military victory and a strategic defeat.

Having personally known both Lincoln and McClellan, Robert E. Lee was able to accurately judge their mental states at the beginning of May. Lincoln would eagerly demand action; McClellan would passively wait for McDowell before attacking Richmond. Lee ordered Jackson to shake things up in the Shenandoah Valley.

With the Union armies of General Banks to his north and General Fremont threatening Staunton to his west, Jackson dazzled them, using the valley as a stage. From 3 through 7 May, the Army of the Valley marched ninety-two miles with no apparent destination. As Banks and Fremont continued their vice-like strategy to squeeze him out of the valley, Jackson put on what may have been his greatest performance.

On 8 May Jackson's Army of the Valley boarded rail cars, seemingly destined for Richmond. With the Confederate capital in imminent danger and the increasing pressure on Jackson from Banks and Fremont, the soldiers had no doubt where the train was going. The mood of the officers and men was dark. As the train got under way, though, those who knew the terrain or took notice of the sun's position realized that Jackson was not taking his army to Richmond, but due west instead.

The train carried the troops twenty-five miles. They disembarked and began marching toward General Fremont's forces. Smashing into Fremont, Jackson took heavier casualties but nevertheless drove the enemy into West Virginia. Panicked by their tangle with Jackson, the Union men set fire to the woods through which they were retreating. The fires became so intense that Jackson had to halt his pursuit. This decisive victory, designed to dissuade Lincoln from sending McDowell to the peninsula, took place, appropriately enough, near the town of McDowell.

Hearing the news of Fremont's encounter with Jackson, Banks' army scrambled toward the safety of Washington. Jackson seemed to have the ability to materialize anywhere at any time. Then, once again, Jackson mysteriously disappeared.

The U.S. Navy finally made a move on Richmond on 15 May. The crew of the *Virginia* had been assigned to man the guns atop Drewry's Bluff, seven miles south of Richmond on the James River. The sharp bend in the James below the bluff had become crowded with old and obsolete Confederate vessels that had been scuttled. Navigating the bend through this maze of sunken ships would be difficult and risky, and such a maneuver under enemy fire might be fatal. As the Federal ships attempted to slip past the artillery on Drewry's Bluff, their own guns were rendered useless by the river's steep banks.

McClellan had pleaded with the navy in the weeks before; the navy now sought help from him. If McClellan would extend his extreme left to Drewry's Bluff, the Confederate gunners would be cut off and forced to surrender or run. Unfortunately for the navy, McClellan would have none of this.

In May 1862, both presidents had lost patience with their commanding generals. Lincoln doubted McClellan's intention to attack Johnston; Davis saw Johnston as a general only interested in retreats. Johnston's failure to pursue the Union army at First Manassas and his subsequent retreat toward Richmond continued to annoy Davis. Now Johnston had retreated to the very doorstep of the capital. Worse, Davis doubted whether Johnston had devised an adequate plan of defense for the capital, and he feared that Richmond might be abandoned as his army continued its flight from the enemy.

As the second weekend of May drew near, an air of apprehension gripped Richmond as its citizens waited for McClellan's hammer to fall. They also expected U.S. Navy gunboats to lay siege to the city. The movement of men and materials through the streets of Richmond was continuous. The mood in the city became increasingly tense with word that the mighty *Virginia* was gone. Johnston's army fell back into the outskirts of Richmond.

His army divided, "almost starved," his supply lines stretched dangerously thin, the critical moment of McClellan's great campaign had arrived. On Wednesday, 14 May, as the crisis in Richmond deepened, President Davis gathered his cabinet for an emergency meeting. After listening to various arguments concerning where the next capital should be and how an evacuation should be executed, Robert E. Lee shocked the room. The usually stoic Lee stood up as if to end any discussion and exploded, "Richmond will not be given up! It will not be given up!"

Lee's display was as much the result of military pragmatism as emotion. He recognized that most of the Confederate states' economies were agriculture-based; the heavy industry in Richmond, such as the Tredegar Iron Works, provided the South with most of its war materiel. To lose Richmond was to lose the war.

As the Confederate leaders agonized over McClellan's presence at Richmond's doorstep, so did the men of the 21st Mississippi. With their backs to the capital, Humphreys' men, including Sam, no longer had retreat as an option.

Will Postlethwaite's days were being spent in an entirely different fashion. Stationed in the Southern Shenandoah

Valley, the 16th Mississippi was finding little glory. Without tents, Will and his comrades had spent the winter and early spring at the mercy of the elements, living "like wild men." Constant exposure to the snow, rain, and sleet of mid-spring had sent more than one hundred of the regiment's number to Richmond for hospitalization. Many of these men would die.

As if their existence wasn't miserable enough, the regiment's rations were reduced by one-third. When not on guard duty or foraging, the men of the 16th were faced with the chore of passing empty, tedious hours. The state of their uniforms ranged from damp to soaking wet for days at a time. Mail call more often than not was a disappointment.

One diversion was the reorganization of the regiment. This shakeup of the 16th was caused by a law passed by the Confederate government which allowed for any soldier under the age of eighteen or over the age of thirty-five to resign from the army if he chose to do so. Will kept his age to himself. Several officers resigned; others who were unpopular were challenged to place their commands before a vote. The result was the active campaigning of candidates throughout the camp. Popularity was the key to success, and few things made a candidate more popular than doling out alcohol. Candidates for captain and other vacant positions plied their prospective constituents with drink. As long as a free taste was in the offing, the candidates had an eager audience.

Carnot Posey, who was eligible to resign, retained his position as colonel, which pleased the regiment. With elections behind them the men of the 16th were eager to perform more meaningful service, but with no enemy in sight they would have to wait.

With one sweeping order the situation changed dramatically. On 20 May great excitement swept through the ranks; the 16th was being assigned to the Army of the Valley. It was the only regiment from Mississippi to hold the distinction. Under Stonewall Jackson's command, army life would be anything but dull.

Having acquiesced to Lee's insistence on making a stand at Richmond, Davis found that his relationship with Johnston was as tenuous as the capital's existence. Riding out to Johnston's headquarters on 17 May, Davis insisted that the general reveal his plans for defending Richmond. If Johnston had a plan, though, he didn't share it with the president. Davis was furious, but Johnston remained tight-lipped. As Davis' fragile relationship with his top general teetered, Lincoln ordered McDowell to march south to join McClellan.

Johnston did have a plan, of sorts. As he had argued weeks before, he believed that McClellan should be handed the peninsula without a fight. With miles of communication and supply lines stretched to their breaking points and the impossibility of keeping more than 100,000 wet, hungry men in fighting shape, McClellan's campaign would be its own undoing.

The opportunity to catch part of the Army of the Potomac vulnerable would probably present itself only once, if at all. Timing, swift action, and a liberal dose of luck were all required if Johnston was to escape McClellan's noose and send a panic-stricken Union army reeling back down the peninsula. But unless McClellan dangled an isolated piece of his army before him, Johnston would be forced to endure a siege.

A year had passed since Sam and Will had joined the army. They had marched hundreds of miles, survived the worst winter in twenty years, and seen countless comrades and enemies sick and dead. Sam passed the days outside Richmond like a prisoner on death row, waiting for McClellan, the executioner, to do his brutal work. Under the rising star of Stonewall Jackson, Will would experience the heart-racing pace of what became one of the most spectacular campaigns in American military history. Westmoreland Plantation seemed a world away. Amazingly, neither of the brothers had seen action in a major battle. A year of suffering, misery, and organized boredom was drawing to a close.

Six miles from the city limits of Richmond, McClellan pondered his situation in much the same way he had at Yorktown. As always, avoiding bloodshed was his main concern. In a telegram to Lincoln he repeated his plea for more troops, stating that it "would be unwise, and even insane" to think that the battle for Richmond would be anything but a bloodbath. He added that the Confederates were "probably entrenched" and "perhaps double my numbers." He closed by stating that fresh troops would make his operation "more perfect." Lincoln replied days later that "General McDowell has been ordered to march upon that city by the shortest route."

The president's fateful order for McDowell to move overland instead of by water opened Joe Johnston's window of opportunity. Lincoln's thinking was that McDowell would march south, keeping an eye on Jackson as he moved; to move McDowell by sea would leave Washington exposed for too long. McClellan grumbled that he had hoped McDowell would arrive via the James River, from whence he could have approached Richmond. Instead he was forced to suffer the "delays and losses incurred in bridging the Chickahominy . . . being necessarily divided by that stream."

Instead of attacking Richmond, McClellan was now forced to concentrate on his rendezvous with McDowell. McClellan sent three of his five corps to the swollen Chickahominy, where they immediately went to work constructing bridges. The flooded stream ruined the first of these bridges, which "were carried off or rendered impassable." The heavy rain "continued to fall, flooded the valley, and raised the water to a greater height than had been known for twenty years."

Even more troubling to McClellan was Lincoln's insistence that McDowell operate independently and not under McClellan's command. This situation irritated McClellan so much that he wired Lincoln a thinly veiled threat that he might resign over the issue. Seeking to soothe the general's bruised ego, Lincoln relented. At last, despite the logistical problems he faced in linking his army to McDowell's, McClellan had everything he wanted and was winning a showdown with Lincoln and Secretary of War Stanton to boot. He referred to these developments as "cheering news" and "felt confident" that his new force would "be sufficiently strong to overpower the large army confronting us."

Will and the 16th Mississippi spent the third week of May in the Luray Valley, a Northern portion of the Shenandoah area, doing little except foraging for food. On the 17th the men began a rain-soaked march in search of their new command. After a nine-mile march, the 16th spent the night without shelter, as was usual. After a two-day delay, the march to meet with Jackson was resumed. The twenty-six miles covered in two days would soon be considered leisurely compared with the pace Jackson would demand from his new troops.

Near Front Royal the 16th halted, close to Jackson's headquarters. Jackson was informed that Posey's Mississippians had arrived and wished to set eyes upon the Confederacy's most famous general. "Stonewall" emerged and spoke briefly to Will and his brothers-in-arms, who gave him the general arousing cheer.

The men of the 16th would find their new assignment a puzzling, often unsettling, experience. Marching orders were given, rescinded, and given again. The army marched and counter-marched, seemingly to nowhere. Speculation as to where their marching would take them soon became moot as the regiment came to accept Jackson's determination to mystify both friend and foe alike.

On Friday, 23 May, the men of the 16th got their first taste of late spring heat and humidity as they sat nine miles outside Front Royal cleaning their weapons. The tone of the idle afternoon changed abruptly when they were ordered to pack up all gear not needed for combat and prepare to move. The roar of Confederate artillery filled the air; with hearts pounding the 16th marched on the double-quick in the direction of Front Royal. The men were "perspiring and eating dirt," only to be disappointed when it turned out that cavalry had already routed a Union regiment.

This force, the 1st Maryland Regiment under Colonel John Kenly, had numbered about eight hundred. In typical Jackson fashion, a sudden and fierce Confederate attack had thrown Kenly's men into a panic, and they were easily routed by Confederate cavalry. More than two-thirds of the 1st Maryland's men were taken prisoner, and Colonel Kenly was severely wounded. This battle saw the 1st Maryland (Confederate) take an active part in defeating the 1st Maryland (Union).

Although Will and the 16th were disappointed not to be involved in the fighting at Front Royal, they performed well under artillery fire and helped gather prisoners. One member of Will's regiment was a Native American who had never experienced the sound of artillery fire. Terrified, he had broken for the rear, only to encounter the firing of Confederate artillery. Just as swiftly as he had fled he returned to his position on the field, explaining that there "was great danger in the rear" and that he felt safer in the middle.

Another unique character in the 16th was an old drummer named Smith. Smith was patriotic and well-meaning but had a tendency to daydream and often fell a good distance behind the column. As the 16th marched through the Shenandoah Valley,

old Smith got some miles behind, and while sitting on the roadside, solitary and alone, resting and eating his beef and biscuit, he observed a full regiment of Yankee cavalry advancing. He jumped into the woods, and as the Yankees came near he thundered away on his drum, beating the long roll with terrible vim. As this was the signal for an enemy at hand, and to form a line of battle, the trick was successful. The Yankees supposing that there was an infantry regiment lying in the thicket, faced about and skedaddled in the regular Bull Run style. Smith replaced his drum, came out in the road again with his beef and biscuit in one hand and his drumstick in the other, and resumed his marching with his usual equanimity (*Confederate Veteran*, 1893–1994).

The rout of the 1st Maryland at Front Royal rocked the White House. Once again Lincoln feared for the security of Washington. Having taken Front Royal, Jackson was now the hunter rather than the hunted in his war of nerves with Banks. If Jackson could position himself north of Banks he would have the choice of making a daring strike on the lightly defended Washington or trapping Banks in the valley and forcing him to fight his way through Jackson's sixteen thousand-man army. Jackson's capriciousness was not lost on Lincoln and Stanton. They swiftly determined that, at least for the time being, McClellan would have to do without McDowell's thirty thousand troops after all.

On the day following the battle of Front Royal the 16th moved on Winchester. Their march was halted close to midnight; a Federal force posted behind a stone wall prohibited any further advance. In an icy rain, the men of the 16th huddled in groups of fifteen to twenty to avoid "freezing to death."

The 16th's initiation to Jackson's tactics was harsh, and exceedingly so. After months of lying about, napping away the hours, the men found that sleep was suddenly a rare commodity. In one sixty-hour stretch during their first week under the demanding general, Will and his comrades were permitted two hours' sleep. Fighting and exhaustion would become part of life under Jackson.

Meanwhile, Jackson was weighing heavily in the thoughts of General Banks, who had positioned his eighteen thousand troops at Strasburg at the time of the Front Royal action. Fearing a trap, Banks marched twenty-five miles north to Winchester. Jackson's foot cavalry raced to meet Banks at Winchester, reaching the outskirts at about

1 A.M. on Sunday, 25 May. At dawn, lead elements of Jackson's army smashed into Banks' retreating men. In a scene reminiscent of Bull Run, Banks' army broke into a panic, discarding much of its equipment, and fled for the safety of Washington.

About mid-morning, while the 16th watched, two regiments were sent to clear the enemy position behind the stone wall. As the skirmish wound down and the Union troops were withdrawing from their stronghold, Will's Company K was sent into action. But to its dismay, Will's company again missed an opportunity to meet the enemy, who had wisely chosen not to tangle with Jackson.

Fortunately for Banks, Jackson's men were human in spite of their growing reputation; fatigue was all that prevented them from annihilating the Union army. His escape notwithstanding, Banks suffered more than two thousand casualties. Jackson lost a relatively few four hundred. Undoubtedly Jackson's reputation had a significant effect on the behavior of Banks' men.

As word of the defeats at Front Royal and Winchester reached Washington, along with reports that the Army of the Valley had once again disappeared into the Northern portion of the valley, Lincoln decided that he had had enough of Stonewall Jackson. Lincoln ordered General Fremont and his fifteen thousand troops to move out of West Virginia in the southern part of the Shenandoah to block Jackson's escape from the valley. Most crucial to the fate of Sam and the 21st Mississippi, he also ordered McDowell to dispatch twenty thousand of his troops to Fremont and Banks in order to trap and destroy Jackson once and for all. Lincoln, in a foul mood, telegraphed McClellan: "I think the time is near when you must either attack Richmond or give up the job and come to the defense of Washington."

The last week of May passed uneventfully for the two anxious armies. The days became hot, resembling August, and each evening, nature displayed her firepower with magnificent electrical storms that added to an atmosphere of foreboding.

Alone in his tent, McClellan wrote to his wife:

> The occurrences of the next few days are quite uncertain. The intentions of the enemy are still doubtful. I go on prepared to fight, but I confess that the indications are not now that he will fight. Unless he has some deep-laid scheme that I do not fathom, he is giving up great advantages in not opposing me on the line of the Chickahominy. He could give me a great deal of trouble and make it cost me hundreds or thousands of lives. God knows that I am sick of this civil war, although no feeling of the kind unsteadies my hand or ever makes me hesitate or waver (McClellan, 1887).

CHAPTER NINE

How Far South Are We Going?

On Wednesday, 9 November 1994, I received a call from a Providence Journal *reporter who said "We'd like to talk to you about all these letters we're receiving from down south." One hundred and eighteen years after his death, Sam was getting a second chance at securing a place in history.*

The reporter brought some of the letters to our first meeting. From Alabama to Texas, Sam's plight had stirred Southern passions. "This lack of human compassion and kindness for our fellow man is beyond my understanding," concluded one letter. Others expressed similar concerns. A letter from Natchez mentioned that "Everyone is buzzing about the plight of Sam's grave, with fear he will be desecrated." Another letter stated, "The problem seems to be the [cemetery] owner. I hope he will change his mind soon. This note is to thank [Mr. Rolston] for caring and his effort in this situation."

There were many other letters urging that the news-paper attempt to influence the cemetery owner, many with touching comments. "Those of us in the South who care about such things consider this veteran to be a brother."

"Mr. Rolston's care of the site of deceased Samuel Postlethwaite CSA is heartwarming. The gravesite is unmarked. It should not be. Let me offer financial help to have the gravesite properly marked."

A writer from California added, "Although we may not always agree with all the values and beliefs of the Confederate South, we must never forget that not so long ago, many people put their life on the line, a concept many of us will never know, because they believed this country's government was not representing them fairly."

A letter from Georgia urged that the Providence Journal *"give any attention possible" to the situation at Greenwood Cemetery. Attached to this letter was a note from one reporter to another stating, "Yet another civil war letter!" Not all of the letters were conciliatory; one was a scathing four-page attack on Northerners.*

Without my knowledge, Southern Heritage *magazine ran an article about my efforts and told Sam's story in some detail.*

It seems that ownership of the cemetery had changed hands over the years. The plot where Pvt. Postlethwaite is buried has been sold to a new customer who is not aware that her plot has a Confederate soldier buried in it. This has led to quite a stir in Rhode Island. Les Rolston has worked diligently to prove the fact that this plot is in fact where the old soldier is buried. So far, the owner of the cemetery has refused to respond. Undaunted, Mr. Rolston proceeded to contact Southerners. His attempt to contact several elected officials from the South was (embarrassingly for us) not successful. Our gallant Northern brother

Rolston is trying to do the proper thing and he needs
our help. He asks us to write to the major paper in
Rhode Island and express our feelings concerning
the owner of the cemetery. Mr. Rolston asks nothing
more. But I ask that you write to him and express
your gratitude for such an unselfish act for our dear,
long suffering, departed compatriot Private Samuel
Postlethwaite of Mississippi (vol. 2, no. 5, 1994).

*I couldn't believe it. Like tributaries flowing into a
river, diverse interest in this lowly private began converging toward a common point, Veteran's Day. An
enthusiastic young reporter interviewed me at my home
on Thursday, 10 November. He put me at ease right away;
"You know, I expected you would be an old guy with a
Winnebago," he confessed. He informed me that his interest in the Civil War itself was limited; like me, he was
more interested in the human side of the story.*

*Fascinated by the bounty of "Sam stuff" strewn across
my kitchen table, Rich Salit and I talked all afternoon. He
eventually asked me to take him to the grave site with a
photographer. I answered, "Well, you probably won't
believe this, but there is a ceremony of some kind taking
place at the grave tomorrow. I'm not involved but I'll be
in attendance." The next morning an announcement
about a ceremony for a "Confederate soldier" appeared in
the* Providence Journal.

*11 November 1994 dawned clear and brisk with a
faint reminder of Indian Summer. Accompanied by my
wife and a friend, I nervously began the twenty-minute
drive to Greenwood Cemetery. Upon arriving, I was surprised by the number of people who had ventured out to
see what was going on. Answering question after question, I tried to explain Sam's plight. "How could something like this have happened?" and "How did he end up
here?" were common questions. And then a column of
gray-clad soldiers crunched through newly fallen oak
leaves on a short march to the grave site.*

John Wrona of the 21st Mississippi reenactors placed a wreath over Sam's grave and offered a prayer for all fallen soldiers. My friend Mark Johnsen-Harris stilled the crowd as he described the horror of Malvern Hill; faces in the crowd flinched, appalled at the image of 4,500 dead and wounded men lying in the rain and then baking in the sun for three days. I remarked that I felt Sam symbolized how often "the efforts and sacrifices of all veterans are quickly dismissed or forgotten." Another friend, Ralph Ciaramello, said he "hoped that we can soon return to this spot when the grave of Private Samuel Postlethwaite is permanently marked."

I read a letter from the Sons of Confederate Veterans Camp 590 in Natchez: "Sam Postlethwaite, like hundreds of thousands of Southerners, fought for their concept of America. Every man who fought and died in this greatest American tragedy, whether Johnny Reb or Billy Yank, considered themselves to be Americans first. When we honor Sam Postlethwaite, we honor every American fighting man.

Ralph closed the ceremony by reading a special message:

Author reads a letter in honor of Sam from the Sons of Confederate Veterans Camp 590 in Natchez, Mississippi.

My heartfelt thanks go to Les Rolston for making this ceremony possible. It would not have taken place except for his tenacity and genuine interest in providing dignified recognition for my cousin Samuel. I am the last male Postlethwaite of our Mississippi line, so the name dies with me, and I particularly regret that short notice and prior commitments prevent me from being present at this event. I expect to visit Greenwood Cemetery in Rhode Island in the near future and would like to take this means to express my deep appreciation for all that has been done for Sam and his memory.

The letter was signed by Alexander Lathrop Postlethwaite.

Rich Salit was so moved by the ceremony that he later stepped out of his role of observer and called the unknowing owner of the cemetery lot, Ruth Cardin, to plead Sam's case. Ruth was moved by the story and, being an avid lover of history, welcomed the opportunity to guarantee Sam's final resting place. "I'd do anything I could to cooperate," Ruth told the Journal. *She called me at home that afternoon and gave me permission to install the grave marker, assuring me that the site would be preserved. We've been close friends ever since. On the morning of Veteran's Day the headline of the* Providence Journal *read "Honoring a Forgotten Soldier." An article told Sam's story, and the story of the effort to preserve his grave site, in detail. I called Alex in Baton Rouge to tell him the good news. I'll never forget how thrilled he was.*

GENERAL RICHARD GRIFFITH'S BRIGADE RESTED ON THE western bank of the Chickahominy, weathering heat and thunderstorms that returned the water to unfordable levels. The men in Sam's regiment watched the rising river, knowing that McClellan's main force had yet to cross. Two isolated Union corps, those of Keyes and Heintzelman, had no hope of reinforcement and could be crushed if Johnston risked a daring strike.

On the north side of the Chickahominy, the men of the 2nd Rhode Island were getting acquainted with war's darker side. Hungry, forced to forage for their food, some of the soldiers began to question the sincerity of McClellan's pledge to "share the dangers of the battlefield with his troops."

McClellan's army was divided by a raging river, waiting for reinforcements that McClellan now knew weren't coming; his situation was precarious. But with nearly 200,000 soldiers congregated in and around Richmond, it was Jackson's tiny contingent that held the attention of America and Europe.

Having devastated Banks' army and driven its remnants across the Potomac, Jackson was ordered to move even farther north, leaving no doubt that Washington was in jeopardy. Reaching Harper's Ferry on 28 May 1862, Jackson's men gathered tons of discarded Federal equipment and supplies. Then a scout brought word of the trap being set by Fremont and McDowell. Jackson's spectacular drive into the northern reaches of the Shenandoah ended there.

On the north side of the Potomac, at Harper's Ferry, Lincoln had assembled seven thousand men under General Rufus Saxton. This force could prevent Jackson's crossing of the river in the immediate vicinity of the town. Twenty-five miles to the north, Banks' demoralized army tried to regroup. It was battered but otherwise ready to fight.

From West Virginia General Fremont's fifteen thousand men began marching east toward Strasburg, fifty miles south of Harper's Ferry. From the east, McDowell sent two divisions of infantry under Generals Shields and Ord totaling twenty thousand men. Should Jackson try to escape from the Shenandoah via the same route by which he had swept north, he would be flanked by the Union army on both sides. The Federal trap consisted of almost forty-eight thousand men; Jackson's sixteen thousand soldiers were the prey.

But Lincoln's plan would work only if properly set up.
Fremont, Shields, and Ord had much ground to cover if
they were to get into position to pounce on Jackson. On 29
May the Army of the Valley was marching south toward
Winchester. In a message to McDowell, Lincoln stressed
that catching Jackson before he escaped the valley was
"for you, a question of legs."

Jackson was willing to gamble that his familiarity with
the valley terrain and the speed of his men would enable
him to slip out of the Federal noose. In this case, however,
the Army of the Valley was hindered by its own successes.
The spoils of war had become a ball and chain as Jackson's
army dragged along a lumbering wagon train of captured
equipment.

While Jackson scurried south and the Federals raced to
intercept him, Will Postlethwaite and the men of the 16th
Mississippi were worn out. Their once-striking uniforms by
now were nearly rags, barely offering protection from the
elements. Will and his comrades rummaged through the
piles of captured equipment, searching for shoes, belts,
shirts, anything that would fit. With many of its men
dressed partially or mostly in Federal uniforms, Jackson's
army resembled a motley parade of vagabonds.

As heavy rain drenched Richmond on 30 May, Joe
Johnston met with his friend General James Longstreet to
share strategies for an attack planned for the following
morning. Although Sam's division was positioned closest to
what would be the field of action, Johnston had decided to
hold it in reserve—possibly because the commander of
Sam's division, Lafayette McLaws, had only recently
attained the rank of major general. In fact, McLaws had
held the rank for only seven days. A forty-one-year-old
Georgian, he was, like many of his peers, a graduate of
West Point and a veteran of the Mexican and Indian wars.
With a long, flowing beard framing intense eyes, McLaws'
presence was striking. This change in command had badly
bruised Prince John Magruder's ego; what had begun as a
sparkling career was sliding into mediocrity.

Four other Confederate generals had major responsibilities in the upcoming action: Longstreet, Gustavus Smith, Benjamin Huger, and Stonewall Jackson's brother-in-law, Harvey Hill. Smith was forty years old, suffered from recurring bouts of paralysis, and was no favorite of President Davis. Huger had held command in Norfolk, overseeing its evacuation three weeks before. Harvey Hill was the ultimate warrior. Unlike his brother-in-law, who was shy and religious, Hill was outgoing, often sarcastic, and hot-tempered. Hill's division would form the extreme right flank of Johnston's attack, the most dangerous position on the battlefield. Three of the generals received written orders describing their roles in the upcoming offensive. Strangely, in light of his impaired hearing, Longstreet received his orders verbally.

Three parallel roads would be used to bring the fourteen Confederate brigades into the vicinity of Fair Oaks Station and a place known as Seven Pines, where the isolated divisions of Heintzelman and Keyes were encamped. Running west to east, the Nine Mile Road (the northernmost), the Williamsburg Road, and the Charles City Road were separated from one another by distances of one to two miles. The 21st Mississippi was camped on the Nine Mile Road. It would take a coordinated march to bring these separate forces onto the field of battle at the same time. Any delay in the attack would give McClellan time to try to get reinforcements across the Chickahominy.

During the early morning hours of the 31st, a division commanded by General William Whiting arrived from Richmond. At that time, General Smith curiously announced that he did not wish to lead his troops into battle, and he relinquished his command to Whiting.

At dawn, Longstreet was to break camp and advance along the Nine Mile Road in the direction of the enemy. Harvey Hill was to advance along the Williamsburg Road and engage the enemy at the same time Longstreet hit the enemy's left flank. Whiting's division would follow Longstreet into action. The remaining brigades would use the Charles City Road, which led to the center of Keyes and Heintzelman's position.

At about 6 A.M., Whiting's division moved onto the Nine Mile Road, where it promptly encountered several of Longstreet's brigades. These soldiers were breaking camp at a leisurely pace, and Longstreet was nowhere to be found. An hour passed, then another. It wasn't until after 10 A.M. that Longstreet and the bulk of his division were located. Longstreet had positioned himself at the intersection of the Charles City and Williamsburg roads, causing another traffic jam. His explanation was that he was waiting for Harvey Hill to pass and lead the way to the battlefield. Longstreet had misunderstood his orders to such a degree that the entire operation was brought to a halt.

In an attempt to salvage what was left of the operation, Longstreet would make another bizarre blunder. Thinking it would somehow save time, he ordered his troops who were on the Nine Mile Road to reverse their march of three-and-a-half miles. After countermarching, he brought these brigades off the road and into the woods heading south, where they encountered a swollen stream known as Gillies Creek.

By an almost comical coincidence, Huger's division was also in the woods, struggling to cross the creek. Although plans called for Huger's division to open the battle, Longstreet asserted that his men, not Huger's, should cross first; this brought up the question of which of the two major generals outranked the other. The fact that both men had been promoted to major general on the same day turned the debate into a farce. Huger finally deferred to Longstreet and the men began crossing Gillies Creek, single file, as the clock ticked.

With the Nine Mile Road once again clear, Johnston could have ordered into action Sam's division, which was camped along that road near Seven Pines; or he could have ordered Whiting to begin a long march. Johnston decided to keep Sam's division in reserve and ordered Whiting to move.

Seven hours had passed since Johnston's army had clumsily begun its offensive, and only a portion of it had reached its designated positions. The surprise attack, scheduled to commence at 8 A.M., was now five hours behind schedule. As early as 10 A.M., Union General Keyes got an inkling that something unusual was afoot on the other side of the Chickahominy with the capture of one of Joe Johnston's staff. By noon, it was reported that the enemy was approaching "in considerable force on the Williamsburg Road." This was Harvey Hill's Division.

At one o'clock, as Union troops were massing to meet him, the element of surprise lost, Hill ordered his division to attack. Hill's men slammed into a small Union force which tried to hold until reinforcements could be brought up. The green Union troops were pushed back and broke for the rear when Confederate artillery came into the fight.

At Confederate and Union headquarters, the sound of battle could suddenly be heard. Each commanding general reacted quite differently. Robert E. Lee was visiting Johnston, and President Davis was on the way to observe; Johnston tried to conceal the fact that he had lost control of his offensive and hadn't a clue as to what was going on. Union General Sumner, on the other hand, didn't hesitate, and by two o'clock he had two divisions crossing the Chickahominy.

Due to Sumner's quick response and the lack of a cohesive assault by Johnston's army, the early Confederate successes were being reversed. Late in the afternoon an anxious Johnston, frustrated at his ignorance of events, rode out from his headquarters only moments before Davis arrived; this, of course, did nothing to improve his relations with the commander-in-chief.

Davis was also determined to view the action; he began riding out to Seven Pines. Twilight was enveloping Richmond as President Davis passed the camp of McLaws' division; he was puzzled because the division wasn't engaged. As fate would have it, after thirteen months of service Sam and the 21st Mississippi were to be sent into their first battle by presidential order.

Griffith led his brigade down the Nine Mile Road for about two miles before finding himself under attack by an unseen enemy. Nothing terrified a soldier more than the prospect of fighting at night, blind. The 21st encountered whirring Minié balls that claimed several victims. Not knowing where the firing was coming from, the men of the 21st had to undergo this initiation into battle without returning fire.

The position of the 21st was relayed to nearby Union artillery, which for several hours poured frightening, but ineffective, fire upon the pinned-down Confederates. The regiment stubbornly withstood this battering as the Battle of Seven Pines came to an end, the artillery fire gradually dying.

As the day's fighting wound down, a jittery Joe Johnston rode back and forth atop the crest of a hill barking orders, hoping to make some last-minute gains in what had been a failed offensive. Consumed by the moment, the general paid little regard to the lead that still filled the air. Almost simultaneously, Johnston was struck in the right shoulder by a Minié ball and by a shell fragment that imbedded itself in his chest.

Thrown from his horse, Johnston briefly passed out. He was being placed on a stretcher as Davis arrived. Upon regaining consciousness, Johnston's first instinct was to locate his sword, which his father had worn in the American Revolution. With the sword safely in hand, Johnston was consoled by President Davis, who expressed concern over Johnston's injuries. Both men knew that Johnston's tenure as commander of the Confederate army in Virginia had come to an end.

The next morning Longstreet made a second assault against the Federals; it also failed. The Battle of Seven Pines can be viewed as a Confederate defeat or as a draw. The fighting claimed eleven thousand casualties from both sides, but the positions of the two armies remained relatively unchanged.

Davis turned to his trusted military advisor, Lee, who had failed in his previous attempt at field command, to somehow stop McClellan from laying siege to Richmond. Upon assuming his post, General Lee gave his command a name: the Army of Northern Virginia; this left no doubt as to where he intended to make a stand.

Throughout the weekend action at Seven Pines, Jackson had driven his men through a steady downpour in the Shenandoah. When Fremont and Shields arrived at their designated positions to wait for Jackson, it became obvious that the Army of the Valley had already passed, slipping by a mere three hours before with its captured supplies and prisoners, legend intact.

The days immediately following the fighting at Seven Pines brought a lull in the battle for Richmond, but they were filled with activity of another kind. For the first time since the aftermath of Bull Run, large numbers of casualties were pouring into the Confederate capital. Empty buildings and private residences were transformed into hospitals. The seriously wounded were treated as swiftly as possible, a difficult task considering the stream of men arriving at these "hospitals." Those in less serious condition found themselves laid out in the streets or wandering the city in search of comfort. Even relatively minor wounds, left untreated, often became infected and were more life-threatening than the initial wounds themselves. Many of the injured didn't even survive the seven-mile journey from Seven Pines. The civilians of Richmond offered what care they could as dead and dying men filled their sun-drenched streets. The concomitants of war were on Richmond's doorstep.

George McClellan, tiring of his supply base on the York River, which forced him to bridge the troublesome Chickahominy, began considering a new base of operations on the James River. But until McDowell joined him, the Army of the Potomac would have to remain astride the Chickahominy. Three miles east of Seven Pines on the western bank of the Chickahominy sat Savage's Station, normally a routine stop along the Richmond & York Railroad line. For the month of June, however, Savage's

Station would serve as a field hospital for McClellan's 3,600 wounded. Hundreds of tents and ambulances filled the area. The surgeons in Richmond and Savage's Station, struggling to care for the wounded, were dealing with only the beginning of a series of bloodbaths to come in the next days and weeks.

As June began, presidents and privates were gripped with anxiety. McClellan and Lincoln anguished as the raging waters of the Chickahominy divided the Union forces. McClellan concerned himself with building new bridges, which would offer "a safer retreat in the event of disaster." As for a sudden bold stroke upon Lee's Army of Northern Virginia, the idea was "never for a moment seriously entertained by anyone connected with The Army of the Potomac." Lincoln wired the general, "I am very anxious about the Chickahominy."

The 2nd Rhode Island could "see the rebel guns." The men passed the days and nights without tents, using only blankets, which were "wet most of the time." The men of the 21st Mississippi endured the torrential rains wondering if and when they would see action.

Unlike the armies clustered around Richmond, Will and the 16th Mississippi welcomed the rain because it impeded Fremont and Shields' dogged pursuit. The speed of Jackson's men had no equal, but under Lincoln's orders the Union armies gave it their best effort, occasionally skirmishing with Jackson's rear guard.

Like a dog with a bone, Jackson refused to cut loose any of his captured stores, even though they hampered his escape. To make up for this handicap his men marched as they had never marched before, placing the emphasis on endurance rather than speed. With hardly a chance to rest, the men of the 16th wondered, "How far south are we going?"

As the first week of June passed, it brought news of Confederate setbacks in the south and west; pleas for more troops came into Richmond from all over the Confederacy. President Davis, with no troops to spare from his embattled capital, entered his fifty-fifth year with little to celebrate. Everywhere the Confederacy was on the verge of collapse. McClellan assured his president that he would strike the final blow as soon as the Chickahominy receded and the landscape, which he described as "a bog," became passable for his artillery.

What Will Become Of Us!

The men of the 21st Mississippi spent the first week of June in a state of nervous distraction. As the distant crackle of skirmishing caught their immediate attention, so did news and rumors of Confederate setbacks at home.

Sam also had his brother's well-being in mind; the Army of the Valley was being hunted like an animal somewhere in the Shenandoah. With the Army of Northern Virginia outnumbered and Richmond about to be besieged, the sight of the 16th Mississippi and the rest of Jackson's army marching through the streets of Richmond would have been welcome to Sam and the rest of Richard Griffith's Mississippians. But not knowing that Jackson's army was racing south to join them, the bored 21st continued to camp, picket, and wait for a chance to get into the war.

Despite Jackson's best efforts and the tenacity of his men, the Army of the Valley was losing its footrace with Shields and Fremont. The Union generals knew they could expect to feel Lincoln's wrath should Jackson escape and join Lee. With their careers on the line, Shields and Fremont were determined to catch and destroy Jackson. On 8 June, Jackson's army would find its head in a Union noose once again.

Basking in the warmth of the morning sun, Jackson and some of his staff had crossed a branch of the Shenandoah River and unhitched their horses to graze. Two messengers delivered reports of enemy movement in the area, but Jackson and his staff ignored them, continuing to admire the peaceful sight of their mounts in the green field.

Sharing this mood of subdued cockiness were Will Postlethwaite and the Wilkinson Rifles, who were enjoying the quiet Sunday by cooking breakfast, attending religious services, and taking advantage of the rare opportunity to write letters and relax. The men mourned the death of their colorful cavalry officer, Turner Ashby, who was killed in a rear guard deployment near Harrisonburg.

About 10 A.M. the shriek of artillery ripped through the spring air. Not only had the enemy caught the Army of the Valley, they had caught it napping. Soldiers broke from their respite and frantically prepared for battle as artillery pieces were hauled to the riverbank. Jackson's men were stunned; no one could believe that the enemy had moved with such alacrity and appeared so suddenly.

Jackson and his staff suddenly were on the wrong side of the river, without their horses. As the general waited for one of his aides to retrieve Little Sorrel, he was offered another horse. Cool as ever, Jackson declined and patiently waited for his horse. Finally securing their mounts, Jackson and his staff made a thundering flight across the bridge into the safety of camp.

Once across the river Will's general immediately acted to seize control of the situation. Turning his horse and gazing across the bridge, Jackson spotted soldiers and shouted to warn of the impending danger. They were Union soldiers; by the slightest of margins the most famous general of the war had escaped becoming a prisoner. As the firing across the river heated up, there was no time to reflect on his luck; the battle of Cross Keys had begun.

In a flurry, the Confederate camps prepared for battle. Confederate infantry double-quicked across the bridge as Union gunners frantically assembled to greet them. Strangely, Fremont, who had so aggressively sought this final confrontation with Jackson, entered it only half-heartedly by throwing only a small portion of his army into action. As if preparing to take a defensive position, the Union general kept nineteen of his twenty-four regiments out of the initial fighting. Jackson's greatest ally, his legend, was at work again.

At first, some of Fremont's troops were successful in overpowering parts of the sleepy Confederate ranks. As Will Postlethwaite was preparing to head for the field, the 15th Alabama, under heavy fire, fell back to the safety of the 16th Mississippi's camp. Loading their rifles and forming a line of battle, the Mississippians stood before the advancing 8th New York.

After thirteen months with no real fighting, Captain Abram Feltus faced the task of delivering his ragtag, even barefoot, Wilkinson Rifles through their baptism of fire. Holding fire as the New Yorkers bore down on them stretched moments into an eternity. Jackson's orders were to "Let the Federals get very close before your infantry fire. They won't stand long." Feltus held his men at the ready. Will Postlethwaite and the rest of Company K listened intently as Feltus tried to steady them. Nervously, the men fumbled through cap and cartridge boxes while trying to steal peeks at the oncoming enemy. The captain's voice, shrill and demanding, became a connection to the events swirling around the infantryman. With other companies' captains shouting similar orders, the sound and pitch of the captain's voice was like that of a shepherd.

Months of seemingly pointless drilling paid off when firing commenced. The 8th New York pressed on until they and Feltus' men could clearly see each other's faces at a distance of a mere fifty feet. The New Yorkers were taking aim on Company K's line. Feltus unleashed the order to "Aim . . . fire!" The rattling crackle of rifle fire sounded in the Sunday morning air. Will Postlethwaite was getting his first taste of battle, and like every man on the field he struggled to load and fire as rapidly as possible. Men of the 16th began to fall as the whirring sounds of Minié balls were punctuated by dull thuds.

The New Yorkers held their ground and poured repeated volleys into the 16th Mississippi, wounding Colonel Posey, but in spite of their gallantry the 8th New

York was getting the worst of it. One extraordinary burst of musketry took a murderous toll on the 8th; as a group the Northern men appeared "stunned" and staggered back.

As the New Yorkers struggled to reorganize their lines, Union fire from a different position rained onto the pursuing 16th Mississippi. The 16th came under sweeping fire as other Union regiments came to the aid of the New Yorkers. With three dozen of its men on the ground, the 16th was in trouble when the 21st Georgia came into the fight.

Fremont's attack fell apart and came to a close with the loss of seven hundred men. The Confederates lost three hundred. Will Postlethwaite and his comrades had their first battle under their belts; they had fought "with much glory."

Having performed so well early in the day, the 16th Mississippi and its brigade were rewarded with what could have been a suicidal mission. As Jackson's main force gathered near Port Republic for an assault on General Shields' army, the 16th was ordered to remain at Cross Keys to keep Fremont in check. As Magruder had done so brilliantly at Yorktown, the 16th was ordered to convince the enemy that it was Jackson's entire army. Of course, if Fremont wasn't taken in by the show he would destroy the performers.

Fremont didn't attack, and in the pre-dawn hours of Monday the 16th Mississippi, forming the rear guard, moved out to rejoin Jackson at Port Republic. As Will and his comrades crossed the Shenandoah, they delivered yet another critical blow to Lincoln's plan by burning the North Bridge; Fremont's only means of joining Shields was gone.

Jackson, eager to get at Shields and to avenge his defeat at Kernstown, wasted no time getting his attack under way. Hearing the sounds of battle in the distance, Fremont raced his army to the North Bridge, only to find it engulfed in flames. Enraged, Fremont could only agonize over the fate of the outnumbered Shields.

Throughout the morning of 9 June, Shields' army refused to buckle under Jackson's relentless attacks; but with no sign of Fremont, Shields' lines began to crack at about eleven o'clock. Jackson's rematch with Shields resulted in a crushing Union defeat. Routed, 450 of Shields' men surrendered; others abandoned their weapons, leaving behind at least one cannon and eight hundred rifles. Stonewall Jackson's Valley Campaign and Lincoln's determined attempt to destroy it was over. General Fremont resigned his command.

As Lincoln's broken army retreated northward up the Shenandoah, the president continued to worry about Jackson. Would the Army of the Valley race up the valley and threaten Washington, or would it march to Richmond to join Lee? Playing upon Lincoln's anxiety was Lee, who went to work making it appear as though he was reinforcing Jackson.

McClellan's relationship with Lincoln now hit rock bottom. The issue, as always, was McDowell. Although a small portion of McDowell's force had been sent to McClellan, there was some question as to who commanded it. McClellan angrily wired Washington, "If I cannot fully control all his troops I want none of them, but would prefer to fight the battle with what I have, and let others be responsible for the results."

In a letter to Ellen, the general seemed contrite.

> It is raining again hard, and has been for several hours! I feel almost discouraged. It is certain that there has not been for years and years such a season; it does not come by chance. I am quite checked by it. The Secretary and President are becoming quite amiable of late; I am afraid I am a little cross to them, and that I do not quite appreciate their sincerity and good feeling (McClellan, 1887).

The next day he closed another letter with "Still raining very hard. I don't know what will become of us!"

As Sam and the 21st Mississippi continued to endure miserable weather, brother Will began what would be a most enjoyable time. With Fremont vanquished, the valley belonged to Jackson and his men. In their defeat, Fremont and Shields had been generous. Food, once scarce, was suddenly plentiful; captured and discarded Union supplies were readily available and the men helped themselves. In addition, the weather in the valley was cool and pleasant, carrying with it a promise of summer. Jackson's men went back to a routine of drilling, relaxing, and light marching. These marches seemed to have no particular purpose; as one soldier in Company K recalled, they "seemed to be marching any old way!"

Events in the eastern theater ground to a halt as McClellan waited for the skies to clear and Jackson awaited orders from Lee. It was during this period of relative calm that another rising star burst upon the scene; he was destined to challenge Jackson for the affections of the South.

At 2 A.M. on Thursday, 12 June, Colonel James Ewell Brown (Jeb) Stuart told his men, "Gentlemen, in ten minutes every man must be in his saddle!" Flamboyant in dress, with a full, flowing beard that concealed a homely face (which had earned him the nickname "Beauty"), Jeb Stuart looked every bit the cavalier. Stuart's appearance contrasted sharply with that of Jackson, who often wore a worn-out private's uniform and cap.

Under Stuart's command, one thousand horsemen left the safety of Richmond, riding north as if to reinforce the Army of the Valley. Encountering little resistance, Stuart daringly veered off to the east, following the south bank of the Pamunkey River, cutting telegraph lines and tearing up railroads that linked McClellan to his supply base on the York River, his umbilical cord to Washington. With no support of any kind Stuart drove deeply into McClellan's supply lines, burning everything he couldn't carry and taking prisoner any unfortunate Union soldier caught in his path. Fighting their way around the Union army, Stuart and his men could have had no idea that this escapade would be praised, reviled, and debated, North and South, for decades to come.

Four days and 150 miles later Stuart's cavalry rode into Richmond with a parade of prisoners and captured supplies in tow. News of Stuart's ride rippled through the ranks of both armies. The Army of the Potomac had been humiliated, and the men of the Army of Northern Virginia were ecstatic. Certainly, an adversary so easily manipulated was not invincible, and the spirits of Confederate soldiers in the Shenandoah and entrenched outside Richmond soared.

No one was affected more by Stuart's expedition than George McClellan. With his supply lines to the York River proving vulnerable, McClellan again considered changing his base to a location on the James River, from which U.S. Navy gunboats could fire into the outskirts of Richmond. In three days, the whole complexion of the Peninsula Campaign was changed, and for the first time, McClellan was watching his back.

On 17 June, the weather at last seemed to turn in McClellan's favor. The rivers had receded, the bridges were being rebuilt, and the roads were "drying beautifully and we shall soon be on the move."

Meanwhile, without pausing to enjoy the fruits of Stuart's ride, General Lee went to work fine-tuning the Confederate war machine. Jackson, encamped at the southern end of the valley, received a letter from Lee: "McClellan is being strengthened . . . . There is much sickness in his ranks, but his reinforcements by far exceed his losses. The present, therefore, seems to be favorable for a junction of your army and this. The sooner you can make arrangements to do so the better." Lee couldn't stress the importance of stealth strongly enough. "The country is full of spies," he added. "In moving your troops, you could let it be understood that it was to pursue the enemy in your front, the movement must be secret."

Once again, Jackson's "foot cavalry" was on the move. This time it seemed to be going everywhere. A small force feinted toward what was left of Fremont's army, while a large portion of the army boarded rail cars bound for an unknown destination. The bulk of the Army of the Valley, including Will Postlethwaite and the 16th Mississippi, took to the road, marching four abreast.

On this march, Jackson's demands on his soldiers were more brutal than ever; at many points along the march and in camp, Jackson demanded total silence. Any discussion of their destination was prohibited; even asking the names of towns they were marching through was strictly forbidden. Few would dare to violate such orders, as these men not only respected the general, they feared him. One soldier recalled, "He would have a man shot at the drop of a hat!" The men also remembered Kernstown, where Jackson had had Richard Garnet court-martialed for taking his troops off the field when they ran out of ammunition.

As the Army of the Valley began its final march, the men whispered about where they might be heading. Only a personality like Jackson could have molded such an army, marching silently and blindly to an unknown field of battle. One small reward for Will and his comrades was the abundance of berries they could easily pluck from bushes lining the dusty roads.

The third week of June found McClellan waiting for his heaviest artillery pieces to be put in place "to make the loss of life on our side comparatively small." Only light skirmishing along the Chickahominy broke the silence of the armies.

At 1 A.M. on Monday, 23 June, Jackson, accompanied by a single aide, slipped out of his headquarters and began a fourteen-hour, fifty-two-mile ride to the outskirts of Richmond. Greeted by Lee at his headquarters on the Nine Mile Road about mid-afternoon, Jackson discovered that he was the first of four lieutenant generals invited to a council of war. His shyness dictated that he wait outside. A short time later, Harvey Hill arrived, witnessing the curious sight of his weary brother-in-law in a dusty private's uniform. Hill's presence put Jackson at ease; with the arrival of Longstreet and General Ambrose Powell Hill, the council of war commenced. (A. P. Hill was no relation to D.

H. Hill; except for service in the Mexican War and the Peninsula Campaign, they had little in common. A. P. Hill was "genial, approachable, and affectionate," but he was a bulldog in battle.)

Lee had devised a plan for the defense of Richmond, but he recognized the importance of delegating. After outlining his plan, Lee left his four generals to debate and work out the logistical details. The fates of the men in the trenches, Richmond, and the Confederacy would rest with the men gathered at Lee's headquarters.

As this meeting was taking place, McClellan wrote to his wife, "The enemy has been making some rather mysterious movements, I don't yet know exactly what it means, you may be sure that I won't be caught in any trap."

The plan was simple. To remain on the defensive would be suicide. McClellan's right flank, which remained on the north bank of the Chickahominy, would be smashed by A. P. Hill, who would be supported by Longstreet and Jackson. This would leave only a token force, which included Sam and the 21st, to protect Richmond from McClellan's left flank, which was located south of the Chickahominy.

Davis and Harvey Hill were gravely concerned that when McClellan's right was assaulted, his left would rise from its trenches and crush the vastly outnumbered Confederates in front of Richmond. The results of such an attack were unthinkable. Lee assured Davis, and later Hill, that McClellan lacked the imagination or the daring to attack Richmond with anything less than his full force. On this assumption Lee was willing to risk everything.

The key to the success of such a bold stroke depended upon the surprise of Jackson's 18,500-man army driving into McClellan's right. Without Jackson, Lee would simply not have enough numbers to succeed, and if McClellan opened his offensive before Jackson arrived, the whole plan would be moot. Longstreet asked Jackson how long it would take his army to reach the Chickahominy and get into position. Not knowing what progress his army had made in his absence, Jackson insisted that his men could be in position the following day. Aware that Jackson was not familiar with the terrain around Richmond, Longstreet persuaded Jackson to allow himself an additional day to reach the field.

A fatigued Jackson left Lee's headquarters and began his ride back to his army; he found his men to be in a similar state. Having emerged from the cool of the Shenandoah, Jackson's men found the woods on the way to Richmond unwelcoming. The dusty roads were hot and the air was thick. Their march was further impeded by the lack of accurate maps. Despite the glory Jackson's men had claimed for themselves in the valley, the weeks of forced marches and fierce fighting had taken their toll.

After months of preparation, it was no coincidence that the Army of the Potomac and the Army of Northern Virginia resolved to attack each other on the same day, 26 June. A deserter from Jackson's army had revealed to McClellan the army's position and its intention to join Lee at Richmond. McClellan couldn't stop thinking about Jackson. If Jackson's army was somewhat off its game, its legend still carried considerable clout.

Not knowing precisely where Jackson was, McClellan further convinced himself of the need to secure a new base of operations on the James River. In what would be the most critical moment of his entire campaign, McClellan faced a decision. Only the unspectacular Huger and the diminished Magruder stood between Richmond and the Army of the Potomac; the rest of Lee's army was massing north of the city on McClellan's right flank. If McClellan attacked immediately there was little doubt as to the outcome.

Jackson once again was the wild card. No matter what action McClellan took against Richmond, it would be disastrous if Jackson attacked McClellan's supply trains as he was moving his base of operations to the James. McClellan chose to focus on changing his base rather than attacking Richmond. So, as they had at Yorktown and Williamsburg,

Sam and the 21st Mississippi waited for a reluctant adversary to attack.

As the last week of June began, Sam and Will lived very different experiences. Will was enduring a slow, sweltering march through the woods of northern Virginia, while Sam dwelled in the trenches. If attacked, General Griffith's brigade, with the divisions of Huger and Magruder, was to hold its ground to the last man.

Beginning with sporadic skirmishing on 25 June 1862, the first week of summer would host the final act of McClellan's Peninsula Campaign "The Seven Days." What was initially planned as a two-week campaign, beginning appropriately enough on April Fool's Day, had lasted a full three months without resolution.

CHAPTER TEN

The Stage Was
Set for Tragedy

On Memorial Day weekend in 1995, one hundred of Sam's "friends and family" gathered at the mansion of Rhode Island's Civil War governor for a reception honoring Rhode Island's Confederate soldier. The proceeds were donated to the Association for the Preservation of Civil War Sites and earmarked for the purchase of Malvern Hill Battlefield. A proclamation from Governor Kirk Fordice of Mississippi and a state flag were presented to Ruth Cardin, who brought down the house when she quipped "A flag, thank goodness! I was worried it might be a tee shirt."

Having following Sam's story closely, my good friend, Ralph Ciaramello, related it for those gathered:

Ruth Cardin accepted a state flag at the governor's mansion where a reception was held in honor of Sam Postlethwaite.

Four years ago, Les and Jane, motivated by a mixture of curiosity and a love of history, ventured into Greenwood Cemetery in search of a Confederate soldier's grave. An obscure reference in a thirty-year-old book proved to be fruitless. There was no evidence of this soldier's presence. It could have ended there in the cemetery, but instead a story was born—the story of Private Samuel Postlethwaite of the 21st Mississippi Infantry, Company D.

As the years went by and Les continued his research, the story began to unfold. As we discussed his progress and learned of this man's life, we affectionately referred to him as "Sam."

Standing here before all of you, I can't help but wonder what Sam would think if he were here today. He probably would be overwhelmed and surprised that so many people, from so many places and so many walks of life, would come together to honor a simple private from Natchez, Mississippi.

One hundred thirty-four years ago, life was less complicated. Young men instilled with a sense of honor and dedication marched off to fight for what they believed in. Many of them died or were wounded and all were witness to the horrors of war.

Sam was one of those men. His wounds, suffered at the battle of Malvern Hill, would change his life forever. Complications in his health brought him to Rhode Island, far from his beloved Westmoreland, and some ten years later proved to be fatal. He was laid to rest at Greenwood Cemetery.

But then something happened—something unconscionable. He was forgotten, a lost soul. No soldier who has fought for his country deserves to be forgotten.

Thanks to the tenacity and dedication of Les Rolston, and to all of you who have given so much to this cause, we have gathered here this weekend to join in a celebration and make amends, to honor Private Postlethwaite, Rhode Island's only Confederate veteran, and to guarantee him his final resting place.

I am very pleased to be here today and proud to have been chosen on behalf of the Honorable Senator of Rhode Island, John H. Chafee, to present Alexander Postlethwaite this flag of the United States of America in recognition of Private Samuel Postlethwaite's service to his state and country.

Also on hand was Catherine Brandon Morgan, the great-great-granddaughter of Sam's first captain, William Lindsay Brandon (who lost a leg at Malvern Hill). Catherine brought with her from Natchez, Mississippi, Brandon's sword. (A year later I visited her home, where I sifted through a box of the old soldier's personal letters.)

Catherine spoke of playing at Westmoreland as a child. "We are here tonight to honor Sam. I knew Sam, I

*Catherine Brandon Morgan held her great-great-grand-
father's sword at Sam's memorial.*

*swam in his creeks and fished in his ponds." The atmos-
phere in the room was electric.*

*I was then flattered and a bit embarrassed as the
United Daughters of the Confederacy presented me with
the Jefferson Davis Medal. In an atmosphere filled with
laughter and patriotism, I couldn't help but think of the
evening as a celebration of the spirit of William and
Mollie Greene, who exemplified the postwar choice of for-
giveness and understanding over bitterness and hatred.
Eyeing the room that night, I was struck by the varied
nature of the audience. People from all walks of life, liberal and conservative, rich and poor, Southerner and
Northerner, had come to remember a forgotten private
from a long-ago war.*

At the end of the evening, as the 2nd South Carolina String Band was packing up, I was approached by the band's banjo player, who appeared somewhat unnerved. I worried that maybe the speeches had gone on too long and had abbreviated their donated performance. Joe Ewers shook his head and said, "Les, something happened here tonight. I don't exactly know what it was, but it was important. Something wonderful happened in this room!" I replied, "I know what happened here. Tonight, all of us shared the experience of feeling good about being American. I think we caught its essence." I still believe that.

The 2nd South Carolina String Band performed at the Memorial Day celebration in honor of Sam.

On 2 June 1996, I drove down the long dirt carriage way of Westmoreland Plantation. With its live oaks laden with Spanish moss, it was just as William Greene had described it to Harry.

IN THE CAMPS AROUND RICHMOND, THURSDAY, 26 JUNE
1862, dawned much like a typical Louisiana summer
morning. The early summer sun beat down upon the
"sacred soil," drawing from it the moisture of the spring
torrents. By late morning, the day had become oppres-
sively hot and humid.

Will Postlethwaite and the 16th Mississippi continued
their march toward Richmond. Despite being delayed by
Union pickets, Jackson's men advanced thirteen miles.
This was slow progress by the foot cavalry's standards;
Jackson, who slept little, was falling behind schedule.
Forced to move through thickly wooded areas teeming with
insects, without reliable maps, the army was marching into
the teeth of McClellan's force; it was hardly the kind of
operation that boosted morale. Only the news of Stuart's
magnificent ride buoyed the spirits of Jackson's soldiers.

As the Confederate battle plan entered its final and
most critical phase, it was already beginning to crumble.
One of Jackson's men had deserted, revealing the Army of
the Valley's position, movements, and numbers. The key
element of Lee's plan, Jackson's sudden emergence to slam
into McClellan's right, was no longer a secret. Immediately,
McClellan's forces destroyed several bridges between
Jackson and the Union position. As Jackson struggled
through the tangled Virginia forests, he had no inkling of
betrayal.

What wasn't known to McClellan was Lee's overall plan.
Lee would leave only a quarter of his army, a mere twenty
thousand troops, including the 21st Mississippi, in defense
of Richmond as he moved the bulk of the Army of
Northern Virginia into position to strike the Northern part
of the Union forces, which were divided by the
Chickahominy River.

As late morning turned into early afternoon, A. P. Hill
nervously waited for Jackson. In one of the Civil War's
countless ironies, Hill and McClellan had been close
friends and roommates at West Point. Both men had fallen
for Ellen Marcy, McClellan eventually winning her hand. At

three o'clock, depending on the arrival of Jackson, Hill would meet his former rival in romance on a military field.

Growing increasingly agitated by Jackson's tardiness, Hill began to lose his composure. At three o'clock, ignoring orders to wait for Jackson, Hill ordered his men into action. Artillery fire erupted near the town of Mechanicsville, and the battle for Richmond began. One Union general recalled the magnitude of the moment: "The curtain rose, the stage was prepared for the first scene of the tragedy."

Along Beaver Dam Creek, at Ellerson's Mill, and in Mechanicsville itself, heavy fighting broke out. Hill's men met early success, pushing the startled enemy back into the town. Had Jackson been on his left he would have engaged the Union artillery; unmolested, it laid a deadly fire on Hill's adrenaline-charged troops. Despite their tenacity, Hill's men were being badly cut up. From a distance, Lee watched and wondered why there was no trace of Jackson.

It was war at its most gruesome. Some of the fighting took place on the ground where the battles of Fair Oaks and Seven Pines had been waged a month before. Scores of partially buried and decomposing corpses exposed by the heavy rains dotted the killing fields around Mechanicsville. The living and the dead endured the Battle of Mechanicsville until darkness brought it to a close.

Jackson never arrived for the battle, which resulted in complete Confederate defeat. Of Hill's fifteen thousand men, ten percent were killed or wounded. Union losses were fewer than four hundred. Desperate to unite his army, McClellan accelerated his efforts to move his supply base to the James River.

In the early morning hours of 27 June, McClellan began moving his right wing over the Chickahominy toward Savage's Station. This move posed a huge logistical problem; a parade of tons of supplies, including 2,500 head of cattle, would be exposed to Confederate attack as it lumbered its way to Harrison's Landing on the James.

As Richmond sat nearly defenseless, McClellan was pre-occupied with his change of base. With Jackson finally in position on his right, McClellan had no doubt that he would be attacked as he tried to unite his army. To General Fitz John Porter, McClellan gave the order every soldier dreads: "Hold until darkness." Near the home and gristmill of a Dr. Gaines, Porter's men felled trees and dug trenches, readying themselves for a Confederate onslaught.

Months of preparation and suffering had brought the church bells of Richmond within earshot of the Army of the Potomac. To the Union men, who were hungry, tired, and disappointed, McClellan's "change of base" had all the earmarks of a retreat. If Lee could crush Porter at Gaines' Mill, McClellan's procession to the James could be turned into a rout and perhaps even an end to the war itself.

The terrain around Gaines' Mill consisted of steeply wooded ravines with a swampy base, making for difficult footing. These slopes were filled with thousands of men intent on killing each other on Friday, 27 June. Porter's men passed the morning hours digging entrenchments and nervously thumbing through newspapers. Blue-clad soldiers continued to fill the swampy woods as noon passed with no sign of the enemy. By early afternoon, the swamp was steamy and filled with tension.

Lee's hope was that Jackson's Army of the Valley would attack, forcing McClellan to stand rather than continue his march to the James. But where was Jackson? Intent on striking Porter's extreme right flank, the Army of the Valley followed its weary commander, seeking the shortest route to a crossroads once known as Cool Arbors; its name had evolved over the years to Cold Harbor.

Midway through his march, Jackson determined that this route would bring his troops into contact with A. P. Hill's, causing a traffic jam and possible casualties from friendly fire. Reversing his march, he added four miles of hiking under a scorching afternoon sun and a delay of several hours. The "valley men" were spent.

As the Army of the Potomac moved past Richmond, McClellan paid little notice to the city's defenses. Having left only twenty thousand men as protection, Lee was gambling that McClellan wouldn't attack the city. To ensure his bet, a ruse belying the city's vulnerability had to be created. Despite misgivings about his leadership, no one was better suited for such theatrics than Prince John Magruder. In essence, Lee called for an encore to Magruder's spring performance at Yorktown; this time, however, the stage was far grander and the stakes incalculable.

The men of the 21st Mississippi were veteran players of Magruder's troupe, and they played their parts with ease. Charging out of the woods, harassing Federal pickets, and firing artillery indiscriminately along the front, Magruder's men did little harm to the Army of the Potomac. Nevertheless, McClellan was once again impressed by Magruder's presentation. Believing that the legendary Stonewall was about to overtake his rear and destroy his supply lines, and that Magruder was attacking his position with "greatly superior numbers," McClellan was in a panic. If only Porter could hold at Gaines' Mill, the Army of the Potomac could reach the relative safety of Savage's Station.

At Gaines' Mill, Porter's men continued to await their adversaries. Shortly after 2 P.M., the crackle of rifle fire was heard over the crest of the ravine. Union pickets began trickling into "Boatswain's Swamp," frantically announcing the arrival of A. P. Hill.

Cruelly beaten at Mechanicsville only hours before, Hill's men were seeking to avenge their fallen comrades. Wild-eyed and shrieking the rebel yell, they charged into the swamp. As Hill's men descended the ravine, they absorbed volley after volley of rifle fire punctuated by thundering artillery that rained iron on them. Undaunted, they slammed into Porter's entrenchments. Men killed each other as they stared into their opponents' eyes. Soldiers on both sides gripped their rifles by the barrels and wielded them as thirty-pound clubs.

Black smoke hovered over the swamp, adding further chaos to the fight. Regiments became entangled and men became lost; confusion reigned in this valley of death. Few had ever witnessed fighting so vicious; soldiers fought like men possessed, killing all who came before them. Many veterans later recalled the Battle of Gaines' Mill as the single most frightening experience of the entire war.

By 4 P.M., the line of battle extended over a front almost a mile long. A. P. Hill's and Porter's men fought desperately; Hill's men got the worst of it. Finally, as Hill's attack was falling apart, the 21st North Carolina and Will's 16th Mississippi arrived leading the Army of the Valley. As the North Carolinians and the Mississippians approached the field, they were greeted by intense artillery fire, through which they advanced. General Isaac Trimble reported:

> The two regiments were ordered to advance, and soon encountered a furious discharge of musketry, shot, and shell from the well selected position of the enemy. Several regiments were falling back and leaving the field. We continued slowly to advance through a dense woods, met by a perfect sheet of fire, under which the killed and wounded were falling fast in our ranks. Still the brave fellows pressed on (U.S. War Dept., 1880–1901).

As the two regiments charged into the ravine, they were met by the remnants of other units which had been battered to pieces. Instead of cheers, shouts of "You need not go in, we are whipped!" and "You can't do anything!" greeted them. Some of the men of the 16th cursed, "Get out of the way! We'll show you how to do it!"

Standing and exchanging volley for volley with a firmly entrenched enemy was folly; tactics were abruptly changed. Fixing bayonets, the two regiments threw themselves at Porter's positions; their colonels led them down the slope, yelling, "Charge men, charge!" Climbing over felled trees and fallen soldiers, the men began the struggle up the other side. As more Confederate units charged into the dark, corpse-strewn site, Porter was also being reinforced.

Will Postlethwaite and his comrades were in the midst of a ghastly scene; whether they were carrying the day or being whipped, there was no means of telling. The battle flag of the 16th was pierced eleven times, and men fell by the dozen. The famed Louisiana Tigers fared no better, becoming demoralized after their colonel was killed; Porter's men began fighting with renewed vigor. (The Louisianans' losses were so severe that their battalion was disbanded after the fight.)

The 15th Alabama and 21st Georgia stood toe to toe with Porter's men and were hurt badly, losing 251 men. The 16th Mississippi and 21st North Carolina, refusing to be stationary targets, lost roughly a third of that number as part of Porter's line broke under the sight of their bayonets.

Mercifully, darkness fell and the battle died away; amidst sporadic firing, the groans of the dying rose over Boatswain's Swamp. One by one, ghostly figures with blackened faces struggled out of the swamp, calling out the names of their regiments and companies. To their horror, Posey's men discovered that more than forty of their number remained in the swamp, dead or wounded. Under the cover of night, Porter began a retreat; his men had held on long enough to secure the safety of McClellan's main army. For each side, the question of whether it had gained victory or defeat was impossible to answer.

The casualties were staggering. Obeying their orders, Porter's stalwarts had made one of the most costly stands of the entire war, losing more than six thousand men. The price Lee's army paid was even greater: eight thousand men were lost; 2,700 of them were A. P. Hill's troops.

One of Will's comrades captured the scene in his diary:

> Death is a terrible thing. Just a few hours ago I was laughing and talking with both Robinson and Barrow. Now they are gone, buried in the ground.
> . . . we were placed on burial detail, a sad, almost

unendurable task. First one digs a hole about 20 inches deep, 2 feet wide, and 6 feet long. Then the limbs of the body are pressed together as straight as possible, the body rolled in a blanket and placed on its back in an east-west position. If no covering is available, a cap or cloth is placed over the corpse's face before it is covered with dirt. I have never done anything like this before and I hope I never have to again (Dobbins, 1988).

In spite of all the casualties, little had changed. McClellan was retreating, his majestic campaign in ruins. But thanks to Porter's stand and Jackson's poor perform-ance, the Army of the Potomac remained intact; Lee had twice failed to destroy it. Lee realized that once McClellan reached Harrison's Landing and the protection of the U.S. Navy he would be replenished and reinforced, able to begin another siege of Richmond. Like a gambler who had come ever so close to taking the jackpot, Lee desperately wanted just one more crack at the Army of the Potomac.

McClellan, like his campaign, was going to pieces. Throughout the battles of Mechanicsville and Gaines' Mill, the main force of his army had not been engaged. Instead, it plodded along toward the James River to establish a base at Savage's Station. Shortly after midnight on 28 June, the general absolved himself of any responsibility for the fail-ure of his campaign. In a rambling, erratic telegram to Washington, McClellan stated:

On this side of the river we repulsed several strong attacks [Magruder's demonstrations]. On the left bank our men did all that men could do, but they were overwhelmed by vastly superior num-bers, even after I brought my last reserves into action. The loss on both sides is terrible. I believe it will prove to be the most desperate battle of the war. The sad remnants of my men behave as men. Had I twenty thousand, or even ten thousand, fresh troops to use tomorrow I could take Richmond, but I have not a man in reserve, and shall be glad to cover my retreat and save the material and personnel of this army.

If we have lost the day we have preserved our honor, and no one need blush for The Army of the Potomac. I have lost this battle because my force was too small.

I again repeat that I am not responsible for this, and I say it with the earnestness of a general who feels in his heart the loss of every brave man who has been needlessly sacrificed today (U.S. War Dept., 1880–1901).

Brightening somewhat he continued:

> I still hope to retrieve our fortunes: but to do this the government must view the matter in the same earnest light that I do. You must send me very large reinforcements, and send them at once. Please understand that in this battle we have lost nothing but men, and those the best we have.
>
> In addition to what I have already said, I only wish to say to the President that I think he is wrong in regarding me as ungenerous when I said that my force was too weak. I merely intimated which today has been too plainly proved.
>
> If, at this instant, I could dispose of ten thousand fresh men, I could gain the victory tomorrow.

In arguably the most acrimonious outburst ever delivered to an American president by a field commander, McClellan concluded:

> I know that a few thousand more men would have changed this battle from a defeat to a victory. As it is, the government must not and cannot hold me responsible for the result.

I have seen too many dead and wounded comrades to feel otherwise than that the government
has not sustained this army. If you do not do so
now the game is lost (McClellan, 1887).

The final two lines were so bitter that the War
Department deleted them before the secretary of war or
Lincoln saw them. "If I save this army now, I tell you plainly
that I owe no thanks to you or to any other persons in
Washington. You have done your best to sacrifice this army."

It is worthwhile to note that McClellan, expecting a
strong rebuke and possible dismissal for these two sen-
tences, received only encouragement from Washington.
McClellan, as field commander, scolded his president and
got away with it. In a telegram to Ellen, McClellan mentioned that he had not slept for two days—a fact that perhaps contributed to the bizarre tone of his telegram to
Washington.

Lee was also having problems. Jackson's failure to reach
the battlefields of Mechanicsville and Gaines Mill in time
to have maximum impact on the outcome agitated Lee. His
other star general, Stuart, was still basking in the glory of
his ride around the Army of the Potomac when Lee
ordered him on an expedition to McClellan's base at White
House Landing on the York River. If White House Landing
had indeed been abandoned, there was no doubt the Union
army was heading for the James.

Arriving at White House Landing, Stuart's cavalry captured a few surprised Union soldiers and scouted the ruins
of McClellan's supply base. White House Landing was
demolished and ablaze. But instead of returning swiftly to
Richmond Stuart lingered, indulging in spoils which, in
their haste, McClellan's men had failed to destroy.

On the 28th, White House Landing was being resur-
rected at Savage's Station. At this base of operations, the
Army of the Potomac struggled to reorganize. Tending to
thousands of wounded men was dreadful work in the midst
of chaos. Tents were erected and taken down. Stragglers,

hungry and confused, wandered about seeking friends or morsels of food. Elisha Hunt Rhodes of the 2nd Rhode Island summed up the mood of McClellan's men: "No one will know how much the army has suffered. No sleep, no food, and tired almost to death." An endless stream of wagons and beef cattle added to the surrealness of the scene.

On the Confederate side, things were also in disarray. Lee struggled to pull his scattered army into a cohesive unit. With Stuart at White House Landing and the bulk of the Army of Northern Virginia lagging behind McClellan's rear guard, only the small force of Prince John Magruder was within striking distance of Savage's Station.

Having fallen out of favor with Lee and Davis just weeks earlier, and with much of his command transferred to Lafayette McLaws, Magruder was nonetheless the man of the hour. Unfortunately for Magruder, he was in a bad state. The strain of defending the Confederate capital with a phantom army had made Magruder's already irritable stomach much worse. Nervous and sleepless, refusing to give up command, he was treated with morphine to relieve his discomfort; this only impaired his judgement and made him irascible. On the morning of the 28th, as the sun burned through a haze, part of his force disobeyed Lee's order of restraint and attacked a Union position. Upon hearing of its success, Magruder gave his blessing. If the fight had gone badly for Magruder he would undoubtedly have faced a court-martial.

Spearheading Magruder's division was the Mississippi brigade of General Richard Griffith, consisting of the 13th, 17th, and 18th regiments along with Benjamin Humphreys' 21st. Magruder worried about a possible attack by McClellan's army as it massed at Savage's Station. Fearing his men would be overrun should McClellan dare to launch a night attack, Magruder ordered his men "to sleep on their arms, and be prepared for whatever might occur." As 29 June dawned, Magruder, intoxicated and sleepless, was as deluded about the enemy as McClellan.

By 7 A.M., a brigade of South Carolinians under General Joseph Kershaw had engaged McClellan's rear guard as it fell back toward Savage's Station. Encountering only light resistance, Kershaw pursued the enemy until he reached the vicinity of Savage's Station, where he was stopped cold. Union artillery tore holes through Kershaw's ranks and an enormous blue line appeared to his front and right.

General Griffith's brigade marched behind Kershaw in reserve. Late in the morning, as Griffith's brigade came upon abandoned enemy fortifications on the Nine Mile Road, rifle fire split the air. Holding his men steady, Griffith coolly ordered his colonels to bring their men into line. At precisely that moment, Griffith was struck in the thigh by a large piece of shell and knocked from his horse. He clenched his fingers and turned gray. Bleeding profusely, he was carried to the rear; he died the next day. The attack ended as abruptly as it had begun.

For the men of the 21st Mississippi, who had not yet seen major action, the sight of their brigade commander being shot down was a major blow. Answering the call as Griffith's successor was the fearless, larger-than-life Colonel William Barksdale. Ironically, Griffith had recently written a letter of commendation for Barksdale, suggesting he be given a brigade command. Barksdale's presence and total contempt for the enemy was contagious; his brigade remained eager for a fight.

Magruder had six brigades at his disposal, and he anticipated the arrival of Jackson as well. Despite Kershaw's early success, Magruder continued to be convinced that he was facing the entire Army of the Potomac rather than a retreating rear guard. As the day wore on, Magruder became even less sure of himself. Believing that McClellan would suddenly take the offensive, Magruder kept more than two-thirds of his force in a defensive position, letting a great opportunity slip away. At the same time, Magruder knew that he must create at least a token impression of attack.

Many a Manly Cheek Was Wet with Tears

The afternoon passed and Jackson's Valley Men still had not arrived. Magruder kept up light, steady pressure on McClellan's retreating army, which stumbled over itself in its evacuation of Savage's Station. By sundown, the brigades of Kershaw and Paul Semmes were worn out. Magruder ordered Barksdale to throw two of his regiments into the fight, and Barksdale ordered Colonel Holders' 17th Mississippi and Humphreys' 21st Mississippi into action. Like a proud father, Humphreys wrote in his memoir, "The 21st regiment fought her first battle at Savage Station." The 17th and 21st charged "under a severe fire across an open field to the support of a battery and engaged the enemy, then strongly posted in the woods beyond the field, and poured several destructive volleys into his ranks."

In his description of the Battle of Savage's Station, Colonel Barksdale neglected to mention that the 17th and 21st Mississippi were in the thick of the fight for more than four hours. In fact, these two regiments spearheaded the attack of two Confederate brigades. Jackson didn't arrive at Savage's Station until the next morning, having had "other important duty" to tend to.

Barksdale continued:

> Messengers arrived and requested that the firing should cease, as danger would result from it to our friends, who were maneuvering between them and the enemy. The men were ordered to lie down (among the dead and wounded), and night coming and the firing having eased, they retired in good order to the woods in rear of the battlefield (U.S. War Dept., 1880–1901).

As the firing faded, it was replaced by the rumble of thunder in the distance. As if demonstrating its own power, nature unleashed a furious storm of lightning and pounding rain. Without tents, Sam and his comrades sought whatever shelter they could find. The Army of the Potomac had been generous in its flight, littering the field with blankets. They provided the men with a small measure of comfort.

First light brought clearing skies and a chance to review the previous day's carnage. Magruder had lost more than four hundred men. Crippled by darkness and Jackson's absence, he had no chance of halting the Army of the Potomac's escape. But this escape wasn't without cost. In his flight to the James, McClellan left a field hospital filled with 2,500 sick and wounded men at Savage's Station to fall into the hands of the enemy. For his men, already anguished by a failed campaign, this was the ultimate indignity. There was no honor in abandoning friends to the mercy of the enemy; many of the wounded begged that they not be left behind and voiced their feelings of betrayal.

As Colonel Humphreys' 21st Mississippi approached the abandoned base at Savage's Station, its men beheld a sight that every one of them would take to his grave—a spectacle of human suffering almost beyond imagination. The wounded from both sides had been brought or had walked to this dumping ground of misery. A Confederate victim described it this way:

> There the torn and mangled lay, shot in every conceivable part of the body or limbs, some with wounds in the head, arms torn off at the shoulder or elbow, legs broken, fingers, toes, or foot shot away. The stifling stench of blood was sickening in the extreme. The front and back yards, the fence corners, and even the outbuildings were filled with the dead and dying (Wheeler, 1986).

As the 21st Mississippi was readying itself for its first major fight and a taste of glory, a recurring intestinal disorder known as "the flux" disabled the fifty-four-year-old

Colonel Humphreys, and he was taken to Richmond for hospitalization. His condition was deemed so serious that he would be furloughed to Mississippi to convalesce. In Humphreys' absence, command of the regiment passed to the man who had mustered Sam into the Jefferson Davis Guards back in May 1861, William Lindsay Brandon. Much had changed in thirteen months.

In two telegrams to his wife on the 28th and 29th, McClellan made no mention of the suffering at Savage's Station; instead he berated Lincoln and Secretary of War Stanton.

> They have outnumbered us everywhere, but we have not lost our honor. I thank my friends in Washington for our repulse. We have fought a terrible battle against overwhelming numbers. We held our own, and history will show that I have done all that man can do (McClellan, 1887).

The last day of June, the sixth of The Seven Days, dawned clear and warm. Sam and the 21st Mississippi resumed their pursuit of the enemy, marching toward the James River. Along their path they witnessed a steady stream of Confederate wounded making its way to Richmond.

The 16th Mississippi marched to the Chickahominy River with orders to protect a railroad bridge. Discovering that McClellan's men had already destroyed it, Posey's men went to work twisting and bending the rails. From the Chickahominy River the York Railroad ran due west for two miles to Savage's Station and continued another thirteen miles to Richmond. While Will Postlethwaite and the 16th alternately mangled the track and rested in the shade, McClellan's rear guard was busy destroying supplies at Savage's Station. Anything that couldn't be carried was burned. Tons of gunpowder and discarded small arms presented a problem, as the Army of the Potomac could ill afford to let these spoils fall into the hands of the enemy.

The answer came on a grand scale. A locomotive and several cars were procured for a one-way trip to the Chickahominy. Loaded with abandoned ordnance, each car was set ablaze as the locomotive built up steam and began a spectacular departure from Savage's Station. Building up speed as it descended toward the Chickahominy, the burning train began to crackle and boom. As Posey's men wrestled with the tracks, the sound of the oncoming train brought some excitement to an otherwise dull afternoon. They scurried for cover as the train, showing no sign of stopping, continued on toward the twisted track and burned-out bridge. To the amazement of the 16th, the train rolled past the men and careened over the remnants of the bridge. Creaking and moaning, the train ground to a stop as cars derailed, some dangling off the bridge.

Although by this time the use of trains in warfare was commonplace, no one had seen anything like this before. Some of Posey's men were eager to investigate the wreckage, but the colonel ordered the regiment to remain a safe distance from the site. In its death throes the train fell still, as if breathing its last, before erupting in a single, shuddering explosion that was heard for miles.

Jackson's army continued to have problems. In another attempt to strike the Army of the Potomac before it reached the James, Jackson was ordered to cross the marshy terrain of White Oak Swamp. The spring rains had turned the swamp into a bog, but it was by no means impassable. Jackson, in spite of his fatigue, slept very little on the 29th and 30th; the result was manifest in another lackluster performance.

For McClellan, things were turning brighter. Only a day's march away was high ground and the protection of the Union navy's heaviest guns. A second day's march would place the Army of the Potomac safely on the James at Harrison's Landing. But McClellan had no doubt that Lee would try to attack again before the Army of the Potomac gained a geographical advantage.

Lee's problem, once again, was organization. Throughout the day, he tried to consolidate his forces, with little success. The biggest disappointment was Jackson, who had reached White Oak Swamp at 11 A.M. but had made no attempt to cross. The afternoon passed as Lee waited for Jackson. At half past four, he could wait no longer and ordered Longstreet and A. P. Hill to initiate an attack. McClellan, relaxing on the U.S.S. *Galena*, calmly listened to the sounds of battle, confident that his army would weather yet another attack.

With the onset of darkness and no sign of Jackson, the battle waned. Aside from its artillery, the Army of the Valley didn't get into battle that day. In a military sense the Battle of White Oak Swamp (also known by seven other names, including Glendale) accomplished little; nevertheless it resulted in 6,500 casualties.

After a day of marching, Sam Postlethwaite's 21st Mississippi reached the battlefield of White Oak Swamp at around 10 P.M. For the second straight night, the men slept amid a sea of dead and wounded "so numerous that it was difficult to walk in the dark. The scene was horrifying." In contrast, Will Postlethwaite's 16th Mississippi spent a relatively pleasant night encamped on the banks of the Chickahominy, about a mile from the site of the train's destruction.

During the night, McClellan's artillery deployed three miles away from White Oak Swamp along the crest of a little-known hill called Malvern. As an engineer and soldier, McClellan understood the ground of Malvern Hill. Nature had created no better ground for the use of massed artillery. A gradual slope of one thousand yards gave his gunners an unobstructed field of fire, with the exception of the extreme left where the hill steepened. The hill's slight crest concealed the muzzles of more than 150 cannon.

Lee would not accept the fact that McClellan had gotten away. As the Army of Northern Virginia slept, Lee, out of options, laid plans for a final assault. His plan was brutal and simple: early in the day, Tuesday, 1 July 1862, artillery massed on the Confederate right and left would pour converging fire on the center of McClellan's line on Malvern Hill. When that line weakened, the entire Army of Northern Virginia (with the exception of A. P. Hill's and Longstreet's divisions, decimated in the Battle of White Oak Swamp) would emerge from the woods at the bottom of the hill and charge one thousand yards to break McClellan's center.

Knowing that McClellan was massing on Malvern Hill, Harvey Hill, never afraid to voice his opinion, warned Lee, "If McClellan is there in force we had better let him alone!" Lee would hear no such talk. Longstreet even found humor in Hill's caution, chiding, "Don't get scared, now that we've got him whipped!"

The next morning would bring July, the last of The Seven Days, and the reunion of Sam and Will.

CHAPTER ELEVEN

It Was Astonishing That Every Man Did Not Fall

The afternoon following the Memorial Day reception, as green leaves rustled under an azure sky, Alexander Postlethwaite slowly and proudly approached the grave of his cousin, Sam. Reaching into a small bag, he gently sprinkled dirt around the shiny bronze marker. Sam would rest forever under soil from his beloved Westmoreland. It is said that Westmoreland has been haunted for decades by a ghost called "Sam." Perhaps that spirit no longer wanders.

Two weeks before, I had called the cemetery to make arrangements for the installation of the marker. I was told by the cemetery's secretary to simply leave it on the ground wherever I wanted it placed. It was the first summery day of a New England spring; as I walked away

Alex Postlethwaite, Sam's cousin, sprinkles soil around the forgotten soldier's grave the afternoon following the Memorial Day reception in his honor.

from the unsecured bronze plaque, worrying about vandals and the possibility that the marker might not be installed by the date of the dedication, I felt as though I was saying goodbye to a friend for the last time. On reflection, though, it was my favorite moment of the entire undertaking.

For me, it had been an amazing journey. I had made many friends and learned invaluable lessons about honor and human nature. I had become more tolerant, more understanding of cultural differences, and perhaps more fatalistic as well. United States Senator Claiborne Pell eloquently put things in perspective in a letter he wrote to me regarding Sam:

How the dead are remembered and honored distinguishes a civilization. Thus your work touches us all. Private Postlethwaite's final resting place is commemorated. The people of his home town are grateful. People today are inspired by recalling the sacrifices of a great war, and succeeding generations are given a precious legacy.

History and historical research are not essentially the stuff of dry scholarship undertaken by academics. History is vital, it lives and gains its meaning in the hearts of ordinary citizens.

A marvelous concatenation is at work: A Civil War soldier dies after reversals of fortune and illness in a place far distant from his home; more than a century later his service and the location of his grave stimulate research by an unrelated man, and by this extraordinary connection between two men, the vitality of history is made manifest.

May peace be with us all.

Three Generations of Postlethwaites: Haine, Cecil, and Alex gather during Memorial Day weekend to pay tribute to Sam.

THE 21ST MISSISSIPPI AND THE REST OF WHAT WAS NOW Barksdale's brigade spent the last day of June marching twenty miles under a scorching sun. Throughout the march, the men were presented with a surreal scene. Their route was lined with knapsacks, blankets, and other gear discarded by McClellan's army on its flight to the James River. The sea of debris left the impression of an army in disarray, on the verge of being routed. Barksdale's men, wanting for almost everything, helped themselves to the enemy's goods. Blankets were a particularly popular find. Despite their good fortune, however, the men found it difficult to gloat. Sharing the dusty roads, stumbling in the opposite direction, were hundreds of men suffering from every imaginable type of wound. It was clear that neither side could claim it was winning.

As June turned into July, the men thought they could make out the rumble of artillery in the distance. But within minutes it became evident that the sounds were of natural origin. Dark clouds rolled in, obliterating the stars and bringing what was at first a light, cooling rain. The blankets abandoned by McClellan's army were put to use as the skies opened, soaking the field. Most of the men sat upright, swathed in their blankets, as flashes of lightning illuminated the scene. For the men of the 21st, it was to be a miserable night.

McClellan was pleased. After spending a comfortable night aboard the *Galena*, he rose early and twice rode out to Malvern Hill to inspect his position. Nothing could have suited the engineer-soldier better than this elevated field. It was a textbook defensive position.

At first glance, Malvern Hill doesn't appear to be a hill at all. In peacetime, the long, gradual slope provides an ideal setting for a picnic or an afternoon walk. From its summit one gets a clear view of an open field ringed by woods one thousand yards away. To the distant right and left, the hill drops off more dramatically, making an approach more difficult. For an infantry assault to be effective, however, the

Malvern Hill today. Sam and the 21st Mississippi reached
the crest pictured in the foreground.

soldiers would have to make their way across the field, in
the open, directly in front of McClellan's artillery.

McClellan had placed a continuous line of artillery
almost a mile long across the crest of Malvern Hill. General
Fitz John Porter, still stinging from his losses at Gaines'
Mill, would seek vengeance by commanding the most critical batteries. To the rear, at the slope's highest point, ten
of McClellan's favorites, the heavy siege guns, were in
place. The navy's heavy guns floated peacefully on a tribu-
tary of the James known as Turkey Creek; they could easily reach the field with two hundred-pound balls. Berdan's
Sharpshooters were entrenched, completing the scene.

The men on Malvern Hill were tired and disillusioned,
giving every appearance of a defeated army. Though
demoralized, however, McClellan's men were tired of running. It was on this perfect killing field, two months after
his arrival at Fortress Monroe, that McClellan was finally
ready to fight.

While McClellan oversaw his defenses, Lee summoned
his generals to his headquarters. Time after time, the
opportunity to destroy McClellan had slipped through his
fingers. Now Lee was determined to land one final, fatal
blow squarely on the chin of the Army of the Potomac.

Although he was bright and coherent, Lee was not feeling well. And the lackluster performance of his generals over the past six days had soured his mood, although he did his best to conceal it. Jackson, in particular, had failed miserably. Lee's other standout, Jeb Stuart, wasn't even present. In his reconnaissance raid on White House Landing, Stuart had exceeded his orders. Enjoying the spoils left there, Stuart lingered, leaving Lee without benefit of cavalry on 1 July. And of course there was Magruder, who, aside from his theatrical talent, did not impress Lee at all.

If the lightning storm had caused Jackson to lose sleep, there was no evidence of it at Lee's headquarters. Jackson appeared refreshed and confident. Having gone several days with only a few hours of rest, Jackson and his staff had managed to get some sleep during the early hours of 1 July. Even the nervous Magruder, in spite of his stomach ailments and excitement, seemed calm. Both generals knew that this would be their last chance to redeem themselves. A Confederate victory would drive the Army of the Potomac into the James River. With McClellan's campaign in ruins, support for Lincoln's war, already fragile, would collapse, bringing with it foreign recognition of the Confederate States of America. It would be a day of glory— perhaps the last day of the war. Every available resource was to be thrown into the fray.

Unfortunately for Lee, his options had been narrowed by the events of the past week. There was no question that during the first six of The Seven Days the best performances had come from Longstreet and A. P. Hill. But now their divisions were worn out and in no condition to fight. Lee had no choice but to place responsibility for his offensive on the shoulders of Jackson, Magruder, and Harvey Hill.

Hill didn't share the enthusiasm of Stonewall and Prince John. In fact, he was worried. As Jackson argued for a flanking movement rather than the frontal assault suggested by Lee and Longstreet, Harvey Hill suggested calling off the attack altogether. A chaplain on Magruder's staff was a native of the area; he understood the strength of

McClellan's position. In Harvey Hill, Reverend Allen found an audience. Allen impressed upon the general the seriousness of the situation: " . . . its commanding height, the difficulty of the approach, its amphitheatrical form and ample area, which would enable McClellan to arrange his 350 field guns, tier above tier, and sweep the plain in every direction." But Hill's was the lone voice of dissent in the war council. He was soon quieted and resigned himself to his duty as a soldier.

Longstreet had found two strong positions for artillery, which, once massed, could place a debilitating fire upon the center of its Union counterpart. Once the center of McClellan's line of artillery was broken or thrown into disarray, a wall of Confederate infantry was to emerge from the woods at the base of the hill and make a charge the length of ten football fields over open ground. If the Confederate artillery didn't achieve the desired results, the plan of battle would revert to Jackson's flanking movement.

Both Jackson and Magruder pleaded their cases for leading the infantry attack. Although Magruder's division was deployed closer to Malvern Hill than Jackson's, Lee chose Jackson's "fresher" troops for the unenviable task. Half of Jackson's division, including Will Postlethwaite's 16th Mississippi, would be held in reserve. Although its men didn't know it, the 16th's duty with the Army of the Valley had come to an end; the regiment was soon to be reassigned.

Lee's orders to Magruder were clear and to the point. He was to advance his division along the Quaker Road until reaching Malvern Hill, where he would form a line of battle on Jackson's right and await orders. Pleased to have such responsibility bestowed upon him, Prince John hurried back to his division; he had neglected to give Lee's map, the only accurate one available, even a glance. Once again, confusion was to rule the day.

Porter's gunners fully understood the import of their position on Malvern Hill, and they relished it. By mid-morning, as the sun began to melt away the haze of the previous evening's thunderstorms, Confederate artillerists were struggling to get their field pieces into position. Problems abounded. It was discovered that Harvey Hill's artillery had been sent to Richmond for refitting. The key to Lee's plan, artillery, was discovered to be a scarce commodity.

Lee needed every cannon that could be pushed or dragged to the field; he wrestled with the problem all morning. But in the rush to gather artillery pieces the inexplicable occurred. General W. N. Pendleton, Lee's chief of artillery, had four battalions of the Confederacy's most effective artillery in reserve. Yet no one thought of using it. Pendleton reported:

> Tuesday, July 1, was spent by me in seeking, for some time, the commanding general, that I might get orders, failing in this . . . in examining positions near the two armies toward ascertaining what could be best done with a large artillery force, and especially whether any position could be reached whence our large guns could be used to good purpose. These endeavors had, of course, to be made again and again under the enemy's shells; yet no site was found. Indeed, it seemed that not one-half of the division were brought into action. To remain near by, therefore, and await events and orders in readiness for whatever service might be called for, was all that I could do (Alexander, 1889).

Lee's failure to use Pendleton's guns was not the only such oversight. Another officer reported that he had a "great superabundance of artillery . . . yet I received no orders." Lacking orders, Pendleton finally resigned himself to watching the battle with President Davis. When the crest of the hill became visible to the Confederate gunners, they noticed that Porter had suddenly upped the ante. Several of Porter's batteries had been pushed forward over the crest of the hill, as if daring Lee to attack.

Magruder was delighted with his responsibilities, but in his haste he blinded himself to blunders that should have been obvious. On the advice of his hired "guides," natives who claimed to know the locale as well as the backs of their hands, Prince John followed directions to Malvern Hill along the Quaker Road. Unfortunately for Magruder, many of the dirt roads skirting Richmond were known by several names; they varied according to who was asked. Roads were sometimes known better for their landmarks than for their names. The Quaker Road invited such confusion.

Had Magruder considered the simple fact that, according to the morning sun, he was traveling west instead of south, the day might have turned out very differently. Instead, he marched his men in the wrong direction for more than two miles. Other divisions that were supposed to follow Magruder along the narrow dirt roads were breaking camp and finding their way to the hill on their own.

The men of Barksdale's brigade, following Magruder, had no idea that they were botching the assault. They dutifully plodded along as the gentle morning sun slowly became a fireball. Longstreet finally could stand the confusion no longer and rode out to find Magruder. When he arrived at the head of Magruder's column, the two generals swiftly fell into argument. For several minutes, the two men hotly debated their whereabouts until one of Lee's couriers arrived and squelched the discussion. Magruder was to reverse his march at once and make his way to the scene of battle. He was already several hours behind schedule.

The men of Barksdale's brigade reversed their march, assuming only that their orders had been changed. Of course, Magruder's blunder would alter their original role. No longer a lead element of the assault, Magruder's division would be fortunate merely to arrive at Malvern Hill before the battle commenced. The morning was lost.

By late morning, the roads around Malvern Hill were clogged with traffic, and among the Confederates, all military cohesion was lost. Troops arriving at the edge of the woods at the base of Malvern Hill encountered a strange scene. As Lee's artillery was pushed and dragged into place, division after division swelled the woods. The officers and men of those divisions, having raced into position, now encountered something they hadn't expected. Instead of the din of battle and the shriek of the rebel yell, there was silence disturbed only by the rustling of leaves amid the treetops or the distant sound of other troops arriving. A haunting, unsettling, yet oddly serene atmosphere fell upon the huddled men.

An hour passed, then another. Many eyes scanned the crest of the hill as the men went about the business of preparing for battle. Most of these men were veterans, and they knew that the enemy's massed artillery, located on good ground, was patiently waiting for their emergence from the woods.

As Barksdale's brigade marched, it encountered more trouble. The roads were filled with other divisions; Magruder and Barksdale would have to suffer the indignity of waiting as other units pushed on to the front. Instead of finding glory and providing inspiration on the battlefield, Magruder's division had become an obstruction. Having had nothing to eat but green apples and hardly any sleep over the last seventy-two hours, the division welcomed an opportunity to rest under trees that lined the road, if only for a few minutes. The men caught a rare glimpse of Lee, who rode out to scold General Huger for his failure to have occupied Malvern Hill the previous day.

General Porter was busy. By early afternoon, it was evident that Lee was establishing batteries on Porter's front and right. The Union general allowed his adversaries to assemble several batteries, leaving them unmolested as they increased in number. Finally he was satisfied with the abundance of fodder to play upon, and he gave the order to destroy Lee's artillery before it could get into action.

Malvern Hill erupted in a fury. The Confederates in the woods huddled together, seeking the shelter of trees and hastily dug trenches. Lee's artillerists made a gallant, defiant stand against Porter's superior gunners, but it was soon evident that the duel was a mismatch. Systematically, clusters of Porter's guns targeted isolated Confederate batteries, smashing them to pieces, frequently killing their crews. The Southern men stayed with their guns as long as they were operational or had ammunition. The Union navy began lobbing two hundred-pound balls into the woods, doing little damage but terrifying Lee's men. A general's horse was decapitated by a ball.

For three and one-half hours, the one-sided fight raged; at no time did Lee get the bulk of his artillery into action simultaneously. Instead, when a single Confederate gun spoke it drew the attention of any number of Porter's gunners, who efficiently quieted it with a deadly crossfire. Hill had the sickening feeling of being right as the disaster confirmed his worst fears. Perhaps now the other generals, and Lee, would heed his warnings. He sent a bitter message to Jackson, informing his brother-in-law that Confederate artillery fire "was of the most farcical character." But if Hill was hoping to find an ally in Jackson, he was mistaken.

Jackson was doing his best to make up for his shortcomings of the past six days, personally overseeing several batteries of artillery on the left flank and placing himself at the most dangerous spot on the field. Displaying the trademark stubbornness he had shown at Kernstown, Jackson fired back a simple message to Hill: "Charge when Armistead's men raise the yell!"

As Jackson remained confident in the success of a massed infantry assault upon the hill, Porter wondered how well his own infantry, tired and demoralized, would hold up under a desperate, suicidal attack on their lines. At about four o'clock, Porter's guns suddenly stopped firing. The Confederate artillery lay in ruins; once again an ominous silence hung in the summer air. Rumors abounded: McClellan was retreating. McClellan was being reinforced. What was happening?

Lee had to know. He realized that his plan for an all-out frontal attack would cost thousands of lives. More importantly, it might fail. Lee reconsidered Jackson's original plan to turn McClellan's right flank. Several hours of daylight remained; if Jackson, already on the Confederate left, could get his foot cavalry into position before being detected, Lee might get lucky. But Jackson, seeing the opportunity, couldn't seize it; he was paralyzed by a complicated and flawed chain of command. As precious minutes ticked away, Lee's left flank was gradually being bolstered.

Ironically, the events of the day would not turn on Lee's anxieties but on Porter's. Fearing an imminent infantry attack, Porter had ordered General Sumner's exposed corps to pull back further behind the crest of the hill. At the same time, Porter ordered skirmishers down the slight slope to harass Lee's massed infantry. Was this a rear guard action? Lee received word that the Army of the Potomac was retreating in great numbers. There was no longer any time to swing his army around to the left. General Armistead sent three regiments out of the woods to chase the Federal skirmishers from the field. The rebel yell and sporadic gunfire resonating along the Confederate line convinced Lee's men that this indeed was the "designated signal" initiating a general advance. It was now about 5:30 P.M.

The hastily repaired remnants of the Confederate artillery renewed the contest with Porter but were quickly crushed. Porter's gunners, as well as the navy, now unleashed a heinous fire on the men in the woods. Trees fell and dirt and human limbs flew amid a constant roar that muffled the screams of the wounded. Regiments became scattered as officers shouted inaudible orders, struggling to keep their lines from breaking. It was through this hail of iron that Magruder, who is rumored to have been drinking, finally arrived.

Barksdale's brigade sheltered itself as best as it could from the firestorm, and the men prayed and pondered their fate; this battle would be like no other. The men of the 18th Mississippi lay quietly beneath a large oak tree, waiting for the order to move. A ball from one of the great navy guns screeched across Malvern Hill; it severed the top half of the massive oak, bringing hundreds of branches directly down upon the frightened Mississippians. The scene was sickening, even for veterans who had seen men killed in every conceivable fashion. Several men of one company lay dying, trapped and impaled, as if in the grasp of some strange monster, "creating a worse panic than if ten times the number had been killed by bullets."

Lee, having been told of Armistead's successful repulse of the enemy and fearing McClellan's escape, was delighted to learn of Magruder's arrival. Lee gave one of Magruder's aides a verbal order to be passed to Prince John: "General Lee expects you to advance rapidly. He says it is reported the enemy is getting off. Press forward your whole line and follow up Armistead's success." It was six o'clock.

Magruder immediately went to work, ordering brigade after brigade out of the woods to begin their fatal ascent of the hill. The result was anything but impressive. At no point was a consolidated assault of massed infantry thrown against Porter's guns. Instead, the units presented themselves before the Union gunners one by one, turning the slope into a shooting gallery. Brigades charged from the cover of the woods, colors flying and hearts pounding. Men fell at each step as the gray line pressed on toward the crest of the hill. The rebel yell filled the air.

Porter's gunners stepped up the pace and "ten (guns) per second" poured down solid shot, shell, and the most feared of all, grapeshot. Grapeshot, a canister containing twenty-seven one-and-a-half-pound iron balls, was invented for one purpose: killing infantry at close range. The grapeshot began shredding ugly swaths through the advancing ranks, but the first brigades charging up the hill met with initial success despite the deadly cost. Then, having reached a point seven hundred yards from the woods and three hundred yards from Porter's guns, the determined men of these brigades were finally pinned down, defenseless. One soldier remembered the initial attempts to reach the enemy's line.

In our next charge we had the support of thousands of gallant men from all parts of the

Confederacy and thousands of dastardly cowards who did us more harm than the Yankees did. It was astonishing that every man did not fall, grapeshot swept the earth, shells burst over us and among us and yet I came from the bloody field walking over the bodies of slain and wounded friends without a scratch (War Dept., 1880–1901).

In the growing confusion friendly fire added to the woes of the men on the field, who were alternately charging and retreating. One soldier recalled:

For half an hour, every possible effort was made to re-form and again advance the charge; but owing to the small numbers, the horror of coming in deadly conflict with our own troops, and the terrible and incessant cross-fire of artillery and musketry, although there was no terror manifested, no demoralization apparent, the effort was unavailing (War Dept., 1880–1901).

Another remembered:

Several of my command were killed by our own friends who had come up on our left and who commenced firing long before they came within range of the enemy. The fire was terrific beyond anything I had ever witnessed; indeed, the hideous shrieking of shells, the whizzing of bullets, and the loud and incessant roar of artillery and small arms were enough to make the stoutest heart quail (Alexander, 1907).

Lt. George Hagar of 10th MA. had a similar account:

the rebs poured out of the woods and charged on us. They came within yards of us when they turned and ran, what was left of them. Pretty soon they poured out in 4 lines and charging our batterys posted on the brow of the hill . . . . We slaughtered them by the hundreds but they again formed and came up to be slaughtered. I kept firing until I could no longer load my gun and threw it away and took up Hemmenway's [another soldier] (Sears, 1992).

Magruder rode to Barksdale's brigade and personally ordered it into the fray. For Barksdale, Brandon, and Private Samuel Postlethwaite, the moment had arrived. As the brigade prepared for its charge into history, the command of its four regiments was entrusted to men of the finest order. Commanding Barksdale's beloved 13th were Lieutenant Colonel James W. Carter and Major Kennon McElroy.

Thirty-year-old Carter had enlisted in Company C of the 13th Mississippi Infantry on 13 April 1861. By 26 April 1862, he had ascended to the rank of lieutenant colonel.

McElroy, a farmer from the town of Lauderdale, had graduated from the University of Mississippi shortly before the fall of Fort Sumter. In March 1861, he joined a local company and at the tender age of twenty-one was elected its first captain. By May 1862, he held the rank of major.

Colonel William Dunbar Holder of the 17th was a native of Tennessee, born there in 1824. When he was fifteen, his family had moved to Mississippi. Holder was smitten by politics and had served as a United States marshal at Pontotoc; by 1854 he held a seat in the Mississippi House of Representatives. When war broke out, he organized a company of infantry, becoming its captain.

Holder's second-in-command was John Calvin Fiser. Another native of Tennessee, Fiser had also spent his formative years in Mississippi. At age twenty-two, this lieutenant in the 17th Mississippi was called to greater responsibility. Beloved by his men, he had displayed a natural ability to lead at Ball's Bluff, earning the respect of superiors and subordinates alike. On 26 April 1862, he was promoted to lieutenant colonel of the regiment.

The colonel of the 18th Mississippi Infantry was forty-six-year-old Thomas Griffin. Griffin had served as a lieutenant colonel at the onset of the war and assumed the rank of colonel after Ball's Bluff. Serving as Griffin's lieutenant was William Luse. At twenty-four, Luse was already a seasoned veteran. At Manassas, his company was one of the first units attacked at McLean's Ford; three months later it drove the enemy into the Potomac at Ball's Bluff at great cost. One out of every five men in Luse's company at Ball's Bluff had fallen victim to Union fire.

Second in command of Sam's 21st Mississippi was Major Daniel N. Moody. Moody was thirty-six years old when the war broke out. He enlisted in what would become Company A on 15 May 1861, at Vicksburg. He would earn the distinction of being the 21st's last colonel.

Magruder's orders to his men were easily understandable: "When going into battle, officers will call the roll of their companies, and in coming out of action the rolls will be called. Any member of the companies absent at the latter call, unless killed or wounded, will be considered as having been derelict of his duty and will be punished accordingly."

With this warning from Magruder, Barksdale instructed his regimental commanders to prepare their men for battle. The men of Captain John Sims' Company D spent their last quiet moments readying for what, for many, would be their last moments or hours of life. Most of these men had grown up together or were cousins or brothers, and there was no place to hide from the duty that called them.

Slowly, Barksdale's stalwarts began making their way out of the edge of the woods. Barksdale recalled that before they left the woods "shot and shell fell thick among [them], several being killed and wounded, and among them Major Daniel Moody, of the 21st Regiment, who was seriously wounded in the foot."

Losing an important officer even before taking the field is a poor omen for any military unit; it was a particularly harsh blow for the 21st, which was already without a colonel. Lt. Colonel Brandon now called upon Captain William Brooks of Company C to assist him in bringing the 21st into action. It was 6:30 P.M.

Marching from the woods, the brigade was "formed in the open field"; the men had a full view of what awaited them. The hill's slope was already littered with thousands of dead and dying, who presented gruesome obstacles for Barksdale's men. The brigade pressed on—one hundred yards, two hundred. The robust Barksdale, holding his sword aloft and shouting encouragement above the din, inspired the men with his apparent disregard for danger.

Will Postlethwaite and the 16th Mississippi were well aware of the events taking place on Malvern Hill and were not unhappy to be in reserve. But as the hours passed and the battle played out badly for the Army of Northern Virginia, the likelihood of Colonel Posey's men being sent into action increased. Along with the divisions of Longstreet and A. P. Hill, the 16th continued to sit and wait.

Porter intensified his firing, and by the time Barksdale's men had ventured out three hundred yards they hit a wall of iron. A cooling breeze wafted black smoke through the ranks. With each roar of artillery, clusters of men disappeared, while others fell mangled and limbless. Berdan's deadly sharpshooters picked their victims and the navy unleashed its huge projectiles. Brandon's men wavered but pushed on.

With Griffin's 18th Mississippi on its right, the 21st reached a slight crest in the hill a mere two hundred yards short of Porter's guns. Through the smoke and confusion, the two regiments lost contact with each other, each believing itself to be isolated. Porter's fire became so deadly that the brigade's soldiers clutched the earth, holding on for their lives; any further advance was suicide. The men waited for orders.

With no sign of support on his right or left, Lieutenant Colonel Brandon decided to move his regiment to safety. He ordered it to fall back several hundred yards. Companies began slithering down the hill as Brandon kept a firm grasp on the men's actions. Porter's men, eyeing the 21st's retreat, unleashed a volley of grapeshot, striking Brandon in the foot; the wound later required amputation.

The other regiments were having similar problems; some lost as many as six color bearers. In the 18th, Colonel Griffin was down and two company captains were dead. Lieutenant Colonel Carter of the 13th and Colonel Holder of the 17th both were seriously wounded and carried from the field.

Harvey Hill had been proved right; his own men took the worst of it. Disgusted, he would later grumble, "It was not war, it was murder!" As Hill's battered division began returning from the field, hollow-eyed and defeated, it passed the 16th Mississippi, which was about to be thrown into the fray. As General Trimble started to give the order to move, Jackson rode up to him. "I guess you better not try it, sir," Jackson warned. The men of the 16th were spared by their former commander.

Having reached a relatively safe position on the field and regrouped to a degree, Barksdale's brigade was ordered once again to take the batteries at the top of the hill. Brooks and his men incredulously went back into the battle. Men continued to fall, including Brandon's son, Lieutenant Lane Brandon, who was shot through the thigh. In a final charge, Sam and the men of the 21st Mississippi threw themselves at Porter's artillery, closing to within 150 yards.

As dire as the situation was, it was about to grow worse. Through the smoke and gathering darkness, a regiment of Union infantry had closed upon the 21st. It began pouring a series of volleys into the 21st's left. Private Samuel Postlethwaite was struck in the chest, a bullet passing through one of his lungs.

Without panic and under the competent command of Captain Brooks, the men "were again ordered to retire and did so in good order, and left the field after dark." The scene was nightmarish. A soldier from the 2nd Rhode Island was appalled at the sight of 4,500 dead and wounded Confederate soldiers lying on the slope: "Oh, the horrors of this day's work. The battle of today is beyond description."

As darkness fell upon the field, a pelting rain washed the blood from the dead and wounded. McClellan's artillery held fire as the Confederates sought to retrieve their casualties. One of Jackson's aides wrote:

> Night, dark and dismal, settled upon the battlefield of Malvern Hill, its thousands dead and wounded. The rain began to fall on the cruel scene and it beat out the torches of brave fellows hunting their wounded companions in the dark. The howling of the storm, the cry of the wounded and groans of the dying, the glare of the torch upon the faces of the dead or into the shining eyes of the speechless wounded, looking up in hope of relief, the ground slippery with a mixture of mud and blood, all in the dark, hopeless, starless night; sure it was a gruesome picture of war in its most horrid shape (Douglas, 1989).

Another soldier remembered that in the dark the hill took on "a singular, crawling effect." There is little doubt that Will Postlethwaite sought his wounded brother on the bloody slope of Malvern Hill.

CHAPTER TWELVE

When Will This State of Things End?

In the fall of 1993, I received a telephone call from Ms. Cherry Bamberg of Marlboro, Massachusetts. In researching her family's genealogy, Cherry had traced the Greene line of her family to Mississippi and Louisiana. Her aunt, Rosalind Colley of Barrington, Rhode Island, had been a close friend of Lenore Greene. Lenore had left to Rosalind a box of letters written by her father, William. The box also contained a collection of photographs of William and his brothers.

William's letters to his young nephew, Harry, told of his adventures in the South, plantation life, and his yearning for Rhode Island and Narragansett Bay. From a yellow fever epidemic to the flooding of the Mississippi River,

William's tales were gripping accounts of his years as a Southern gentleman. William's brother, George, had also corresponded with Harry. The tone of these missives evolved as Harry grew into manhood and entered Brown University. Tragically, the letters ended in 1867, when Harry's life was cut short by typhoid fever; he was eighteen.

Fortunately, this rare glimpse into postwar plantation life didn't end with Harry's death. While reading Michael Wayne's fascinating book, The Reshaping of Plantation Society *(University of Illinois Press, 1983), I was stunned to find a Samuel Postlethwaite listed in the index. I assumed that it referred to Sam's grandfather; instead, it was our boy! I was thrilled to learn that a series of Sam's letters was located among the James A. Gillespie Family Papers at Louisiana State University. I read these letters in awe as Sam finally spoke, telling his own story of hardship and optimism. Sam's affection for William Rogers Greene is evident in these letters, which end shortly before failing health brought Sam to Rhode Island, where he would spend his last days.*

Tying William and Sam's letters together was yet another source. A young girl from Woodville, Mississippi, wrote a series of letters that serve as a moving narrative of the war's last days. Describing the daily life of starving citizens who were futilely resisting the approaching Union army, Kate Blount paints a portrait of fear and dashed hopes. In a reference to Reverend Adams, she completes the connection; Adams is mentioned in both Sam's and William's letters. It was not altogether surprising for me to learn that Kate, William, and Sam were somehow connected through acquaintances. The excitement for me was in discovering their entirely different stories.

In Lenore Greene's letter to her "cousin," Mary Postlethwaite, she inquires as to the whereabouts of the portraits of "Uncle Sam" and "Aunt Sue." Mary's response, unfortunately, has not been found (if it indeed exists), and through eight years of research, a photographic image of Sam has eluded me.

ON THE MORNING OF 2 JULY 1862, TWO HUGE ARMIES EYED each other like battered prizefighters across the ring—proud, but unable to stand. Between them lay a sea of mangled humanity. Some of the living would come to envy the dead: wounded men lay in the summer sun for as long as three days before being taken from the field.

When Sam Postlethwaite was finally carried from Malvern Hill, the Army of the Potomac was already making its way to Harrison's Landing on the James River. The refreshed divisions of A. P. Hill and Longstreet braced for an attack that would never materialize. Jackson, convinced that "McClellan will be gone by morning," closed his eyes for some much-needed sleep. The Seven Days were gone, taking with them thirty-five thousand casualties. Aside from a largely ineffective pursuit by Jeb Stuart, McClellan had gotten away clean.

Barksdale's brigade had distinguished itself. Of the units attacking up Malvern Hill, it had advanced among the farthest, and it had taken some of the heaviest casualties as it followed its commander, who carried the colors himself for a time. For his valor, Barksdale was promoted to general.

Will's brigade commander, General Trimble, remembered:

> The next morning by dawn I went off to ask for orders, when I found the whole army in the utmost disorder, thousands of straggling men asking every passer for their regiments; ambulances, wagons, and artillery obstructing every road; and altogether in a drenching rain presenting a scene of the most woeful and disheartening confusion. This was the first time in the war that this army had been entirely repulsed, and it jarred the troops badly (*Confederate Veteran*, 1893–1994).

Another general reported:

> As soon as it was light enough, next morning an appalling spectacle was presented to our view in

front. The field for some distance from the enemy's position was literally strewn with the dead and wounded. The parties of both armies in search of comrades gradually approached each other and continued their mournful work without molestation on either side, being apparently appalled for the moment into a cessation from all hostile purposes by the terrible spectacle presented to their view (*Confederate Veteran*, 1893–1994).

Sam Postlethwaite's role in the American Civil War was over, his life irreparably changed. With thousands of faceless, nameless wounded, he lay in a Richmond hospital bed, struggling against death. Aside from homeopathic medicines and quinine, doctors had few allies in the treatment of war injuries and deadly infections. Men with seemingly minor wounds sometimes succumbed to fever and infection while others, apparently beyond hope, might miraculously recover. The official report on Sam's wound, from the National Archives Service Record stated that a Minié ball had passed completely through one of his lungs, rather than lodging in his chest. The fact that the lead projectile had exited his body would provide at least a modest chance of recovery.

The Confederacy had paid a dear price, but Richmond had been delivered. During the last three days of fighting, close to eight hundred Union soldiers had been killed—a number that paled in comparison with the nearly eight thousand Confederate dead. Despite the outcome of Malvern Hill, though, the capital was full of good feeling. The restaurants and theaters were open, and for the first time in months, it was safe to roam the countryside or enjoy the mountains of Virginia. Will Postlethwaite and the 16th Mississippi regiment remained in Richmond for several days after the battle, allowing Will to stay close to his brother.

The Mississippians in Richmond established a social club of sorts that was open to any soldier from Mississippi looking for relaxation, news from home, or special treatment for a nagging wound. Way Side Home was a partial remedy for homesickness. The news from home was almost always bad, however. New Orleans and Corinth, Mississippi, had been occupied, the brutal siege of Vicksburg had begun, and the Federal stranglehold on Mississippi was being tightened. From privates to field commanders alike, Mississippians in the Army of Northern Virginia shared their worry and anguish.

The fallout from The Seven Days campaign immediately brought changes on both sides. Davis was pleased that he had found a fighter in Lee, and the Army of Northern Virginia set its sights on Northern soil. On 11 July, Lincoln, distraught with McClellan, removed him as general-in-chief of all United States ground forces, replacing him with Henry Halleck. Little Mac would spend the next two months overseeing the return of his beloved Army of the Potomac to Washington.

Two weeks after the Battle of Malvern Hill, the 16th Mississippi was reassigned to the brigade of forty-three-year-old Winfield Scott Featherston, a lawyer and former Congressman who had gained a reputation as a "Yankee Killer" at Ball's Bluff. Completing the brigade, which was now part of Longstreet's overall command, were the 12th and 19th Mississippi infantry and the 2nd Mississippi battalion. The brigade was sent north to Manassas, where Will returned to the business of war.

As events unfolded rapidly in the Deep South, the Virginia theater temporarily fell quiet. Throughout the summer, Sam Postlethwaite's painful recovery progressed, but doctors could make no long-term prognosis. By the end of August, Sam's condition had improved enough that he was officially discharged from the Confederate army to recuperate in the care of his family. The war would continue, but for Sam, life as a soldier was over.

The Mississippi that greeted Sam Postlethwaite upon his return home barely resembled the proud state he had left only sixteen months earlier. If Virginia had been scarred by war, Mississippi had been ravaged by it. Like poison coursing through a vein, Northern troops had poured into the state via the Mississippi River. What had been a lifeline now strangled the devastated state.

Crops, even entire plantations, were indiscriminately destroyed on the whim of Union officers. Property was stolen. Slaves were freed, some not comprehending their freedom, some hiding in fear from the events swirling around them. Money became worthless, food was scarce, and material goods from the North and Europe were practically nonexistent. The citizens of besieged Vicksburg lived like moles in a subterranean world. Natchez itself, the jewel of Mississippi, suffered the indignity of becoming Union headquarters in the southern part of the state. To this day, the floors of the antebellum mansion, Rosalie, bear scars from the spurs of Union officers. The worst fears of those who opposed secession had come to pass. The Old South lay dying.

Yet, there was resistance. In northern Mississippi, Confederate General Earl Van Dorn wrestled with Ulysses S. Grant in what amounted to a fight for time—an attempt to stave off the inevitable. A recuperated Joe Johnston devised an overall strategy for the defense of Mississippi, only to be rebuked by Davis. The entire state was a battleground; skirmishes flared spontaneously in the north and along the banks of the Mississippi River. Small bands of roving calvary provided the only means of protection for plantations, such as Westmoreland, which were otherwise at the mercy of Union raiding parties. These cavalrymen struck with a vengeance at any Union outfit that had the misfortune of becoming isolated or cut off from the river.

Among the more notorious of these cavalry battalions was that of Colonel Edwin A. Scott. In reality, these units were mounted infantry that traveled very lightly, refusing to fight pitched battles. Scott's battalion was repeatedly reorganized under various designations but was commonly known as Scott's Cavalry. Scott was admired by his men and adored by civilians; his presence was a reassuring one to the besieged natives.

The Westmoreland plantation grounds of Samuel Postlethwaite in Natchez, Mississippi.

Thirty-nine-year-old, Scott was a cotton planter from East Feliciana, Louisiana, with a wife and five children. He owned more than fifty slaves and 1,600 acres of land. Colonel Scott was smart and as slippery as a snake. Once, after being captured near New Orleans, he and a number of other Confederate prisoners were being ferried to Point Lookout Prison in the Chesapeake Bay, on the steamer *Maple Leaf*, when they overpowered the crew and made their escape.

Just a year and a half before, no one could have imagined such a nightmare as the Federals' raids from the Mississippi River. Now, at any given moment, anywhere along its winding route, blue-clad soldiers might come ashore in search of provisions and sometimes an opportunity to plunder unprotected towns, such as Woodville. The citizens went to elaborate lengths to alert themselves to the presence of Union troops, who usually appeared in small numbers, fearing to venture too far from the safety of the Mississippi.

The arrival of Union soldiers in these sleepy towns was as subtle as a flying mallet. They seized cattle and often personal items, such as art or family heirlooms, in spite of the pleadings of their defenseless owners. Worst of all was wanton vandalism. Absolute power brought out the worst in men who were otherwise decent. The more honorable officers in command of these forays would, at the request of a resident, post a guard at the door of a house to prevent looting while its owner was questioned about Colonel Scott's whereabouts. For the most part, however, whatever the Union troops needed, they took, whether courtesy was involved or not.

Back to Manassas

On the morning of 21 August, Will Postlethwaite's Wilkinson Rifles and another company were posted as pickets along the Rappahannock. They were there to protect a crossing known as Kelly's Ford. The woods were alive with Federal troops, and the day's work promised to be contentious. Sure enough, the two isolated Confederate companies were pounced upon by Yankee skirmishers and cavalry. Recognizing their numerical advantage, the blue-clad soldiers ordered Will and his comrades to surrender. The reply, "Surrender be damned! Mississippians don't know how!" was punctuated by a volley of riflery.

The Confederate companies fell back, keeping up a steady fire as the Federals took the bait and ran headlong into the entire 16th and 12th Mississippi regiments, which stopped the Union advance cold. By the time the small affair of Kelly's Ford was over, the Federals had been badly cut up and had learned firsthand of the unpleasantness that accompanied shooting at Mississippians.

Lincoln was wasting no time. As a result of the successes in the south and west, he was more intent than ever on seizing Richmond. Furthermore, he had a brand-new army, the Army of Virginia, commanded by the universally disliked John Pope. Pope had a unique talent for handling all matters in a condescending fashion, but Lincoln, having few options, believed he was the man for the job.

For Stonewall Jackson, Pope was merely a plodding new adversary against whom he could perform his magic. During the middle of August, as Pope rested his army on the banks of the Rappahannock, Jackson marched his valley men east, apparently toward the Shenandoah. Upon reaching Salem Court House, Jackson, in conjunction with Longstreet, marched thirty miles due east along the Manassas Gap Railroad into Manassas Junction. With the simplest of maneuvers Pope had been outgeneraled and unraveled. With Lee's army at his front, Jackson and Longstreet to his rear, Washington unprotected and the Army of the Potomac resting back at Harrison's Landing, Pope was finished before he got started.

Like a cornered animal, on 30 August, Pope went after Jackson at Manassas, unaware of Longstreet's presence. Pope's men fought fiercely, repeatedly slamming into Jackson only to be beaten back with heavy losses, "a sad, tragic, and moving sight." By nine o'clock in the evening, Pope had ordered an organized retreat to the safety of Washington. Jackson and Longstreet put up a token pursuit, but their men were worn out.

With this second victory upon the field of Manassas, the future of the Confederacy suddenly shone much more brightly. Two months after McClellan's campaign had failed, the Army of Northern Virginia now sat on Lincoln's doorstep. For Posey and his men, these were heady times. The 16th Mississippi had performed admirably, earning Posey the command of the brigade.

After Second Manassas, one of Jackson's aides noted a macabre contrast between the two armies:

> The next day, Sunday, was one of incessant rain:
> the heavens weep over every bloody battlefield.

The day was spent by our people in burying the dead, caring for the wounded, collecting arms and ammunition. It was noticeable in how much better condition were the Confederate dead, who had been lying on the field for several days, than those of the Union army. The latter were nearly all discolored, some black, some much decayed, while the Confederates were but little affected by the exposure. The Federal troops were well cared for, well fed, fat, and in good physical condition; upon them decay and discomposition made quick work. The Confederates had little flesh upon them, no fat, nothing to decay. The difference was so marked that in places the lines of battle could be distinguished by the color of the dead. The horrors of war are innumerable (Douglas, 1989).

On 2 September, as Lee looked longingly at Maryland and Pennsylvania, Lincoln fired John Pope and reinstated George McClellan.

On Saturday, 6 September, Posey's brigade, looking like a parade of misfits and vagabonds, crossed the Potomac River near Leesburg. The Army of Northern Virginia was invading the North, a maneuver unthinkable just a few weeks earlier. Four days later, the 16th Mississippi was in Frederick, Maryland, much to McClellan's chagrin. Although Confederate plans had fallen into his hands, McClellan was urged by the White House to proceed with caution. In the days that followed, sporadic fighting and skirmishing broke out north of the Potomac as McClellan moved to intercept Lee.

On the 15th, Jackson seized Harper's Ferry, boosting Lee's confidence and hopes for a Confederate victory on Northern soil. The political results of such a victory would be immeasurable. Lee chose a dilapidated little town called Sharpsburg, on Antietam Creek, as his field of battle. Outnumbered by three to two, the Army of Northern Virginia waited for McClellan.

On Wednesday, the 17th, McClellan crashed into all points of Lee's line. Early that morning, in a light rain, the 16th Mississippi raced toward the sound of gunfire. The wounded were already streaming out of the town. Plunged into combat, Posey's men hadn't seen fighting so intense since Gaines' Mill. Seeking shelter from the sheets of flying lead, Will Postlethwaite and the 227 other men of his regiment gathered in a sunken road eroded by years of wagon traffic.

The fighting broke off into separate battles. Etched into history that day were such innocuous names as the Cornfield, Burnside Bridge, and the Sunken Road. Posey's men shared the Sunken Road with remnants of scattered regiments. Confusion reigned as units intermingled and cohesion was lost. Federal charges upon the road were driven back by murderous bursts of Confederate fire. Eventually, though, the road turned from haven to hellhole as Union units finally managed to position themselves on a flank of the road so as to fire along its length. A shot that missed one man more often than not hit another farther down the line. The men in the road desperately tried to hold their position as the "bloody lane" began to fill with bodies.

Antietam Sunken Road on which Will Postlethwaite fought his final Civil War battle, 17 September 1862.

Command of the 16th fell to Will's captain, Abram Feltus, who described the scene in his report:

> About 10:00 A.M., being ordered to advance in the direction of the enemy, did so in good order. Passing by a large barn, we proceeded, under a heavy fire of artillery and small arms, several hundred yards farther, and came upon (two other brigades) lying down in the road beyond the first corn field after passing the barn. The regiment, as did the brigade, passed over these troops and confronted the enemy in line of battle, who were drawn up some 300 yards from the road, pouring a destructive fire in our ranks. During this time the losses in the regiment had been heavy. A murderous fire of grape, canister, shell, and small arms played on us.
> Notwithstanding, this regiment gallantly held its position until ordered to retire, which it did in good as order as could be expected from its thinned ranks. The number of men carried into the battle 228; of them, 144 were killed or wounded, leaving only 84 men (U.S. War Dept., 1880–1901).

The 16th's casualties were a stunning sixty-three percent. In one day's fighting there were 25,000 casualties overall, yet the battle had been a draw. Will Postlethwaite was among those spared. It was the worst experience he had ever suffered. In the coming days, Lee would cross back into Virginia, Lincoln would fire McClellan once and for all, and Will Postlethwaite would go home.

Home

On 29 September, Will was informed that, due to the conscription act, which was not applicable at the time of his enlistment, he was "underage" and not eligible to remain in the service of his country. Ironically, this hardened veteran of the Valley Campaign, Gaines' Mill, Second Manassas, and Antietam was discharged from the Army of Northern Virginia on the grounds that he was just a boy. Westmoreland would be a welcome sight.

The situation at Westmoreland was no different from that of any other plantation in the Woodville area. Cotton was worthless because it couldn't be sold. Whole crops were seized by Northern troops, and plantation owners took it upon themselves to burn their cotton rather than let it fall into enemy hands. The rare planter who strove to make a go of it faced not only the Yankee threat but that of Confederate troops, who were also burning cotton fields.

Sam and Will's father, William Dunbar Postlethwaite, was a broken man at fifty-two years of age. In failing health, he watched over the remnants of a once-thriving cotton plantation, knowing that a way of life was lost forever. The bluster of patriotism had been replaced by muted talk of survival. There was little to eat and no indication that things would improve anytime soon. On the positive side, the area had not been totally occupied by the enemy, but that provided little solace. There was fear, worry, and a longing for loved ones far away. When a soldier returned safely from Virginia, the community had a rare reason to rejoice and count its few blessings. The sight of seventeen-year-old "Willie" walking up the dusty carriage way of Westmoreland brought a measure of joy to a father who was suddenly an old man and a mother, Sophia, whose boy had come home. Will's older sisters, Nancie (Anna), Mollie (Mary), and Amelia undoubtedly embraced him as the little ones, Fannie (Frances), Nen (Helen), and Georgie (Georgiana) wondered what all the fuss was about. What kind of questions did they ask? Could Will ever tell of the horrors of Boatswain's Swamp or the Sunken Road, or the senseless destruction on Malvern Hill? Sadly misplaced and aloof was the true family matriarch, Susan, now twenty-eight, her only full sibling incapacitated by a terrible war, her family forever incomplete.

On 12 December 1862, the Battle of Fredericksburg was fought and events looked suddenly bright for the Confederacy, at least in the east. Rhode Island's own Ambrose Burnside had risen, mostly through the incompetence of his predecessors, to command the Army of the Potomac. But Burnside, although well-intentioned, was way out of his league. This fight was Malvern Hill with the roles reversed as America once again showed its darkest face to the world. Almost thirteen thousand Union men were slaughtered during an ill-conceived assault upon an entrenched Confederate position behind a stone wall. Burnside repeatedly sent men out to die needlessly; the Confederates could not be budged from their killing nest. In one of the most bizarre episodes of the war, men of Barksdale's brigade found a baby on the battlefield. The infant was rescued and survived. Again Barksdale, the bold secessionist from Mississippi, would see his legend continue to grow as he led the 21st Mississippi.

Perhaps no one captured the feelings of betrayal and helplessness of civilians in war as stirringly as a young woman from Woodville, Mississippi, Kate Blount. In her early twenties, Kate didn't make history, she lived it. In letters to her cousin, a Confederate soldier, Kate wrote an indelible account of life in the Natchez District at the time of Will's return home. In a letter written early in 1862, she reported:

> We have taken down our church bell to send to General Beauregard. [We live a life] pretty destitute of ways, but I am ready to live on beechnuts if it comes to that so our soldiers can be clothed and fed.
>
> The Yankee gunboats are quietly sailing up and down our noble river. When they come to Woodville, and place their stars and stripes over our Courthouse, I will join the band of spirited women who have resolved to tear it down, if the men will stand and quietly look on. I do not despond, and always look on the bright side, but every night brings the heartache.

Regarding the raids from the river, she expressed her innermost fears:

> We had quite a stirring time about two weeks ago. The Yankees are getting near to us. [One of their gunboats] ran aground [and our men] went aboard the boat and brought off everything that could be removed and then burnt the boat. Another gunboat came up that day [and its men] came ashore with torches and set fire to the town [Bayou Sara]. They say they owe Woodville a grudge. I will never bow or shake hands with them. [They are] a tribe of the meanest kind in this portion of the country . . . huge monsters . . . spreading terror and destruction wherever they go.
>
> I have just one sheet of paper left, don't be shocked if I write to you on the margin of a newspaper. Our country has been revolutionized and torn to pieces. When will this state of things end? (Blount Letters, 1861-1865).

Will Postlethwaite found the situation intolerable. Within weeks of his return to Westmoreland, he was riding with Colonel Scott's cavalry. The only requirement to join was an eagerness to fight. As 1863 began, the citizens of the Natchez District refused to bow to the persistent Union raids. Those too old or infirm to ride with the resisters found other means of contributing to the lost cause. In an attempt to boost morale and take people's minds off their hardship, "Some of the gentlemen gave a picnic about six miles from town. It is the first time I have participated in any amusement since the war commenced. We danced all day . . . I nearly wore my feet out," wrote Kate.

Grant continued to pound away at Vicksburg. On 13 March 1863, during what would have been planting season in peacetime, William Dunbar Postlethwaite died at Westmoreland. His body was taken to Natchez for embalming. The following day a large contingent of friends and relatives gathered at Westmoreland, forming a funeral procession that would take them to the family cemetery at The Forest. Everyone was there except the deceased, who was detained in Natchez. The Postlethwaite Family Papers at the Department of Archives and History in Jackson mention the late Postlethwaite patriarch as being "late for his own funeral." Sam's father was eventually buried at The Forest, a few miles south of Natchez, on what is now Highway 61. His monument reads:

> I Will Both Lay Me Down In Peace And Sleep The
> Eternal God Is Thy Refuge And Underneath
> Are The Everlasting Arms.
> Blessed Are The Pure In Heart
> For They Shall See God

With Sam and Will both taken by the war, and with six sisters and a widow to look after, the responsibility for running Westmoreland fell to Susan. A true steel magnolia, Susan was determined to make Westmoreland survive the worst of times.

Throughout the winter and early spring of 1863, General Robert Edward Lee dreamed of giving a measure of the hardship his compatriots had endured to their Northern opponents. A bold stroke on the heels of the victory at Fredericksburg before summer of the new year would surely drive Lincoln's administration to compromise.

Lee was determined to keep the Army of Northern Virginia's momentum intact. Because he was unable to offer any support to Johnston in Mississippi, success in the eastern theater was imperative; Lee had to take the pressure off Mississippi. His newest opponent was Major General Joe Hooker of Massachusetts.

On 1 May, a new season of battle opened. At Port Gibson, Mississippi, 24,000 Union troops crushed a Confederate force to one-third their number, firming Grant's grip on the already staggering state. More impor-

*The headstone of William Dunbar Postlethwaite,
Sam's father, at Forest Cemetery.*

tantly, Hooker had moved the Army of the Potomac's 70,000 men into the vicinity of Chancellorsville; this force was primed for an attack on Richmond. Lee, denied the luxury of caution, went after Hooker immediately. Already outnumbered, Lee boldly divided his army to send his ace, Jackson, to slam into Hooker's weak right flank. Jackson outdid himself, giving the performance of his life. It was also his last.

As Hooker's broken army tumbled back toward Washington, Jackson explored the dark woods around Chancellorsville. As after any major battle, there was confusion. On the evening of 2 May, it was rumored that the woods around Chancellorsville were alive with Yankee cavalry; Confederate pickets had very itchy fingers. Returning to camp, Jackson and his staff were greeted with a volley of friendly fire. Eight days later Stonewall Jackson was dead.

Two months after Jackson's death, as North and South celebrated the Fourth of July, Lee's Army of Northern Virginia staggered out of Gettysburg, Pennsylvania, nearly destroyed. Vicksburg surrendered to the relentless Grant. For the Confederacy, the war was lost. All that remained was survival.

The Great World

During the first week of October, Will Postlethwaite was in northern Mississippi participating in a series of raids on Federal camps and supply lines. A few miles outside of Corinth, on the 5th, Will found himself in a desperate fight against the 3rd Michigan. Underestimating the size of the force they were up against, Scott's men were forced to stand and fight, hanging on as the rear guard while the bulk of the Confederate regiments slipped away. The colonel of the 3rd Michigan reported that "We formed a line, but the panic was so great that the enemy withdrew, left a rear guard of one regiment, which I attacked and drove 3 miles toward Okalona. We killed 2, captured 11 with arms, and 15 horses and equipment."

Will Postlethwaite, a prisoner of war, was taken to Memphis, where he was held until the third week of October 1863. On a train loaded with other prisoners, he was sent to Alton, Illinois, a suburb of St. Louis, Missouri. Early in the war, when holding prisoners had become a growing concern, Lincoln had procured a nearly empty prison in Alton for Federal use. Will arrived at Alton Prison in the middle of a smallpox epidemic. He was immediately issued his "Jeff Davis uniform," "a pair of old blue pants with a large hole cut in the seat and an old army overcoat with the tail bobbed off in an unshapely manner." For the next five months, Alton Prison would be Will's home.

Despite the North's abundance of medicine and supplies, one out of every five prisoners at Alton died, a shocking ratio. The death rate in Southern prisons, despite shortages of everything, was under nine percent.

As 1864 began, the citizens of the Mississippi-Louisiana area found themselves with little protection from the

Federal raids. The prospect of a full-scale Federal invasion and occupation was a daily topic. Kate Blount described the hopelessness of daily life:

> It is a 'a pity for the young people' to be cut off so early from all pleasure. Their youth is something they cannot keep for better times. I have changed a great deal in five years. I am wearing my hair back, I am so thin now, so if I ever happen along you won't know who it is. Ah me. I cannot realize that this week I will be twenty-four, I do not feel as aged as I did when I was seventeen (Blount Letters, 1861-1865).

In spite of their sorrows, the people of Woodville put on a brave front for the tired remnants of their defeated army. "Our little Woodville . . . every soldier coming home says it is the most cheerful looking little town in the Confederacy." Despite this noble effort, the town had fallen into despondency by late winter. "I have been hoping for better times and brighter days but it seems like hoping against hope." By spring, the Yankees had still not materialized, only heightening the anxiety.

On 4 March 1864, Will Postlethwaite was shipped farther north, to Fort Delaware Prison on Pea Patch Island in the Delaware River (near Delaware City). As miserable as prison life at Fort Delaware was, it was a marked improvement over the conditions at Alton. The prisoners' diet was abysmal, sometimes consisting of rotten vegetables, and disease was rampant. The prison population swelled to a staggering 7,700. To alleviate the situation, many of the prisoners who had dependents and were willing to sign an oath of allegiance were released and sent home. However, Will Postlethwaite, having twice taken up arms against the United States, would be going nowhere.

Within Fort Delaware Prison, a microcosmic world evolved. There were chess clubs, debating teams, bands, and a Christian Association. An elaborate newspaper, aptly titled the *Prison Times*, began to circulate late in the war. The *Prison Times* carried advertisements announcing every kind of service from laundering to dentistry. A poetry column was a regular feature.

In an article titled "Our Prison World," the editor mused:

> A glance at our advertising columns will show that to call our barracks a miniature world is not so much of a misnomer as it might seem to be at first to the uninitiated.
>
> Except for the want of two grand essentials (women and children) our prison world is quite a good abridgement of the "Great World" outside.

One of the more unusual advertisements in volume 1 of the *Prison Times* read:

RATS
All who are able to indulge in luxuries can be supplied with fat-Rats by immediate application to Fox at the Entrance.

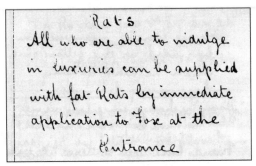

A portion of the original Prison Times.

At home, things continued to worsen. By the end of June, residents along the Mississippi River were living in squalor.

> I have been told by several gentlemen to hurry up and write all the letters I wish to send or I will

lose the opportunity. They say that the Yankees are going to take possession of all this part of the Country. I cannot think that it will be so but everybody believes it, so there must be some great probability of it. But this I do know—there is nothing now to keep them away when they choose to come. They are expected every day.

Everyone is supplying themselves with the poisonous greenbacks. I will not murmur at anything if we can be free from the molestations of our detested merciless foes. (I hear) the Yankees will be among us in less than two weeks. I trust it will not be as bad as we anticipate.

Apparently untouched by the war—in fact, prospering—William Greene wrote the following letter to his nephew in late July:

Vicksburg July 30, 1864

Dear Harry,

Some days since I received your letter, and I was very glad to hear from you. I suppose you are enjoying the salubrious breezes of Newport, which I imagine contrasts favorably with the close, hot weather of the Sunny South, which I am now enduring rather than enjoying. I wish you were here to take a tour around with me and visit my plantations.

I am cultivating upwards of 2000 acres of land which would be quite a respectable size for a farm in Rhode Island, don't you think so. An immense amount of labor is required to cultivate cotton successfully. I have to provide for the sustenance of upwards of 900 people, great and small. This is rather a large family for a bachelor, what do you think? It takes of course large amounts of provisions to feed so many people, and I am kept very busy, ordering supplies and distributing to the various plantations.

It would amuse you to visit a plantation, and see the people at work in the cotton fields, men and women, the latter plowing and hoeing with nearly equal facility to the men. We do not allow them to leave the field to go after water when they are dry but have a cart which hauls water to the fields in bbls [barrels], then we have boys and girls to "tote" the water to the field hands. They dip it out of the bbls in buckets or water pails and carry it over to the field on their heads. The custom of "toting" articles on the head is very customary among the Negroes of the South. In the course of a month we shall commence picking cotton. It is already in full bloom and the bolls are forming rapidly. The cotton plant is peculiar in this respect, that it commences blooming very early and continues to bloom and form until frost comes to check the growth, therefore the later the frost the better the crop.

I am now busy preparing my gin houses as on some of the plantations they are very much out of order. I have got one new gin house to build 80 by 40 ft and two to partially build as they have been very much torn and injured by the soldiery.

Last week I went up to Goodrich's Landing in [Louisiana] 60 miles up the Miss River above here, where I had business and was detained there 3 or 4 days. On Saturday night the scouts came to the town, where there is a military post and fort occupied by some 200 negro troops, and reported that there were three regiments of Rebs coming in to attack the place that night. The house where I was stopping was in the outskirts of the town where the outer pickets were stationed and on the main road where they would come in. I felt somewhat uneasy, but concluded I would see the fight but about 9 o'clock, as all was quiet, I went to bed. I was roused at 1 o'clock by the gentleman of the house with whom I was stopping, who said a man had just come in through the pickets who reported the enemy only 8 miles off, and a fight would occur before morning. Our forces drew up in a line of battle in front of the house where I was stopping. I waited until 3 o'clock and as I again got sleepy went to bed and slept until morning when I found out our forces had gone to their quarters, and everything quiet.

The next morning a cavalry scout went out to learn where the enemy was, and succeeded in hearing they were just 15 men that were in the day before and raided a plantation some ten miles out. The rumor spread rapidly that there had been a fight, and in Vicksburg it had been announced the Millikens Bend was captured and that I and my friend Mr. Alexander were taken prisoners. Wednesday my friends thought it was true, and were greatly surprised to see me. (Greene Letters, 1850-1870).

In late August 1864, Kate Blount wrote, "I have heard much of the hardship of the prisoners at Ft. Delaware and I cannot bear the idea of one of our loved ones being there to suffer." Describing life at home, she went on:

Communications is cut off and it is very evident they are after Scott and want to drive him out of the country. Last Friday . . . the Yankees were ten miles (away) on the Woodville Road. The news came about six o'clock and caused a great excitement. Mr. Adams came home with us from Church to help us hide the horses. He and sister rode the horses off and tied them in the woods. I am just writing this to give you some idea of the constant fuss we are kept in. Our trials and troubles have been great, but I trust the end is coming.

On the first anniversary of Will's capture, Kate wrote the last letter she is known to have written during the war.

> I have had a great tramp this morning and am very tired. Mr. Adams told us the Yankees were expected in half an hour. As quick as the horses could be saddled, we mounted them, and rode off to the woods, where we wandered until we found a secure place, and tied our steeds to the trees, hid the saddles and bridles and walked back. The Yankees returned to the river without coming out so far as Woodville. I am not afraid of anything but Yankees and fear we might be caught napping" (Blount Letters, 1861-1865).

The following morning, 6 October 1864, a small force of Confederate soldiers appeared at Bowling Green Plantation in Woodville, the home of the Honorable Judge Edward McGehee. Half-starved, they asked for something to eat. The seventy-eight-year-old judge responded with a breakfast on the lawn. Soon after these grateful guests had departed, Federal troops came crashing through the woods.

The judge was swiftly dragged from the house, pistol-whipped, and informed that Bowling Green would be burned to the ground in twenty minutes. As the McGehee family desperately struggled to remove family heirlooms and valuables, Federal soldiers absconded with them. Within an hour, the house was gone. Today, the columns of Bowling Green still stand as a reminder of the events of that day.

By 30 December 1864, the war had all but ended. William Tecumseh Sherman had cut the South's heart out, introducing the world to the concept of "total war." In the coming spring Grant would hunt down Lee's once-glorious Army of Northern Virginia. With all hope for victory or European recognition gone, the Confederacy could only fight for a conditional surrender. Even that cause was to be wasted optimism.

In an effort to win Will Postlethwaite's release from Fort Delaware, a relative of the Postlethwaites who had political ties to President Lincoln, tried her hand at persuading the president. Mrs. C. J. Harris of Paducah, Kentucky, wrote the following on the next-to-last day of 1864:

Mr. Lincoln, My dear sir,

The unfortunate occurrences of this war are not a few and notwithstanding your brain may be kept ever busy and a good time employed with great affairs, things that concern this mighty nation's life and future glory and destiny—yet I venture to intrude a woman's characteristic prayer for your notice—and a request that is urged from a feeling of deep sympathy for the unfortunate and from the confidant belief and satisfaction that the president will not be deaf to a woman's request. Willie Dunbar Postlethwaite, I have my dear President as relative, confined at Ft. Delaware as prisoner of war. He belonged to the 9th La Cavalry Company A as private. He is very anxious to be released on parole that he may visit us in Kentucky. He has been in confinement for fifteen months. I am very anxious for him to be paroled, that he may visit us here. I am almost certain that a change can be effected if he should visit us, which he will do if you can and will grant my humble prayer. And I do further make my request upon the grounds of my father being one of your warmest supporters in Western Kentucky. I will look earnestly for the coming of your favorable answer to my simple request. And until then I will remain, My dear President with the profoundest Respect.
Yours very truly,
Mrs. C. J. Harris
(National Archive Record Collection, William Postlethwaite, 9th Louisiana Calvary.)

Perhaps it was Mrs. Harris' political ties to Lincoln or even her reference to Will, for the first and only time, as Willie—an overt tug at the heartstrings—that prompted Will's transfer to City Point, Virginia, on 7 March 1865. Five days later, at Boulwares and Coxes Wharf Virginia, Will Postlethwaite was exchanged for a Federal prisoner.

On Sunday, 26 March 1865, as Lee was preparing to abandon Petersburg and make a stand somewhere near Appomattox Court House, Virginia, William Greene was in Vicksburg writing to Harry.

> Some days since I received your note enclosed in a letter from your Father to me, and as I have a few moments of leisure this quiet Sunday afternoon, I will write you in reply. Another Sunday and I can expect it to find me on my way to St. Louis as I now think of leaving for that city by Saturday next . . . . I shall be right glad to see your Uncles Kit and George, as it will be a year next month since I went to St. Louis.
>
> I call myself a Mississippian now having resided here for nearly a year and a half. I am so much of a cosmopolitan that I really can't say where my home is. Some times I call Mr. Morancy's house at Millikens Bend Louisiana for there I am actually keeping house, although I stay but little. Then again Vicksburg seems more of a home, for I am so pleasantly situated in the family of my dear friend Mrs. Merwin and when I go to St. Louis, I say "I am going home" for there I have my bachelors hall, and when I go to the dear old state of my nativity then I am "going Home"—so if you never knew what a cosmopolitan was before, you see one in me.
>
> But enough of this, as it can scarcely be of much interest to you. I shall probably remain in St. Louis a month, as I want to be back here by the first of May. I am a great farmer you know and I can't stay away as I like to look after my interests here.

Where a farmer in Rhode Island cultivates acres by twenties and fifties, I cultivate by hundreds and even thousands, as I have had to attend to the management of nearly or quite three thousand acres this year, not all in one place to be sure but divided into four or five plantations. I hope to make a good crop this year, but we can't foretell beforehand, although everything now looks propitious.

Kiss your brothers and sisters for me. I long to see you all, but I am afraid I shall have to deny myself the pleasure for another, as I am apprehensive I should be too anxious to enjoy myself, so desirous am I of having my interest succeed here this year.

Nine days later, Sam Postlethwaite turned thirty-one years old as he continued his recuperation at Westmoreland. The American Civil War would end in less than seventy-two hours.

CHAPTER THIRTEEN

I May Go Up to Vicksburg

Lionel Joseph "Pete" Cardin and Sam Postlethwaite lived nearly one thousand miles and one hundred years apart. They now rest together in Greenwood. Both men answered their country's call in time of crisis, one that began with Fort Sumter and the other with Pearl Harbor. War took them to places far from their homes.

Lionel Joseph Cardin came into the world on 21 February 1910, the son of Canadian immigrants Elie and Anna Cardin. Settling in Warwick, Rhode Island, Elie worked in the mills of Phenix, a village adjacent to Riverpoint.

As a boy, Lionel worked at People's Drug Store, a center of the villagers' daily routines. Ruth Cardin told me how she regularly purchased gum at the store as an excuse to see the young man who worked there. While making his daily deliveries to the drugstore, the postman would ask Lionel, "How's it goin', Pete?" The name stuck.

Pete Cardin (shown here in Navy uniform) was buried next to Sam Postlethwaite. Today the graves of both men are marked with similar bronze plaques.

While earning a degree in pharmacology at what was then Rhode Island University, Pete continued to work part-time at People's Drug Store. He was still in school when the store's owners decided to sell it. With some financial help from his mother, Cardin was able to buy the store, and People's became known as Cardin's Drug Store. Business flourished and expanded, the store soon featuring a full-service restaurant. America was struggling from the depths of the Depression, and for young businessmen like Pete Cardin, the future seemed bright. Three weeks before Pete and Ruth were to be wed, however, the Japanese attacked Pearl Harbor.

The business of war requires skills and talents from all aspects of civilian life, medical knowledge being near the top of the list. Men being wounded in the thousands need treatment and medicine. Pete Cardin served as a pharmacist's mate in the U.S. Navy and Marine Corps in both the Atlantic and Pacific theaters of World War II.

At the war's end, Pete, an honorably discharged veteran, resumed his career at Cardin's. He and Ruth raised two daughters, Bette and Elsie, and purchased a home only a few streets from Corotoman Farm (then known as the Quinn House). Pete Cardin was a respected figure in the community; Ruth describes him as a "quiet gentleman with a passion for golf."

When Pete Cardin died at the age of sixty-one, he was unknowingly laid to rest next to Sam Postlethwaite, whose grave was then unmarked. Today the graves of both men are marked by identical bronze plaques, issued by the Department of Veterans Affairs, that recognize their service as American soldiers.

The war's end was punctuated by the assassination of Abraham Lincoln and the arrest of Jefferson Davis. Jackson, Barksdale, Posey, and Jeb Stuart were all dead. At the scene of surrender, on 9 April 1865, men on both sides laughed and cried while Union soldiers shared rations with their defeated adversaries. At Appomattox Court House,

The gravestone of Frank Greene at Swan Point Cemetery in Providence, Rhode Island.

the 16th Mississippi, numbering about seventy men, surrendered. The once-proud Wilkinson Rifles had been
reduced to a band of fifteen skinny, worn-out soldiers.

The 21st Mississippi had fared even worse. The regiment was about one thousand strong at the war's outset;
fewer than fifty men were left on 9 April 1865. Company
D, the Jefferson Davis Guards, was represented by a mere
eight privates. Upon surrendering, the regiment's color
bearer refused to surrender the flag, instead wrapping it
around his waist beneath his shirt. (It is displayed today at
the Old Court House Museum in Vicksburg.) The Southern
men were fed, paroled, and told to start walking home.

In the coming weeks and months, there were parades
and celebrations throughout the North. The South would
also have a parade: a stream of wounded, broken soldiers
slowly finding their way home.

By summer, Sam Postlethwaite's health had vastly
improved, and his full recovery seemed quite likely. He
once again immersed himself in the running of
Westmoreland, which was now his, with the help of
brother Will. The South's men went about farming as if
there had never been a war at all, although most farms had
suffered severe neglect. Men who had for four years been
preoccupied with sword and rifle were once again concerned with the plow and the mule. A major difference,
however, was the lack of slave labor, although many former
slaves remained on their plantations as hired hands or
sharecroppers, knowing no other way of life.

William Rogers Greene had spent the war in the right
place. With so many planters removed by the conflict, he had
successfully managed several plantations for handsome fees.
Being from a prominent New England family, he had been
treated favorably by the Yankee raiders. William had made
no attempt to conceal his pro-Union sympathies, particularly
in light of brother Frank's severe wounding at First Manassas.

In early December 1865, William wrote to his nephew
Harry, who was at that time sixteen years old, encouraging
his pursuit of an education at Brown University:

It must be a matter of pride with you to reflect
that you are now studying in the same institution
that your father was pursuing his studies thirty
years ago . . . I hastily look back upon it and think
of the time when we "boys" tried to tease your
father by calling him "Dandy Ed dancing up
College Hill" as it was considered quite aristo-
cratic in those days for one to attend college.
Accept the advice of one who realizes the advantages of acquiring a thorough education before
embarking in the busy pursuit of life, and who
has regretted more than once that he importuned
his Father to allow him to leave school at too
early an age, at an age too when what he could
have learned would have been of substantial
value to him. Let it also be your pride to lead a
good and virtuous life, imitating your Father and
I may add his Brothers in the life they have led
and which I assure you affords real pleasure and
a glorious satisfaction to look back upon.

Yes, I am now a resident of New Orleans and a
citizen of Louisiana where I think I shall become
a fixture but I have so long enjoyed a cosmopoli-
tan life that it seems difficult for me to remain in
one place very long. I like New Orleans however
and like the nature of my business here and as I
prefer a warm climate to a cold one, I believe I
will permanently settle here. I would like to see
you here some one of these days. I am looking for
your Uncle Kit to come here and stay a few days,
so that I may go up to Vicksburg on a short tour
and business.

I am shipping some cotton to your Father
today and will send with the Cotton a bag of
pecans and oranges which I trust will reach you
before Christmas so that you can all have a feast
(Greene Letters, 1850-1870).

Two weeks after William wrote this letter—two days after Christmas—Frank Greene died in Riverpoint. Although he had endured a variety of illnesses, the official cause of death was listed as tuberculosis. He was twenty-three. Frank is buried on a bluff high above the Blackstone River at Swan Point Cemetery in Providence. He is joined there in death with his former brothers-in-arms Ambrose Burnside, John Slocum, Elisha Hunt Rhodes, and Sullivan Ballou.

The Greene family, North and South, passed the winter months grieving the loss of their youngest. For William, Christopher, and George, Frank's death hit particularly hard. They had last seen their crippled brother in the fall of 1864 when he and brother Henry visited the South for a voyage up the Mississippi. Frank had attempted to help with William's business but soon realized that his health was not up to the task.

In mourning, William Rogers Greene ventured to Vicksburg, as he mentioned in his letter to Harry. Also on her way to Vicksburg was Mollie (Mary) Postlethwaite. As William and Mollie's daughter Lenore later recalled, Mollie and her Aunt Jennie (Merwin) "were about the same age and always great friends." Jennie's mother ran a boarding house in Vicksburg at which William Greene occasionally stayed. Word quickly spread among the guests that a Northerner was in the house, displeasing many. Among them was Mollie, who "refused for a long time to come down to the dining room as she would not eat with a Yankee." Both William and Mollie carried the deep scars of civil war. During the war, Mollie had lost her father, seen one brother imprisoned, and the health of another ruined. The life of William's nineteen-year-old brother had been destroyed in an instant by a Confederate Minié ball.

In a 1958 letter to a friend, Lenore Greene told the family story:

> One day, while eating her solitary meal up in her bedroom, my mother looked out of her window and saw my father coming down the street with Aunt

Jenny's small son and daughter perched on either shoulder clutching his thick hair and shouting with laughter as he 'galloped like a horse'. She thought he might not be such a bad fellow, after all, and that night she came down to dinner.

Mary Carter (Mollie) Postlethwaite, Sam's half-sister, and William Rogers Greene fell in love at first sight.

It was a genuine case of love at first sight, and William wasted no time in asking for Mollie's hand in marriage. Mollie accepted, becoming engaged to a Yankee. George Greene announced the news to his family back home in a letter to Harry in February 1866; it included news of yet another surprise: the engagement of his other brother, Kit.

> I know you will all love her very much she is so kind and good. I shall be proud to call her sister as your Uncle Wm is proud of paying his devotions to her. Then too another nice, kind lady whom you have been accustomed to call Miss Pratt you will some of these days address her as Aunt Maria. Isn't it funny how such changes will occur sometimes. What a radical change for each of your two old bachelor uncles. Now I shall be the only bachelor uncle. Wm thinks he may go on

East this week to be home two or three days and return in time to accompany the ladies home. I have not said who the others are. Well, I will tell you the names of the whole party. They are Mrs. Postlethwaite, her daughters Mary and Fannie and Miss Cobb their cousin. Miss Fannie intends staying here to attend school. I am making preparations to return with Wm. to [New Orleans] as we have decided to break up business here and I shall locate in N.O. In some respects I rather regret leaving St. L. but upon the whole I think I would prefer living in N.O. than anywhere else; excepting New York. Now Harry, Father and Mother have kindly desired that I should wear the watch and chain that your Uncle Frank used to carry, I have a good watch with a great chain which I shall send you the first opportunity, which please accept with much love from your uncle (Greene Letters, 1850–1870).

In early March, George shared with Harry an account of the riverboat journey he and William had made down the Mississippi from St. Louis with the same ladies. An incident had occurred just south of Memphis.

. . . we ran to see what the matter was and right in front of our boat about 600 yds we saw the wreck of the Steamer *R.P. Lockwood* which had exploded its boilers. The cries of the living calling for help and the groans of the wounded and scalded were truly heartrending. The scene was truly awful. Presently we were alongside the wreck. Not a light could be seen. We passengers thought the Capt[ain] ridiculously cautious as we could not see a spark of fire, but hardly had we launched our lifeboats ere a flame burst forth from the midst of the ill-fated steamer and spread with such rapidity that it seemed as if it would be impossible to rescue all, but we did & it seemed but a work of a moment when we pushed away when the wreck was but one sheet of flame.

The flames rose to a very great height, and great clouds of smoke were curling upwards it seemed miles. The trees and brush on either side of the river presented an appearance of phantom, weirdlike forms, and while we were beholding this grandeur, we could faintly hear the cries of some wounded man left on the wreck who could not be extricated.

The cause of the explosion was a patched & leaking old boiler. They were running slow endeavoring to reach Memphis to have the boilers repaired the next day.

We are having a very pleasant day. Wm went on with the ladies to Bayou Sara. The grass is quite green & peach trees are in blossom. In two weeks I expect to be feasting on strawberries (Greene Letters, 1850-1870).

On 26 April 1866, William and Mollie were married at Westmoreland. George was William's best man. At the wedding, he met Julia Dunbar, Mollie's cousin and brides-maid, of Natchez. On 17 May, Sam Postlethwaite wrote to his Uncle James Gillespie:

I arrived home only a day before the wedding. Everything came off well, & I think we had quite a pleasant party, though I suppose you heard all about it by this time.

I hope you have not been considering me forgetful of my promises, on acct. of not having sent you the peas I promised. As soon as I got home, I examined them carefully. I found them too bad to risk planting myself. So of course, I would not make you pay freight on them, on an uncertainty. So please excuse me if you are disappointed. We are all well. I wish you could have been at the wedding. I know you would have enjoyed it. Love to you all from your affec. nephew (Postlethwaite Family Papers).

During the summer of 1866, William introduced Mollie to his family on a visit to Rhode Island. That September, Kit Greene married Maria Pratt.

In mid-October, George passed a lazy Sunday afternoon aboard The SS *Grey Eagle*. He took the opportunity to write to Harry, describing changes in the Greene brothers' lives:

> On the first of the month we acquired the office in our new building and we are very much pleased with the change, being comfortably and permanently fixed are quite prepared to attend to any business which may be offered to us of which we feel quite assured that it will assume to a pretty large amount notwithstanding the failure of the cotton crop this year.
>
> You would like to know perhaps why I am on this boat, and I will explain to you. Mollie's sister Miss Nancie Postlethwaite was married on Thursday last to Mr. John Fletcher of Natchez, and as Mr. F. had kindly extended to me an invitation to act as one of the groomsmen on the happy occasion, I left N.O. on Tuesday evening last by this same boat, arriving at Bayou Sara at noon the next day where I met Wm. and we took a carriage and drove out to Westmoreland, a distance of 21 miles, first however partaking and excellent dinner at Maria Wicker's Hotel, Bayou Sara. Maria is an old darky, and she keeps a firstrate house, and she thinks a 'heap' of us as William has stopped there so often during his courting times. Wm. arrived at B.S. with the guests from Natchez early in the morning, and they all drove out early leaving Wm. behind to go with me. We arrived at Westmoreland about 6 PM where we received a cordial greeting.

The weather was beautiful, and the next morning's sun never rose to a more beautiful cloudless day. It was exactly similar to the day Wm. and Mollie were married. Rev. Mr. Adams [who is mentioned in Kate Blount's letters] Episcopal minister from Woodville Miss was the person to marry them, and he was very pleasing. The groomsmen were Gen'l Z. Yorke, a rich planter, a distinguished Confederate General, and a very fine man about 40 years of age born in Connecticut & came South to teach school about 20 years ago. Mr. Henry Garrett and intimate friend of Mr. F's, a young & quite wealthy planter and a fine fellow. Mr. Will Postlethwaite and myself. The bridesmaids were Miss Fannie P., Miss Beverly Jenkins, a young and pretty cousin of the bride, Miss Georgie P. and Miss Julia Dunbar another pretty cousin (Greene Letters, 1850–1870).

George neglected to tell young Harry that he was courting Julia Dunbar with keen interest and that his own bachelor days were coming to an end.

By mid-winter of 1867, William was a father-to-be. While inquiring about events at home, he hinted at Mollie's condition in a letter to Harry:

> I would like to see the new office when it is newly fitted, but I don't (know) whether I shall see it this year, as I do not anticipate that I shall go east this year. We will let your Uncle Kit and Aunt Maria represent us all this summer, as they anticipate spending at least a portion of the summer in Rhode Island.
>
> Your Aunt Mary has been intending writing you for some days but you must excuse her if she does not write promptly as she is not very well, but she will write you soon. She speaks & thinks of you all very often and learned to love you all when she was with you last summer with an affection that will

never waver—and looks forward anticipating with
pleasure the day when she can welcome any or all
of you to her own sunny South, as well as to that
time when she can make you another visit to your
own Home.

Remember us both to all with our warmest
loves, and whenever you can write, remember your
letters are always read with the keenest pleasure
and if you do not receive a prompt reply—do not
get discouraged but keep on writing—and we thank
you for the promptness with which you have kept
the promise you made us when we left R.I.—by
writing us often (Greene Letters, 1850–1870).

By early spring, Sam, recovering from what was probably
a bout with malaria, described to his uncle the recent events
of his life and his plans for the coming planting season:

Your welcome letter of Feb. 18th only came to
hand on March 9th. I read it on the afternoon of
said day just as I was out after one week's illness,
this was Saturday & on Monday I had to go to
Bayou Sara where I have been on the Jury until last
Saturday 23rd, so you see my dear Uncle that this
is about the first chance I have had of answering
your letter for the last three weeks. I have just paid
off my hands & made a new contract for the present year. It runs thus, I give them one third of the
cotton & corn, two thirds of the potatoes & hogs
raised the present year. They feed and clothe themselves. I have three squads under separate drivers
or foremen, one of 21 hands, one of 16 hands & one
of 17. I came out last year about even, mules plows
and hoes over expenses, which was doing only tolerably, but so many did worse that I can't grumble.
I am planting about two hundred acres of corn,
plenty of potatoes, pumpkins & peas & will then
make what cotton I can.

I think with you that our situation is anything but encouraging. My only hope now is that Thad Stephen's confiscation bill will not be passed until I get all my cotton to New Orleans, have it all sold & put the money in my pocket. The Yankees are certainly the most ungenerous people in the world & the more they get a man down the more they will hit him, & there is no more calculating as to what will probably be done in congress than there would be in surmising what One Hundred Lunatics would do, were they suddenly convened from an insane asylum. When I read the Congressional Proceedings, I don't blame Mr. Stratton of Natchez for thinking the world is about to end, as I am told he now preaches (Postlethwaite Family Papers, 1867).

In the spring of 1867, William described the beauty of Westmoreland in its spring glory, and he tried to convey his respect for and fear of the mighty Mississippi River to his young reader in Rhode Island:

I have been with your Aunt Mary to Westmoreland, her country home to which she is so much attached, and justly so, as it is certainly the most attractive place in its natural beauties of any place I have ever visited and is the perfection of rural retirement, completely isolated as it is from the outside world. As you approach Westmoreland from the highway—you turn down a lane, which is about a mile and a half away from the house, and for a half a mile or more before you approach the house you drive through a dense and beautiful old forest, and finally suddenly bursts upon you, concealed among the trees, beautiful Westmoreland. In front of the house are beautiful irregularly grouped shade trees, amidst which they have a splendid croquet ground, still farther beyond is their large flower garden, which was in the zenith of its bright spring beauty when we first arrived there. The beautiful snow white spirea, lilys & other flowers in fine contrast with the scarcely less beautiful, but more showy flowering peach. They have an immense quantity of the spirea, here & there, through the garden in large bushes. The white flowers in graceful curves, blending with the beautiful delicate green leaves in the greatest profusion, made a sight pleasant to behold, in contrast with the dusty, swarthy City we left behind. Here indeed we could commune with 'nature and nature's God' undisturbed by any mundane thoughts.

"The great old river has been playing its annual ugly pranks, being on its spring rampage and running over its banks everywhere, the Levees not being in sufficient order to confine the river to its channels, carving numerous crevasses and extensive inundations with great loss of life, property and the dash of the hope of thousands, a picture sad to contemplate, the River being 10 to 16 feet above its banks. You can readily imagine how it tears when it breaks loose from its bank, like a beast of prey breaking from its cage, seeking whom it may devour. We have been very much favored by Divine Providence and have received but little damage from the flood, and as it is now at its greatest height we may dismiss almost all of our apprehension. We ought to be & are daily thankful while thousands around us have so seriously suffered that we have been spared." (Greene Letters, 1850–1870).

We Live As You Say You Do, Very Poorly

From New Orleans, on the day after the Fourth of July, William wrote again to Harry, introducing him to his new cousin:

I wish you could see your cousin Helen. We think her a pretty sweet little child, and if all is well to introduce her next summer to Aunts, Uncles & Cousins without number.

In about ten days we expect to close our house & your Aunt Mollie & baby will spend the summer at Westmoreland.

In the fall of 1867, a yellow fever epidemic struck along the banks of the Mississippi. William described its effects in a letter to Harry:

. . . in order to check the pernicious fevers, with which we have been so much afflicted, and which in New Orleans especially has caused the deaths of thousands, bringing sorrow and distress to many a household, and causing us all to breathe the prayer of "God stay the plague." Among others who have fallen a victim of to this fearful disease is my dear friend Miss Nina Cobb, lovely as she was in all virtues that constitute a true woman; I am thankful, deeply thankful that your Uncle George has passed through the trying season unscathed.

Two weeks ago today I left this place to visit your Aunt Mollie and your little Cousin Helen. I arrived at Bayou Sara on Sunday noon, finding there a letter from your Aunt writing that in consequence of yellow fever being epidemic in Bayou Sara, that they had decided to not send a carriage for me, but for me to hire a Buggy & ride out 6 miles, where I would find the carriage waiting for me, so I started out, arriving at the place about 3 o'clock. I found the carriage and occupying it, were my good wife & her sister Nellie, who came to meet me, and accompany me home. I remained at Westmoreland until Friday morning.

I left at an early hour (boarding a boat at Bayou Sara). I had a very comfortable trip up the river.

There were but 6 or 7 passengers aboard, as since the epidemic has prevailed people are afraid to travel.

On arriving here on Saturday AM, I found the quarantine had been removed and that yellow fever had become epidemic here, and one of my near neighbors & an old St. Louis acquaintance and friend, had died & several others that I knew more remotely; there are about 100 cases under treatment here at this time, but I am told that since the frost Wednesday night no new cases have developed.

Remember me with much love to all at home & with the hope of hearing from you soon (Greene Letters, 1867).

This would be William's last letter to Harry. One month later, on the second anniversary of Frank's death, Harry contracted typhoid and died at the age of eighteen. Tragedy sent the Greene family reeling as yellow fever claimed Kit's young bride, Maria, at about the same time.

In early September 1868, Sam Postlethwaite, struggling to sound optimistic, wrote to his uncle:

I write according to promise to let you know how we got home. We got an early start from Holly Wood & were congratulating ourselves upon how well we were getting on when in crossing the broad sandy bayou about a mile from the Farrars, snap went the double tree. I patched up with part of a fence rail & drove on to A. Farrars where we were accommodated with a set of plow double & single trees, which did us good service the rest of the day. Hard rains at home Tuesday Wed & Thur but no wind. Rain made cotton very trashy. I have out 18 bales tonight. 1500 to a bale & expect to get out 3 bales per day for some days to come. As yet, I have not had time to hunt out a suitable stalk of Dixie Cotton for you. Mr. Greene & I in riding out this evening selected one of medium size for John

Fletcher. It was 3 ft high & had 46 full bolls, but you can take my word for its being the best old land cotton that ever grew. The worms have not eaten a leaf of cotton for me yet & I hope they will keep off four weeks longer, as my crop seems to be taking faster now. I never saw a crop so green at this season of the year, but there are plenty of worms scattered throughout the fields everywhere (Postlethwaite Family Papers, 1868).

William Greene fared little better. As more and more planters failed, the William R. Greene Company suffered. Adding to William's concerns was the added responsibility of a second child, William Reginald Greene, who was born on 16 October 1869, in New Orleans.

By January 1870, Sam's outlook was growing increasingly bleak:

> Since my return from N.O. I have been in a whirlwind of trouble & annoyance, paying off hands & trying to make new contracts. So I have done the best I could but am not pleased. This contract will force me (to) watch close during picking season, but as I am again enjoying good health that won't hurt me. But I feel new energy since I got rid of my inheritance of debt by going safely through Bankrupt court. They were hard on me & though I hated the unprincipled rascals to get my money I considered it was really worth $250 to me & determined to go through. Love to all (1870).

By fall, Sam expressed his concern for the market and the health of his sister Susan:

> My two best pickers got 400 & 436 lbs ea which is the best picking I have done since the war. But the price of cotton bothers (me) considerably & there seems to be no prospect of any improvement

for some time. Mr. Greene, Miss Jennie & Nannie's two children go up to John's (Fletcher) tomorrow. Sue will probably come up to make you a long visit which she very much needs as she is looking badly, in consequence of her trying summer (1870).

His success dwindling in New Orleans, William Greene terminated his business relationship with Sam in the spring of 1871. Anxiously, Sam wrote to his uncle:

Mr. Greene is going to close up in N.O. & go to Vicksburg & of course I must transfer to another house my business for present year. I thought it would be a simple matter & that any merchant would jump at my business as I ship 200 bls & and only require about 1000 or 1200 $ in supplies & money, but I found no one willing to touch it. So I think my best plan is to negotiate a loan of 1200 a(t) about 11 1/2 per c secured by mortgage payable in Decem. which will render me independent of all merchants & I can ship to whom I please. If I can negotiate a loan we will have a laugh at all the merchants.

I hope this year will be the last that I have to apply to any one for money as I believe in the safe and simple (1870).

Sam continued his struggle the next year:

I have 35 regular hands this year & 3 others, 2 carpenters & a blacksmith. I expect the blacksmith will make me about 2 bales of cotton in my time. I give him and each of carpenters 8 acres of land for themselves & I am thus getting the place in good order. You probably won't believe me when I tell you I have had to issue stringent orders to prevent their [Negroes] taking the mules to the fields to plow before daylight. That is not generally the case in these parts I assure you. The great drawback this year is that the corn crop did not turn out well last year & I expect I will have a little to buy (1872).

Sue, described by Mollie as "being a very bad correspondent," wrote to her Uncle in March 1872. She described her family's meager existence and her deep affection for her brother Sam:

Brother's health is, I am thankful to say, better than it has been for many years. Brother has had a good deal of building to do. He is putting up some quarters and will dig a cistern too this year, so it keeps him busy, and he is glad to get Will to attend to the crop. Brother weighs more than he has done since he went to the army, and he never gets sick even at our extremely plain and coarse fare, for I can tell you nobody can beat us there, we live as you say you do, very poorly. Maybe we'll all do better this year, everybody says it will be a fine crop year, though how they know I can't tell.

Our girls keep up their health and spirits wonderfully. They always seem to be in good humor, and though Fan assured me she is falling off every day, I can't see it. I suppose my eyes must be getting dim. Mollie and her two children are here yet. Mr. Greene comes down occasionally, though he is very busy near Port Gibson, making brick for the bridge he and Maj. Haisie are going to build. Mollie was very much disappointed in not being present at the Golden Wedding of Mr. Greene's parents, which took place on the 13th of this month. I expect we will soon hear grand accounts of it. Mollie wanted to be there very much.

The boys are very much encouraged to see how well the hands are working. There is no difficulty in getting them out, and they work without urging. I am ever Your affectionate niece Sue (p.s.) Please ask Aunt Jane if she has any Bell Pepper seed. I want some for Brother very much.

Sam's efforts to survive in difficult times took him to highs and lows:

The crop is very fine & the season so far is almost perfect (June 1872).

I suppose times are as tight with you as they are with us. I have never seen anything equal to them here. A large number of our Bayou Sara & Woodville merchants are flat broke and shut up (Winter 1874).

As a diversion from his bleak world, Sam sought comfort in a hobby:

I am still reading up on bees in my leisure time & hope to turn out enough honey with the help of a good season to keep people from laughing at my hobby. I find it necessary to have something of that kind on hand as an amusement for I believe in the old law 'All work & no play' etc (1874).

William Rogers Greene, who had desperately tried to keep his businesses afloat in a devastated economy, decided it was time to go home. Grieving the loss of his Maria, Kit returned to Rhode Island. George had married Julia Dunbar and resided at The Forest, "never coming North except for summer visits to his parents." "Aunt Jule" became a favorite among the Greene children. William suggested that his wife's entire family leave the impoverished Westmoreland and live with them in Rhode Island. Sam, Susan, and Will would hear nothing of it, but Mollie's sisters, Helen and Amelia, and their mother, Sophia, welcomed the opportunity of a new start. Even their young housekeeper, Evelyn Moncrief, decided to go.

William's grand adventure in the South, ruined by a war-ravaged economy, a worm infestation of the cotton crop, and the Vicksburg fire that destroyed what little was left of a major center of interstate commerce, had come to an end.

By 10 June 1874, as he battled hard times and a festering war wound that manifested itself in recurring episodes of malaria and the onset of tuberculosis, Sam Postlethwaite's life as a planter was nearly finished. Putting a brave face on a desperate situation, he wrote:

> Nothing that I can think of at present would give me greater pleasure than to come up with Sue & spend some time with you & Aunt Jane, but I must tell you that at present the thing is not possible. Bill (Will) is away & no one here to leave things in charge of.
>
> True I am leasing this year, but I am to get a third & am to be paid out of the other two thirds, for my advances, mules, supplies etc, so I need not tell you that this is a very interesting crop to me. I also have ever in view that I may have to take back some of the mules, so I am looking after them this year closely & making sure the negroes take good care of them. My object in selling out this year is to try & pay up every cent to my merchant & have if possible enough over to run myself next year.
>
> That is my plan at present any how. This was a poor season for honey, but I got 26 gals. of Beautiful extracted honey from 12 stocks of bees, over 2 gals. average. A new style of hive I am trying this year gave 4 gals. 1st extracting & they have enough now again for all they require.
>
> Love to all.
> Sam Postlethwaite (1874)

Upon his return to Rhode Island, William, along with Mollie and their growing family, moved into the "mansion house" on Fairview Avenue facing Greenwood Cemetery.

Corotoman Farm, as it was known, consisted of several acres with tennis courts, croquet lawns, and a trout stream. William, now a "calico printer" by occupation, enjoyed his daily walk down Woodside Avenue to his place of employment, S. H. Greene & Sons, and he was soon a welcome fixture in Clyde. Kit also found employment with the family firm. On 20 May 1875, Henry Aborn Greene was born to William and Mollie.

By summer of 1875, Sam's health had deteriorated severely. Will had left for New Orleans, where he had married Miss Anna Buhler (she would bear him two sons, Peyton and William Dunbar 3rd). Susan, penniless, could offer her brother little comfort. William and Mollie, deeply concerned, "brought him North to their home in Rhode Island to recuperate from malaria and hoping that something might be done for him by surgery."

Thus, Confederate veteran, Samuel Postlethwaite, moved North, leaving Westmoreland and its way of life forever. His health shattered, he had less than a year to live. On a cool, breezy Sunday afternoon, Sam Postlethwaite, consumed by tuberculosis, died at Corotoman Farm. On the following day, 21 August 1876, Sam was buried at the front of Greenwood Cemetery—his grave marked by a simple marble block with the inscription "S.P." This tiny monument would not survive the years. First, the inscription was eroded by time and the elements; eventually, the block itself disappeared.

Sam's obituary read:

> a man of unblemished reputation, a citizen of unsullied purity. A friend whose fidelity knew no variableness nor shadow of turning. A son whose life was one long offering of filial love; a brother who had no equal in fraternal devotion. His departure has left in the State, society, and the family circle a void which cannot be filled. The hand of friendship is all too feeble to pen a fitting tribute to one of such immeasurable worth in all the relations

of life. It remains but to draw the curtain over a sorrow which cannot by human hands be appeased.

Deeply do we deplore this loss; reverently, tenderly we offer our sympathy to the bereaved family (Postlethwaite Family Papers; Gillespie Papers).

So it was that Frank and Sam, two soldiers divided by war, both died not on the battlefield but of tuberculosis in the sleepy mill village of Riverpoint, Rhode Island, long after the guns had fallen silent, members of the same family.

The Department of Veterans Affairs issued this bronze marker for Sam's grave to recognize his service as an American soldier.

EPILOGUE

WILLIAM ROGERS GREENE LOST A LONG BATTLE WITH BRIGHT'S Disease on 23 September 1889. He was fifty-nine. He had sought various treatments for his condition, traveling as far as London. He is buried next to his four-year-old son, Christopher, on the cemetery lot adjacent to Sam's.

Mollie Carter Postlethwaite Greene bore William eight children. In addition to the aforementioned Helen, William Reginald, and Henry, there was Lenore, Barney (who survived only a few days), Marion Eleanor, Benjamin Allen, and Christopher. Upon William's death, Mollie lived for a time in Europe. She made her final residence in Los Angeles, California, where she died in 1901. Her place of burial is unknown.

Susan Postlethwaite sold Westmoreland to Dr. T. Woods on Christmas Eve 1885. Nothing else is known of her.

Will Postlethwaite's life after Westmoreland was filled with tragedy. He and his wife, Anna, lost their first son, Peyton, as a young boy to drowning. Their surviving child, William Dunbar III, was a deaf-mute. While visiting the Greenes in Rhode Island, he was struck and killed by a train. Will died, a widower, as "an indigent soldier" at the Beauvior soldier's home in Biloxi, Mississippi, on 23 September 1925. He was seventy-eight years old. It had

Anna Postlethwaite with her son,
William Dunbar III.

Will Postlethwaite's headstone at Beavior
Cemetery in Biloxi, Mississippi.

been sixty-four years since he had joined the Wilkinson Rifles. His name is misspelled on his headstone.

Jane and I visited Beauvoir in 1996. As we walked up the front steps, a loud thunderclap came from the sky. We joked that it was Will saying hello.

In a soaking downpour, we said goodbye to this story standing in front of Will's misspelled gravestone. I touched it gently saying to myself, "I know what you did my friend."

George Greene died in Natchez at the age of seventy-five. He is buried with his wife, Julia, at Forest Cemetery, just south of Natchez on Highway 61. His stone bears the inscription: "Blessed Are The Pure In Heart For They Shall See God." Julia outlived him by three years.

Graves of George and Julia Greene at the Forest Cemetery, south of Natchez, Mississippi.

Simon Henry Greene died at home in Riverpoint in 1885 at the age of eighty-six. His wife, Cornelia, died two years later. They are buried in Swan Point Cemetery, Providence. His home and Swedenborgian church (now a cellular phone store) still stand. Simon Greene's house and William's house at Corotoman Farm were nearly identical.

Christopher "Kit" Greene died on 13 March 1885, his father Simon's last birthday, in Riverpoint. He was fifty-seven. Kit never remarried and had no children.

Headstone of Simon Henry Greene at Swan Point Cemetery in Providence, Rhode Island.

William Lindsay Brandon died at his home, "Arcole" on 8 October 1890. He was eighty-nine. He is buried at Arcole.

Benjamin Humphreys survived the war, attaining the rank of brigadier general. After the war, he was elected governor of Mississippi. He had fourteen children. He died on 23 December 1882, at the age of seventy-four. He is buried in Port Gibson.

"Prince" John Bankhead Magruder survived the war. He refused a parole and became a general in the Mexican Army. Returning to the United States, he briefly made a career on the lecture circuit by telling tales of his military experiences. He died in poverty in 1871.

George McClellan was defeated by President Lincoln in his bid for president in 1864. He was later elected governor of New Jersey. He died in 1885.

Helen Postlethwaite (Aunt Nen), Sam's half-sister, married Mr. James Simmons of Rhode Island. She died in 1913 and is buried with Sam in Greenwood Cemetery. There is no marker.

298

Kate Blount survived the war. Little else is known of her.

Lenore Greene, William and Mollie's fourth child, was born a month before Sam's death on 18 July 1876. She eventually became something of a family historian.

> Our house was always filled with Southern relatives in the summer, coming to escape the hot weather or to recuperate from malaria. My father was very hospitable and generous and did everything he could to help my mother's family and friends, many of whom were impoverished due to the war.

Lenore died in California during the 1960s.

Westmoreland was destroyed by fire in the late nineteenth century. The property, now known as Westmoreland Farms, is presently the residence of Miss Dorcas Woods Brown.

At the close of the nineteenth century, the Greene family moved to Forest, California, where they began a new venture: the Corotoman Mining Company. The meaning of the word Corotoman remains a mystery.

Corotoman Farm was sold to Patrick Quinn during the 1920s. It was the residence of the Quinn family until the early 1970s, when it was sold to Downing Associates. In 1974, during renovations to turn it into a museum, the house was destroyed by fire. In its place today stand several ranch-style homes. Only sections of Corotoman Farm's impressive stone walls remain as a reminder of another age.

A section of Corotoman Farm's stone wall.

BIBLIOGRAPHY

Abbot, Willis John. *Battle-fields of '61: A Narrative of the Military Operations of the War for the Union up to the End of the Peninsular Campaign.* New York: Dodd, Mead & Co., 1889.

Alexander, Edward Porter. General. *Military Memoirs of a Confederate: A Critical Narrative.* New York: Scribner, 1907.

Baker, Jean H. *Mary Todd Lincoln: A Biography.* New York: W.W. Norton, 1987.

Barker, Harold R. Brigadier General A.S.U. (retired). *History of the Rhode Island Combat Units in the Civil War, 1861–1865.* N.p., 1964.

Billings, John D. *Hardtack and Coffee: The Unwritten Story of Army Life.* Lincoln: University of Nebraska Press, 1993.

Blount, Kate. Letters, 1861–1865. Collection of the Woodville, Mississippi Civic Club (601) 888-3998.

For more information write to:

Woodville Civic Club
P.O. Box 1055
Woodville, Mississippi 39669

Boatner, Mark M. III. *The Civil War Dictionary.* New York: David McKay Co., Inc. 1988.

Bowman, John S., ed. *The Civil War Almanac.* New York: World Almanac Publications, 1983.

Brandon Letters. 1862. Used by permission of Catherine Morgan Brandon, Natchez, Miss.

Bridges, Hal. *Lee's Maverick General: Daniel Harvey Hill.* Lincoln: University of Nebraska Press, 1991.

Catton, Bruce. *Mr. Lincoln's Army.* Garden City, N.Y.: Doubleday and Co., Inc., 1951.

Commanger, Henry Steele, ed. *The Blue and the Gray: The Story of the Civil War as Told by Participants.* New York: The Bobbs-Merrill Co., Inc., 1950.

Cross, Harold A. *They Sleep Beneath the Mockingbird: Mississippi Burial Sites and Biographies of Confederate Generals.* Murfreesboro, Tenn.: Southern Heritage Press, 1994.

Cullen, Joseph P. *The Peninsula Campaign, 1862: McClellan and Lee Struggle for Richmond.* Harrisburg, Pa.: Stackpole Books, 1973.

Denney, Robert E. *Civil War Prisons and Escapes: A Day-by-Day Chronicle.* New York: Sterling Publishing Co., 1993.

Dinkins, Captain James. *1861-1865: By an Old Johnnie, Personal Recollections and Experiences in the Confederate Army.* Cincinnati, Ohio: Robert Clarke Co., 1897.

Dobbins, Austin. *Grandfather's Journal: Company B, Sixteenth Mississippi Infantry Volunteer's Harris Brigade, Mahone's Division, Hill's Corps, A.N.V. May 27, 1861–July 15, 1865.* Dayton, Ohio: Morningside House, 1988.

Douglas, Henry Kyd. *I Rode With Stonewall.* St. Simons Island, Ga.: Mockingbird Books, 1989.

Dowdey, Clifford. *The Seven Days: The Emergence of Lee.* Boston: Little, Brown & Co., 1964.

Foote, Shelby. *The Civil War, A Narrative.* New York: Random House, 1958.

Farwell, Byron. *Ball's Bluff: A Small Battle and Its Long Shadow.* McLean, Va.: EPM Publications, 1970.

Fisher, John E., ed. "The Travels of the 13th Mississippi Regiment: Excerpts From the Diary of Mike E. Hubbert of Attala County (1861–1862)." *Journal of Mississippi History* 45 (1983): 288–313.

Freeman, Douglas Southall. *Lee's Lieutenants: A Study in Command.* New York: Charles Scribner's Sons, 1970.

Fuller, O.P. *The History of Warwick.* Providence, R.I.: Angell, Burlingame and Co., 1875.

Gillespie, James Dr. Papers. Louisiana State University, Baton Rouge.

Gragg, Rod. *The Illustrated Confederate Reader.* New York: Harper & Row, 1989.

Greene, William Rogers. Letters, 1850–1870. Used by permission of Rosalind Colley, Barrington, R.I.

Harwell, Richard Barksdale, ed. *Cities and Camps of the Confederate States.* Urbana: University of Illinois Press, 1958.

Hassler, Warren W. Jr. *Commanders of the Army of the Potomac.* Baton Rouge: Louisiana State University Press, 1962.

Haythornthwaite, Philip. *Uniforms of the Civil War in Color.* New York: Sterling Publishing Co. Inc., 1990.

Henderson, G.F.R. *Stonewall Jackson and the American Civil War.* New York: Da Capo Press, 1988.

Hesseltine, William B., ed. *Civil War Prisons.* Ohio: Kent State University Press, 1962.

Johnson, R.U., and C.C. Buel, eds. *Battles and Leaders of the Civil War, Being for the Most Part Contributions by Union and Confederate Officers.* New York: The Century Co., 1887–1888.

Johnston, David E. *The Story of a Confederate Boy in the Civil War.* Portland, Ore.: Glass & Prudhomme Co., 1914.

Jones, Terry L. *Lee's Tigers: The Louisiana Infantry in the Army of Northern Virginia.* Baton Rouge: Louisiana State University Press, 1987.

Lewis Papers. University of North Carolina Library, Southern Historical Collection, Chapel Hill.

Lightsey, Ada Christine. *The Veteran's Story.* Meridian, Miss.: Meridian News, 1899.

Long, E.B., and Barbara Long. *The Civil War, Day by Day.* Garden City, N.Y.: Da Capo Press, 1971.

McClellan, George B. *McClellan's Own Story: the War of the Union, the Soldiers Who Fought it, the Civilians Who Directed it, and His Relations to it and to Them.* New York: Webster & Co., 1887.

Mitchell, Joseph B. Lieutenant Colonel. *Decisive Battles of the Civil War.* New York: Putnam, 1955.

Mitchell, Reid. *Civil War Soldiers.* New York: Viking Press, 1988.

Mounger Letter. Private collection of Dr. William Mounger, Greenwood, Miss.

National Historical Society, The. *The Image of War: 1861–1862.* Garden City, N.Y.: Doubleday Press, 1981.

Nevins, Allan. *The War for the Union: The Improvised War 1861–1862.* New York: Charles Scribnerís Sons 1959.

Patrick, Rembert W. *The Fall of Richmond.* Baton Rouge: Louisiana State University Press, 1960.

Posey Family Scrapbook. Private collection of Mrs. James Gross, Woodville, Miss.

Postlethwaite Family Papers. Mississippi Department of Archives and History, Jackson.

Priest, John Michael. *Antietam: The Soldier's Battle.* New York: Oxford University Press, 1989.

Rand, Clayton. *Men of Spine in Mississippi.* Gulfport, Miss.: Dixie Press, 1940.

Rhodes, Robert Hunt, ed. *All For the Union: The Civil War Diary and Letters of Elisha Hunt Rhodes.* New York: Orion Books, 1985.

Rowland, Dunbar, ed. *Encyclopedia of Mississippi History.* 2 vols. Madison, Wis.: Selwyn A. Brant, 1907.

_____. *History of the Mississippi: The Heart of the South.* 2 vols. Jackson, Miss.: The S.J. Clarke Publishing Co., 1925.

Sears, Stephen W. *To the Gates of Richmond.* New York: Ticknor and Fields, 1992.

Stiles, Robert. *Four Years Under Marse Robert.* Dayton, Ohio: Morningside House Inc., 1988.

Swanberg, W.A. *First Blood: The Story of Fort Sumter.* New York: Charles Scribner's Sons, 1957.

Tanner, Robert G. *Stonewall in the Valley: Thomas J. "Stonewall" Jackson's Shenandoah Valley Campaign, Spring 1862.* Garden City, N.Y.: Doubleday, 1976.

United States. War Department. *The War of the Rebellion: A Compilation of the Official Records of the Union and Confederate Armies.* Washington,

D.C.: Government Printing Office, 1880–1901.

Ward, Geoffry C. *The Civil War: An Illustrated History.* Based on a documentary by Geoffry C. Ward, Ric Burns, and Ken Burns with contributions by Don E. Fehrenbacher, et al. New York: Alfred A. Knopf, 1990.

Wayne, Michael. *The Reshaping of Plantation Society: The Natchez District, 1860–1890.* Baton Rouge: Louisiana State University Press, 1983.

Wert, Jeffery D. *General James Longstreet: The Confederacy's Most Controversial Soldier, A Biography.* New York: Simon and Schuster, 1993.

Wheeler, Richard. *Sword over Richmond: An Eyewitness History of McClellan's Peninsular Campaign.* New York: Harper and Row, 1986.

_____. *Voices of the Civil War.* New York: Thomas Y. Crowell Co., 1976.

Wiley, Bell Irvin. *Embattled Confederates: An Illustrated History of Southerners at War.* New York: Harper and Row, 1964.

_____. *The Life of Johnny Reb.* Garden City, N.Y.: Doubleday, 1971.

Wilson, Legrand James. *The Confederate Soldier.* Tenn.: Memphis State University Press, 1973.

Woodbury, Augustus. *The Second Rhode Island Regiment.* Providence, R.I.: Valpey, Angell and Co., 1875.

_____. *The Campaign of the First Rhode Island Regiment.* Providence, R.I.: Sidney S. Rider, 1862.

Yeary, Mamie, comp. *Reminiscences of the Boys in Gray, 1861–1865.* Dayton, Ohio: Morningside Press, 1986.

ABOUT THE AUTHOR

Author with his dog, Keith.

LES ROLSTON WAS BORN IN 1954 AND HAS STUDIED American history for most of his adult life. His greatest interest is in the lives of ordinary people, who in times of crisis go on to do extraordinary deeds.

From 1990 through 1995, Mr. Rolston worked to preserve the unmarked grave site of the only Confederate soldier known to be buried in Rhode Island. For this effort, he gained national attention, telling his story in the pages of the *Rhode Islander, Confederate Veteran* magazine, *Civil War* magazine, and other publications. The story was also covered by the Associated Press and television programs.

As a result of his work, Mr. Rolston received a citation from the Rhode Island House of Representatives and a letter of commendation from U.S. Senator Claiborne Pell. He was also presented with the Jefferson Davis Medal, the United Daughters of the Confederacy's highest literary award.

Some of Mr. Rolston's other work has been published in *Civil War* magazine, *Our Heritage*, the *South Reporter*, and the *New Orleans Times-Picayune*. *Lost Soul* is his first book. He is currently at work on a second.

Other titles available from

Ancestry®

By James C. Neagles
#186 Softbound
286 pages
5 1/2" x 8 1/2"
ISBN 0-916489-16-7
$15.95

CONFEDERATE RESEARCH SOURCES:
A Guide to Archive Collections

Nearly one million Americans served in the Confederate military. This book gives detailed descriptions of records available in the Confederate and border states and in the National Archives. It also provides valuable insights into Confederate historical and family history background.

U.S. MILITARY RECORDS:
A Guide to Federal & State Sources, Colonial America to the Present

From the earliest days of the United States, millions of Americans have served their country in a military capacity. Thus, most families have one or more members who served in America's armed forces.

For this reason, genealogists look to military records to enhance their research. Enlistment records, muster rolls, pension applications, and other records are extremely valuable because they often contain detailed personal information. *U.S. Military Records* describes the records that are available and where they can be found.

By James C. Neagles
455 pages
8 1/2" x 11"
ISBN 0-916489-55-8
#180 Hardbound
$39.95

THE SOURCE:
A Guidebook of American Genealogy, Revised Edition

The Source sets the standard for genealogy reference books. It identifies and describes the rich body of original research materials—birth, marriage, census, and many other kinds of records available for family history researchers. Further, it explains how best to use these materials to discover and enjoy your family history.

When it was originally published in 1984, *The Source* was a groundbreaking work. This 1997 edition has been thoroughly updated and includes two new chapters. The information and practical advice combine to form one of the best genealogical resources ever created.

Edited by
Loretto Dennis Szucs
and Sandra
Hargreaves Luebking
846 pages 8 1/2" x 11"
ISBN 0-916489-67-1
#101 Hardbound
$49.95